TROUBLE IN STORE?

RETAIL LOCATIONAL POLICY IN BRITAIN AND GERMANY

ABSTRACT

This report discusses locational policy for retail developments in Britain and Germany over the last 20 years, set in the context of their North American origins. Two national chapters examine retail planning, structure and development in each country, and are each followed by three case studies to illustrate particular retail issues. British case studies focus on South Hampshire, Wolverhampton and York; German case studies on Dortmund, Köln and Regensburg.

It is explained that the US flight to suburbs and out-of-town locations has left many 'downtowns' a shadow of their former selves; for many, what was there before was not particularly distinguished in social and urban design terms so a restructured city was not seen to be a particular problem. Now there **is** a problem - of traffic moving in patterns unconceived when journeys-to-work were unidirectional and radial, requiring orbital roads to be built through the most expensive residential land.

With an uncontrolled development of out-of-centre retail (and leisure) complexes, Britain could look forward to similar situations. But following US trends could be worse for Britain, because many existing town centres are of a high urban quality, sustained by activity and the exchange of goods and ideas. While others are of a poorer quality, **all** existing centres have been structured by walking, and not the private car: in London this is still substantially the case.

Construction laws in Germany, and consequent retail development patterns, show that rational control is possible in order to secure the future of town centres. In many cases these laws combine with public transport and environmental improvements to enhance the rôle of existing centres.

It is argued that it is foolhardy to encourage any development which encourages car travel in congested urban areas, for it destroys these powerful and stable central city structures, creates a demand for new road infrastructure and generates a host of problems which are against the interests of the community at large. 11 recommendations recognise these issues and suggest it is crucial for Britain to learn from Germany, France, the Netherlands, Sweden, Canada... all of which have placed legal constraints on excessive and inappropriately located retail development.

a report by TEST for the ANGLO-GERMAN FOUNDATION
with additional support from the English Department of the Environment

The Anglo-German Foundation for the Study of Industrial Society was established in 1973 on the initiative of the late President Heinemann by an agreement between the British and German governments and incorporated by Royal Charter. It was initially financed by the German government, but since 1979 has been supported by both governments.

The Foundation aims to contribute to the understanding of industrial society in the two countries and to promote contacts between them. It funds selected research projects likely to be of practical use to policymakers in the industrial, economic and social field, mostly bilateral comparisons, and organises and finances Anglo-German conferences and meetings.

****

Transport & Environment Studies (TEST) was founded by John Roberts in 1972. It has a wide research base, being interested in transport planning and the interface between transport and the environment; urban and rural planning, and applied research into leisure attitudes and behaviour also figure significantly in the list of close to 100 projects undertaken by TEST in 17 years. Clients have included the World Bank, UNDP, OECD, the English Departments of the Environment and of Transport, the Transport & Road Research Laboratory, London Regional Transport, various Passenger Transport Executives, local government, the Countryside Commission and the Sports Council. TEST has worked in Egypt, Iraq, Malaysia, Portugal, Singapore, Venezuela and the United States, and has undertaken three international studies covering several European countries.

****

Wordprocessing, laser printing and graphics by TEST

Final artwork printed and bound by
Imediaprint Ltd   1 Memel Street   London EC1Y 0SY

Copyright © TEST 1989
Extracts may be reproduced provided TEST is acknowledged as the source

TEST Report No 80
ISBN 0 905545 23 0

This report may be obtained from
TEST   177 Arlington Road   London NW1 7EY   England

February 1989

C O N T E N T S

TABLES AND FIGURES

PREFACE

The Anglo-German Foundation for the Study of Industrial Society (A-GF)(*Deutsch-Britische Stiftung für das Studium der Industriegesellschaft*) agreed to support this study in October 1986. Dr Hans Wiener was the Project Director at that time. His successor Dr Nicholas Watts saw the project through to the publication stage. During the course of the study, the English Department of the Environment gave additional financial support. Mr Robert Chubb, the nominated officer, and Dr Watts, critically appraised the draft report, which eased the task of producing the final version. Neither organisation necessarily endorses all the report's findings. Our gratitude also extends to Manfred Sinz in the Federal German research institute, the *Bundesforschungsanstalt für Landeskunde und Raumordnung* (BfLR), in Bonn, who collaborated with aspects of the German research programme.

John Roberts of TEST directed the project, but such an appellation must not disguise the major contributions made by Nicholas James, who undertook most of the English case study and national work and helped with final editing, and Carmen Hass-Klau, who researched most of the German case studies and the German national study. Also within TEST, Bryan Lipscombe, Peter Rawcliffe and Mark Goodwin prepared the graphics, while Ruth Silman and Ann Whipp carried out literature searches. Linda Kocks, a student at Bonn University, was employed to review literature which had been recommended by BfLR. Susie Ohlenschlager then translated Fraulein Kocks' findings.

Terence Bendixson was commissioned to provide a paper on retail developments in Britain and Dr Alan Hallsworth advised on the South Hampshire study. John Lillywhite of Wolverhampton MBC helped advise the Wolverhampton study and John Rigby of York City Council the York case study; both also read drafts of the relevant chapters. Additional help was given by planning officers at Birmingham City Council, Fareham DC, Hampshire CC, North Yorkshire CC, Portsmouth City Council, Southampton City Council and York City Council.

In Britain, we are grateful to Rory Joyce of Drivers Jonas, Professor Dawson at Institute for Retail Planning University of Stirling, Dr David Thorpe at The John Lewis Partnership, Dr David Kirby at Lampeter University, Tony Cumberbirch of LSPU, Dr Keith Thomas at Oxford Polytechnic, Dr Stephen Plowden, Mr Brisbane of Roger Tym and Partners, Dr David Quarmby of J Sainsbury Plc, Sarah Bassett-Johnson of SEEDS, David Hurdle at SERPLAN, Graham Percival at Surrey County Council, Dr Ross Davies, Elizabeth Howard and Jonathan Reynolds of Templeton College Oxford, Stuart Moore of Tesco plc, and Dr Bryan Wade at URPI Reading.

In Germany, a similarly large number of people deserve our gratitude. Among the, we must mention (alphabetically by agency) Dr Wichmann of Bundesverband der Selbstbedienungs Warenhäuser, Bonn; Dr Scharmer, DIfU, Bonn; Herr V Hatzfeld, private consultant, Dortmund; Dr Weitz, Hauptgemeinschaft des Einzelhandels, Köln; Dr Hermanns, IHK, Köln; Dr Bundgen, Institut für Landes- und Stadtentwicklungsforschung des Landes Nordrhein-Westfalen, Dortmund; Dr Halliers, Institute of Self-service, Köln; Herr Hötteke and Herr Schubert, Kaufhof Department Store, Köln; Dr Kläsener, Karstadt Department Store, Essen; Herr H-P Heidebach, Referat für Stadtplanung und Bauordnung der Stadt München; Herr Dipl-Volkswirt H Dauerer, Amt für Stadtentwicklung und Statistik der Stadt Regensburg; Professor H Heineberg and Dr Mayr, Westfälische Wilhelms Universität, Münster.

CONVERSIONS

1 metre = 3.28 feet; kilometer = 0.621 miles; m^2 = 10.764 ft^2; hectare = 2.471 acres; 1 km^2 = 100 ha = 0.386 square miles

GLOSSARY

A-GF	Anglo-German Foundation
AMA	Association of Metropolitan Authorities
BBauG	Bundesbaugesetz (Federal Construction Law)
BAG	Bundesarbeitsgemeinschaft (Federal Work Association)
BauNVO	Baunutzungsverordnung (Construction Use Regulation)
BfLR	Bundesforschungsanstalt für Landeskunde und Raumordnung (Federal Research Institute for Regional Studies and Environmental Planning)
CBD	Central Business District
CC	County Council
Central Place Theory	A theory of the hierarchy of cities developed by Christaller in 1933 specifically for Southern Germany but since widely applied in Germany and elsewhere
Comparison goods	Also called 'durables': all goods other than convenience goods bought to satisfy medium to long term needs
Convenience goods	Also called 'perishables': food, drink and tobacco goods, for short-term needs
DC	District Council
DCPN	Development Control Policy Note
DEZ	Donaueinkaufszentrum (Danube Shopping Centre)
DIfU	Deutsches Institut für Urbanistik (German Institute for Urbanistics)
DIY	Do-it-yourself
Fachmärkte	Retail warehouses
EKZ	Einkaufzentrum (Shopping Centre)
GLC	Greater London Council
HGZ	Handels und Gaststättenzählung (Trade and Catering Census)
HGZL	- shops and stores only
HGZT	- all retail trade
Hypermarkets	In Germany >3 000 to 4 000 m^2; in Britain, >5 000 m^2 net floorspace selling (self-service) convenience and comparison goods
Innenstadt	Inner City (approximately)
LPAC	London Planning Advisory Committee
LSPU	London Strategic Planning Unit
MBC	Metropolitan Borough Council
Plc	Public Limited Company
Regional Shopping Centres	Purpose built centres with a range of goods comparable to those found in traditional town centres; abbreviated to 'Shopping Centres' in Germany. Net floorspace >50 000 m^2
Retail warehouses	Net floorspace >2 500 m^2; sell DIY, electrical white ware, carpets, furniture, shoes, fabrics; often group in 'retail parks'
RTPI	Royal Town Planning Institute
SB Warenhäuse	Hypermarkets
SEEDS	South East Economic Development Strategy
SERPLAN	The London & South East Regional Planning Conference
SMSA	Standard Metropolitan Statistical Area
Superstore	In Britain >2 500 m^2 net floorspace, selling mainly convenience goods; in Germany, >1 000 m^2 net floorspace
TEST	Transport & Environment Studies
URPI	Unit for Retail Planning Information
VAT	Value Added Tax
Verbrauchermärkte	Superstores

0 SUMMARY

0-01
This book is about the accommodation of retail change in Britain and Germany. It uses extensive numerical data and a wide literature in Germany, and a similarly large literature in English with less adequate numerical data, for problem definition and policy formulation. It ends with a number of recommendations. There are three main sections. The first provides a North American and European context. The second considers West Germany and Britain and three case studies in each country. The third attempts some cross-cultural comparisons, draws conclusions and constructs recommendations.

0-02
The 'retail revolution' in the United States and Canada has a history starting in the 1920s, when the first out-of-town shopping center was opened in Kansas City in 1926; by 1984 there were nearly 25 000. This trend has accompanied the rise in car ownership and the demise of 'downtown'. As many of the more youthful downtown areas had little intrinsic interest, did this matter particularly? This may simply be answered by pointing to the trends which parallelled and still parallel the loss of downtown: voracious consumption of time, space, energy and environment by those who can afford it, a dearth of facilities for those left in the central city, and no focus for the wider community. These are important pointers to one possible future in a space-intensive Europe.

0-03
At least, these are the concerns with which most people are familiar, and the large-scale reconceiving of the functioning of urban areas which could be emulated in parts of Europe. To-day's trends will take longer to absorb, but they are potentially more lethal. They are exemplified in downtown office 'clones' which appear in subcentres or deeper into the suburbs. Related movement is orbital in contrast to established radial patterns, and there are few adequate roads (and fewer quality transit systems) to accommodate these movements. To build new ones means buying up some of the most expensive real estate in the city - within outer residential areas.

0-04
Canada became an acolyte of the US concept, though there were considerable differences between its general acceptance in the west and the controls applied by cities like Toronto in the east, to safeguard its downtown. Many European nations also followed, only to discover the concept's marked imperfections, and to take corrective action. France was an early follower in the 1960s, because it wanted to stimulate a stagnant retail sector; as early as 1973 restrictive legislation against out-of-centre retail developments had been introduced. Its legacy, in 1976, was 305 hypermarkets (the UK had 4, West Germany 538). Belgium introduced restrictions in 1975, the Netherlands followed in 1976, and 'disincentives' were introduced in Italy, Luxembourg and Eire. Germany, a principal concern of this book, introduced restrictive legislation in 1977 and tightened it further in 1986.

0-05
The British chapter is the longest in the book. It describes Britain's slow adoption of fundamental locational and size changes in retailing. By the time it relaxed controls over out-of-centre retail development most European nations had been through that stage and substantially rejected it. Britain made up for this by sheer scale: almost every day a very large new shopping centre project was announced, more often than not unintegrated with the pattern of retail development that had taken hundreds of years to establish, and which had strong

affinities with Christaller's Central Place Theory, a theory with large numbers of adherents in Germany. As is happening now in the United States and to a lesser extent in Germany, the British experiment had all the appearance of overkill - too many centres chasing too few shoppers. But this is an experiment which will take many years to amortise; during that time it will determine transport, energy, environmental, residential and job location policies for many years - even though it could, conceptually and in other terms, be wrong.

0-07
One benefit of out-of-centre developments is that they have stimulated the redevelopment of existing town centres. Those who have cars, time and money also benefit, if such centres are not viewed holistically. That is to say, they provide a wide range of choice, many aspects of shopping under one roof, and low prices. On the other hand, the study shows a number of structural, locational, social and transport problems which may be overlooked in the pursuit of profit. In Britain, whose traditional urban centres are much more at risk than those in Germany, some of the issues arising are that retailing is becoming developer- rather than retailer-led; that (in both countries) there are continuing trends toward concentration of suppliers, and a corresponding reduction in small, independent retailers; that what we have termed a 'spatial monopoly' is taking place as large retail outlets such as superstores dominate a local market and reduce a consumer's choice of store.

0-08
Locational and transport problems go together: out-of-centre retailing invites low-density residential development which together increase travel and reinforce a dependence on the car - which cannot be sustained in countries with a high density of population, if the original attractions of that country are to survive; social problems are more to do with access than price. Chapter 11 considers how cities grew organically around walking as the dominant mode of transport. Extraordinarily, this tenet still holds in traditional urban shopping centres, but it cannot do so with the concentration of retail (and leisure, educational, health and office) facilities in other than a traditional town centre and perhaps one or two more in the largest cities.

0-09
The three British case studies - South Hampshire, Wolverhampton and York, each have particular lessons. Both Portsmouth and Southampton are strongly opposed to out-of-centre retail development. Both are countering these trends with city centre improvements which include new shopping centre development, pedestrianisation and even glazing over streets. Both believe they should mimic outer centres by increasing car-parking in their own city centres: TEST argue this is counter-productive. Portsmouth has found that land ownership rather than planning regulations may be the most effective form of control. However neither have any say over what happens in adjacent District Councils, and the County has inadequate powers to control such developments. The Districts, in the absence of regional or sub-regional powers, are often happy to welcome new retail developments to boost their own economies. Developments in Eastleigh and Test Valley threaten to undermine Southampton's retail base.

0-10
Wolverhampton, second only to Birmingham in the size of its city centre, is set in the midst of a metropolitan area where survival depends on the resolution of conflict and administrative chaos. Since the abolition of the West Midlands County Council there is no strategic authority. The adjacent Metropolitan Boroughs of Dudley and Sandwell are each proceeding with very large retail developments; Birmingham has grand plans for uplifting its city centre to regional stature; and the new town of Telford, only 40 km northwest, has its own vast town centre, with free car parking and a direct motorway link with

2

Wolverhampton. The Borough are renewing parts of their extensive pedestrian network, and their existing Mander Centre (within the town centre) is having a face-lift. Wolverhampton is also due to be connected to Birmingham with the first stretch of the West Midlands light rail; this may not be entirely good news, for it would pass through Sandwell's retailing and leisure centre.

0-11

York, one of Britain's finest cities, is rapidly developing two shopping markets - one for tourists, and one for residents. The tourists benefit from upmarket shopping in what is probably Britain's largest pedestrianised area, but their shops are either too expensive or inappropriate to the residents' needs. The latter are increasingly being satisfied by large out-of-centre retail developments. The County plus York and the District Councils surrounding it put considerable effort into devising an 'out-of-town' policy, in which they considered that one major development near York would suffice. No sooner had this been agreed when one of the Districts broke the agreement by giving permission for the development of a new large centre.

0-12

The German picture is very different, containing a substantial element of *déjà vu*. As we have seen, Germany early permitted a large number of out-of-centre facilities and then increasingly placed controls on development. The pressures for such development have not changed greatly, however and, to get around the restrictions, they are today either below the size maximum of 1200 m^2 gross, or are located on outer industrial or mixed use zones, or they are integrated with existing shopping. There certainly has been a reduction in unintegrated retail store construction. Apart from the law on retailing, the other major difference between British and German retailing concerns statistical data. Germany has an irregular census of retailing; the last three to be undertaken were in 1967/8, 1978/9 and 1984/5. These are used extensively where it is clear what they are representing. A problem with the last census is that retailers are demanding more information security - this has led to a wider use of gross rather than net floor area, and data on all retail trade, rather than just fixed shops. Often the data are not comparable.

0-13

Three case studies were undertaken, in Dortmund, Köln and Regensburg. Dortmund has affinities with Wolverhampton - both are less prosperous cities, Dortmund's industrial base of coal having subsided, leaving brewing as the main industry. With about 19% unemployed, the economic support for the city centre is worse than many cities. The Chamber of Commerce is not particularly effective and all these factors have contributed to a less successful city centre than in the other two case studies. Out-of-centre pressures are also quite significant, and the largest out-of-town shopping centre in Germany is on the boundary of Dortmund and Bochum, in the northwest of the city.

0-14

Köln is altogether different. It has a strong Chamber of Commerce which involves itself in everything to do with the city's economy - and its culture, as it recently supported the building of a new museum near the main railway station. Köln's city centre has always been one of the most important in Germany and, to a considerable degree, that importance has been retained. Remarkably, the power of the city was sufficient to deter major retail developments outside its boundary until 1976; even since then there have not been as many as there are in the surroundings of most other large cities. Within Köln many integrated and unintegrated new retail centres have been permitted, but far less than the number applied for, so control has been achieved there too. The result is that the city as a whole showed a -7.3% fall in retail turnover in real terms 1978 to 1984. Bonn, as capital city, improved on this with -4%. Köln's other neighbouring city, Leverkusen, reduced by -12.2% and Stuttgart, in the

3

prosperous south but with severe pressures from four surrounding towns and many out-of-centre retail projects, lost -15.5% of its retail turnover.

0-15
Regensburg, a city similar in size, history and architectural quality to York, is almost unique in Germany in not having had its centre destroyed in the second world war. It is located approximately half way between Nürnberg and München but has the same central place status as those two larger cities. Some irreparable damage was done to the city centre to extend retailing up to 1976 when the whole of the city centre was made a conservation area. The other unique characteristic of Regensburg is the very high city centre residential population who have helped retain its trading viability. Nevertheless, expansion had to be accommodated; the city controlled this through ownership of most of the suitable sites in the city. Eventually it was decided to allow development close to the city centre, across the Danube to the northeast. This has been successful from the start and has increased in size twice until it now has almost the same floorspace as the city centre. The two centres share the majority of the city's retail spending with a large degree of harmony - from the City Council's point of view partly because they required any expansion of the new centre to be accompanied by improvements to stores within the old centre.

0-16
The book's recommendations are as follows:

1 A standard set of criteria for evaluating retail planning applications should be established.
2 National planning policy and advice should be based on clear definitions of acceptable levels of impact on trade, employment, environment and transport
3 National planning advice should encourage retail applications to be evaluated holistically, with reference to social as well as land use effects
4 Clear but flexible land use zoning policies together with the powers to implement would reduce uncertainty and could benefit society, retailers and developers alike
5 Where local authorities own land, they should be given reasonable discretion to use this in the best interests of the locality
6 A quinquennial retail census should be reintroduced in Britain to lessen planning uncertainties and remove the advantage enjoyed by developers and retailers. In Germany, retail census data should be available in a nationally consistent manner
7 Counties or new statutory sub-regional or regional bodies should invariably consider applications whose impact extends beyond the boundaries of an individual District
8 Trends toward retail concentration and sectoral and spatial monopoly should be carefully monitored to ensure they are not against the public interest. The remit should be kept as wide as possible to look at indirect effects which may result from concentration
9 Retailers should form strong Chambers of Commerce, on the model of Köln and Wolverhampton, to protect their interests, and to lobby for sensitive conservation of traditional town centres
10 Local authorities should bring together local and national agencies such as Chambers of Commerce, Tourist Boards and Historic Building Agencies to develop a town centre's character, to raise public awareness and to develop integrated local design schemes
11 Local authorities should be wary of redesigning their town centres to accommodate the car, in an attempt to compete with out-of-centre retail On the contrary, they should introduce traffic restraint, environmental improvement and better public transport. A substantial residential population, within walking distance, complements such policies.

4

1 BACKGROUND

SUMMARY

1-01
This book is about the accommodation of retail change in Britain and Germany. While it is policy-oriented, it needed to sift a mountain of empirical data before the effects of existing policies could be understood, and the requirements for normative (or less deterministic) future policies could be arrayed. While a high proportion of the book is about Britain and Germany, some of the roots of current issues needed to be examined - at second hand, as that field has been well-trodden by others. This first chapter therefore scans the 'retail revolution' and its origins, sees what has happened in and to the United States and much of continental Europe, and finally lets these outcomes frame the objectives and hypothesis of this study.

1-02
The 'retail revolution' is but one of several consumerist responses to substantial changes in Western society. In brief, most people now enjoy higher disposable incomes, better education, more mobility and shorter hours of paid work than fifty years ago. Those who still work long hours cherish their free time, trying to maximise it through reductions in household labour. Some results of these trends are increases in comparison goods buying, lower density housing, large increases in car ownership and use, deterioration of public transport, greater congestion on routes to traditional centres, and establishment of new out-of-centre shopping - which has substantial car parking. Stores have become larger, stocking wider ranges of goods; they are more often parts of multiple chains, leaving the small shopkeeper to try and survive in traditional centres. The explanatory variables and their consequences are not endorsed by significant sectors of society, even though they may be participating in them.

1-03
In the United States, the results of accommodating (often, initiating) these trends has been a radical run-down of traditional Central Business Districts (CBDs) and a reduction of public transport to pathetic levels in many cities. In others there has been lavish expenditure on 'downtown' renewal and on transit in the hope, not always successful, that these trends could be countered. There remains unrelenting expansion, at low residential and employment densities, in most cities. Using the Los Angeles model, clones can now be found in Denver, Phoenix, Atlanta and many other cities. As Europe is generally considered to be at least 10 years behind the US, and Britain often further removed, many lessons could be learnt here and future problems avoided. In fact the response varies. France, Germany and several other European countries, have attempted to control, if not reverse, laissez-faire policies of the 1960s and early 1970s. Britain has only comparatively recently **introduced** laissez-faire policies, let alone gone full circle in attempting to control them.

1-04
Present-day political ideology in Britain is explained in a Command document (HM Government 1985). This explains two key elements in government economic policy: 'to keep down inflation and offer real incentives for enterprise, in order to generate jobs.' The document is about 'one important aspect of helping enterprise to grow - by reducing burdens imposed on business by administrative and legislative regulation.' It sets out 'the case for more freedom in the business sector and the need to deregulate.' It notes that these actions 'must be done with care. The line between liberty and licence is fine and can easily be crossed. We have to bring about the conditions to promote growth but not abuse.'

NORTH AMERICAN ORIGINS

The United States

1-05
Changes in retailing have been dramatic over the last 25 years. Most started in USA, were adopted somewhat later in continental Europe, and hit Britain later still. Cox (1978) said the first out-of-town shopping centre was County Club Plaza in Kansas 1923; Lord (1988) said Kansas City 1926. He noted a lull until the 1950s, when significant expansion took place. By 1984 there were nearly 25 000, two thirds of which were under 100 000 ft^2 (9 290 m^2).

1-06
Why did these shopping centres appear? Writing in the early 1970s, Thomas (1972) said 'In the US, towns have a traffic problem that becomes worse every day, with a growing number of private cars and a deterioration of public transport.' No doubt true up to the time Thomas was writing, but changes since that time have meant a further increase in cars, though urban transit has improved taking the US as a whole. In 1972 there were 97.1 million cars. By 1985 there had been a 34% increase to 130.3 million; bus and rail accounted for 2.61% of intercity passenger-miles, and 2.01% in 1985. On the other hand, the number of public passenger transit vehicle-miles increased by 12.4% from 1 883 million in 1970 to 2 117 million in 1983 (the latter set of figures includes urban transit. US Department of Commerce 1986).

1-07
Thomas continued 'In spite of an attempt by local authorities and retail stores to provide parking space, the problem has not been solved, owing to the expense of land in town centres and the great number of car owners attempting to find spaces near the shops. Because customers could not get to the stores, the stores moved to the customers and were (incorporated in) shopping centres outside the towns with an abundance of parking space ... Most of these shopping centres have been planned and built by developers, who granted leases to stores, charging rents calculated on a percentage of sales. Such has been the demand for tenancies that shopping centres have sprung up in the countryside close to many large towns.'

1-08
Thomas considers that US shopping centres took three forms:

* Neighbourhood shopping centres of 10-15 stores selling food and convenience goods, with parking for 500-1 000 cars;
* community shopping centres with 15-40 stores + parking for 1 000-3 000 cars;
* regional shopping centres, with 40-100 stores including department stores, plus parking for over 5 000 cars.'

Nowadays the classification of such centres is more likely to be by area than number of units. However, Thomas' reasoning for the development of out-of-town shopping centres is inadequate. Cox (1978) enlarged. He noted increasing suburban populations and real income; central area decay through movement of affluent US citizens to the suburbs, leaving the most disadvantaged groups in the centre, through retail trade following purchasing power, and through the inability of city governments to cope politically or financially; the decline of public transport and the high level of car ownership.

1-09
Then, possibly because the subject is increasingly well researched, Lord (1988) suggested a wider range of explanations for the decline of CBD shopping in the US. He considered the competition not just to be regional malls, but also smaller shopping centres and ribbon developments. Downtown suffers not only

from traffic and parking problems, but a negative image, obsolete physical plant and fragmentation of land use. Lord also discussed the importance of office workers to CBD retailers and cited a study by the Urban Land Institute which showed that an increase in 1 000 downtown office workers was accompanied by a $3.32 million increase in retail sales. But catering for a lunchtime peak means an inefficient use of shop labour; furthermore not every city has experienced office expansion - in many cases offices have accompanied retailing to the suburbs. As examples, Denver now has three 'downtowns' and several suburban centres; Washington DC is surrounded by satellite office/residential/ retail centres; Atlanta has two downtowns (see para 1-17) and Houston more than one.

1-10

Yet the US retail industry was also changing. The number of firms scarcely changed from 1963 to 1982 - from 1.53m to 1.57m - but the number of multiunit establishments (owned by firms which operate at two or more locations) nearly doubled from 220 to 415 in that period. Those firms took 36.6% of total retail sales in 1963 and 53.2% in 1982. The number of retail employees doubled from 7.1m in 1954 to 14.5m in 1982. Total retail sales expanded 78% in 1982 prices, 1967 to 1985 - a very real increase as the US population only increased by 20.4% over that period. The US statistics are not uniformly presented in terms of years, but an attempt was made to compare sales in current terms between 1970 and 1985 according to the British classification of convenience (defined in Britain as food, beverages and tobacco, though tobacco cannot be disaggregated in the US statistics) and comparison (including durable) goods. This suggests that sale of comparison goods increased by 297% over the period, and of convenience goods by 209% (all above data from US Department of Commerce 1986).

1-11

But, who benefits and who loses? Lord (1988) quoted figures showing that CBD sales as a percentage of a sample of 59 Metropolitan Area sales were 34.6% in 1948, and 7.9% in 1972. He quoted from a national sample of 159 Metropolitan Areas to show changes from 1972-1977: the CBD lost 23%, the Central City experienced no change, and the suburbs gained 19% in retail sales. In terms of employment changes in CBD retailing Lord examined 20 large cities and found that all except New Orleans lost jobs 1977-1982, all the others losing between 16% and 52%. The number of establishments fell almost everywhere (Miami being the only city to gain), with losses from 2% to 27%.

1-12

Lord (1988, quoting from Shopping Center World January 1985) noted the size distribution of planned shopping centres in the US, which suggested that it is the smaller ones that dominate:

Table 1-1 : Distribution by Floorspace of US Planned Shopping Centers

Size group, sq ft GLA	US Centers in 1984	
	Number	Percent
less than 100 000	16 469	66.6
100 000 - 200 000	4 812	19.5
200 000 - 400 000	1 888	7.6
400 000 - 800 000	975	3.9
800 000-1 000 000	265	1.1
greater than 1 000 000	308	1.3
Totals	24 717	100.0

1-13

Lord also detected overkill, saying the growth in planned shopping centers had outstripped growth in retail demand. Between 1972 and 1984 growth in US population was 13%, in total personal income 44%, and in planned shopping centers 86% with a roughly equal increase in retail floorspace. Lord drew the inescapable conclusion that to survive these new centers must draw trade from CBDs, as well as competing with each other. He noted that Charlotte, North Carolina with a retail market of 450 000 people has **93** centers built or planned, with a total area of 11 million square feet: there is one center of 100 000 square feet or more per 13 600 people; in Britain Lord noted one such centre per 190 000 people. There are powerful lessons here for the discussions below of retail trends in Britain and Germany.

1-14

Similar and partly related trends may be detected in offices. The Conservation Foundation (1987) provides a figure on existing and proposed offices according to location within an urban area. The data have been translated:

Table 1-2 : US Office Location in Selected Cities, 1986 (mill. sq. ft. and %)

| City | Existing | | | Under Construction | | |
	In CBD	Outside CBD	% Outside	In CBD	Outside CBD	% Outside
New York	125	62.5	33	4.5	9.5	68
Chicago	95	60	39	7	6	46
Houston	37	100	73	0.6	0.4	40
Los Angeles	20	115	85	2	11	85
Washington	60	60	50	6	15	71
Dallas	30	80	73	2.5	8.5	77
Boston	30	50	63	4	5	56
Denver	20	40	66	-	2	100
Atlanta	15	45	75	4	6	60
San Francisco	35	15	30	2	3	60
Miami	12.5	12.5	50	2	3	60
San Diego	10	15	60	2	-	0
Kansas City	10	15	60	2	3	60
New Orleans	4	1	25	0.5	0.5	50

The (rough) figures above, both of existing office space and that under construction, show a distinct movement away from the CBD toward other parts of the city. In terms of existing floorspace, the movement is less pronounced among the old eastern cities (New York and Chicago for example), though Washington shows an equal division between CBD and outer areas. This is probably because of height restrictions in Washington, where no tall buildings are allowed - the 'under construction' data show a flurry of building, 71% of which is outside the centre. The 'newer' cities (Houston, LA, Dallas, Atlanta for example) all show more than 70% of the existing stock is outside the CBD. When it comes to offices under construction, all but four cities (Chicago, Houston, San Diego and New Orleans) show over 50% being outside the CBD.

The quantity of existing office space is reflected in the ordering of the cities - New York with nearly 190 million square feet easily leads with Chicago (155 million) and Houston (137 million) following. However, it has to be remembered that the cities were selected - a brief glance shows the absence of Philadelphia, Baltimore, Pittsburgh... Of the cities listed, Washington has the largest construction programme followed by New York, Chicago and Los Angeles.

1-15
Schwartz (1984) listed what he called Downtown Vitalization. Los Angeles might come into this category. Some examples are provided in Table 1-3 on the next page. It is interesting that Schwartz included Santa Monica in his list (not included above because no investment cost was given); it has two department stores and 163 other stores. The interest is that a pedestrianised 'main' street near the ocean evidently was not enough to revive downtown - it appeared underused when visited in 1981.

Table 1-3 : Recent or Ongoing Downtown Retail Developments in some US Cities

City	Investment million $	Retail floor-space 1000ft^2	City	Investment million $	Retail floor-space 1000ft^2
Boston	120	40	Los Angeles	1 200	185
	400	385		360	63
Chicago	2 000	1 300	New York	1 000	293
	1 000	100		1 000	100
Detroit	50	85	Philadelphia	500	380
	427	544	Stamford	500	1 000
Harrisburg	150	115	WashingtonDC	150	150
Lexington	40	80		154	130

Note: Investment is for the whole scheme, often including large quantities of office space, hotel, etc. Source: Schwartz 1984

1-16
Morrill (1987) confirmed the trends away from the CBD with a study of the Seattle sub-region.

Table 1-4 : Change in Retail Trade 1954 to 1982, in $m at 1982 prices, for selected parts of the Seattle Area

Location	1954 sales	as % of total	1967	%	1982	%
Metropolis	3 928	100	7 239	100	9 140	100
King County	3 485	89	6 294	87	7 553	83
Seattle	2 812	72	3 930	54	3 080	34
Rest	673	17	2 364	33	4 473	59
Downtown Seattle	1 216	31	1 390	19	925	10

Not only did the CBD's share of retail expenditure fall from 31% to 10% over the period, but Seattle itself fell from 72% to 34%, the rest of King County climbing from a mere 17% to 59%.

1-17
Dent (1985) discussed the decentralisation of retailing in Atlanta, a city 'as close to free-market principles as possible'. The latter comment may be true for retailing, but the city, in association with some surrounding counties, has 'imposed' a cross-shaped metro network on the transport market of the sub-region. Retailing has been linked to freeway construction (Interstate sections of which would achieve considerable Federal funding), and this has induced a

precipitous downtown decline. Thus, in 1954 downtown's share of SMSA (Standard Metropolitan Statistical Area - in 1983 they became MSAs) sales was 28.9%; by 1977 this had fallen to 4.0%. At roughly the same period, the Atlanta suburbs had a 38% share in 1963 and a 69% share in 1977.

1-18
Dent then said 'With the fragmentation of local government in the Greater Atlanta metropolitan area (47 independent municipalities and 18 counties) each striving to preserve local planning efforts and autonomous control, with no central planning agency with region-wide authority to co-ordinate planning efforts, growth management is lacking. In case after case we are seeing the rise of additional physical growth around these "suburban downtowns".' Is this a foretaste of Britain's metropolitan authorities in a few years time?

1-19
As a final comment on the US retailing scene, Orski (1987) has illustrated a particular problem concerning one of the prime movers of change - the automobile. He noted that not only have CBDs suffered as office and retail functions have decentralised, but traffic congestion - the primary reason for relocation - is now no longer confined to city centres and radials connecting them with the suburbs, it now pervades the whole network. Often traffic on orbital roads (usually with much less capacity than radials) exceeds peak flows on the radials. This introduces a major dilemma for the road builders as property values along these orbitals are very high.

Canada

1-20
Hallsworth (1988), when discussing Canadian regional shopping centres, noted that the west was laissez-faire inclined while the east - typified by Ontario - preferred to plan its retail development. Developers in the east are happy with this, having built their centre, for it prevents excessive competition. Hallsworth continues 'Retail innovations tend to be drawn towards areas of high spending, attractive environment and good accessibility. In Canada, many such locations are downtown and have been made more attractive with inputs of public money.' Another significant difference from the US is the vital rôle that department stores play as 'anchors' in shopping centres: few free-standing department stores are built these days. Hallsworth suggests such stores can virtually become a surrogate for shopping centre development:

Table 1-5 : Canadian Department Stores by Province and City

Province	No. of department stores	City	No. of dept. stores
Ontario	324	Toronto	96
Quebec	157	Montreal	72
British Columbia	103	Vancouver	42
Alberta	88	Edmonton	34
Nova Scotia	38	Ottawa	33
Manitoba	37	Winnipeg	29
Saskatchewan	31	Calgary	26
New Brunswick	30		
Newfoundland	14		

Source: Statistics Canada (1987)

Related to the above Table, department store sales in the first six months of

1987 increased by 1.4% over the comparable period in 1986, while the retail sector as a whole increased by 7.6% in the first five months. So, while department stores remain important as anchors, their market share is decreasing.

1-21
Hallsworth understandably devoted much time in his report discussing the West Edmonton Mall, currently the largest non-traditional shopping centre in the world. The four Ghermezian brothers, who own the centre, moved from Iran to Montreal in the early 1950s and moved into Alberta in the 1960s when the oil boom began. Rising land prices are the principle explanation for the growth in their wealth. The wealth was not accompanied by shopping centre development expertise, however: the first stage of the centre had no car parking provision. Its growth to 1.2 million square feet still did not place it apart from other shopping centres in Edmonton, but this happened when the brothers decided to double the size of the centre and add a wide range of leisure facilities. By this stage the centre had parking for 20 000 cars, and 400 000 people might visit on a weekend. By 1985, the Edmonton Mall contained 11 department stores, 826 other stores and had reached 5 million square feet, almost twice the size of the next largest shopping centre of the kind in Torrance, California. A 1985 visitor survey showed that 30% came from Edmonton, 28% from elsewhere in Alberta, and 42% from beyond the Province.

1-22
Moving east, Toronto's city council has shifted its views about major retail developments (Shaw 1985). In 1956 there were 64 shopping centres accounting for about 2% of retail trade. By the mid-70s such centres accounted for over 23%. In Toronto as elsewhere in North America retail development followed residents to suburban areas (though the latter could also have followed the former after a certain period), creating a major impact on city centre stores. In 1980 the Official Plan signalled a significant change in attitude away from the laissez-faire 1970s toward positive planning for areas suffering from the development of the new shopping centres. Now new shopping centres are discouraged in certain areas to allow traditional shopping streets to survive (heresy to market economists), but they are encouraged where they complement existing retail provision. This has been achieved by rezoning purely for residential use or by adjusting densities. It is proposed that the local authority should gain the right to preview major projects of 1 800 m^2 or more, except in the city centre.

1-23
These new policies reflect Toronto's earlier policies of not providing support infrastructure in outlying areas, and of attempting, with some success, not to replicate US sprawl through higher density residential development. All these policies were oriented toward retaining a strong city centre. That centre was beginning to decline in the 1960s, but Thomson (1978) stated 'the trend was reversed after building the metro.' Toronto achieved fame among urban transport planners and economists through studies of the Yonge Street metro, which stimulated urban development of offices, shops and residential accommodation around its stations.

CONTINENTAL EUROPE

1-24
In Western Europe various countries show different responses to entrepreneurial demands for change. France was one of the earliest to echo North American trends of a move of some types of retailing from traditional 'downtowns' to suburban or exurban shopping malls. This was central government strategy to stimulate a sluggish retailing sector; when its consequences were fully realised there was a policy reversal (according to Davies [1984] restrictive legislation was introduced in 1973) with investment encouraged in traditional centres. These were also being improved environmentally through pedestrianisa-

11

tion, public transport improvements, and other measures. Davies also noted that West Germany had built the greatest quantity of superstores and hypermarkets, though the worst excesses in terms of suburban intrusion were associated with France:

Table 1-6 : Hypermarkets in Europe in 1976

Country	Number	Country	Number
W Germany	538	Netherlands	12
France	305	Finland	11
Belgium	72	Italy	8
Sweden	36	Spain	5
Austria	23	Denmark	4
Switzerland	22	UK	4

Source: MPC Associates 1976

France's restrictive legislation may have controlled the number of hypermarkets: Table 1-6 shows 305 in 1976. According to Davies, in 1981 there were 433 hypermarkets and superstores in France. France's restrictive policies were followed by Belgium in 1975 and The Netherlands in 1976, and disincentives were introduced in Italy, Luxembourg and Eire.

France

1-25
Delobez (1985) explored the development of shopping centres in the Paris region and gave some data for such centres in France. Thus, she enlarges on the data given above for centres larger than 3 000 m^2 GLA:

Table 1-7 : Rate of Opening of New Centres >3 000 m^2 Gross Land Area in France

		Before 1969	69-71	72-74	75-77	78-80	81-82
Cumulative	Paris Region	7	24	69	86	90	99
	France	22	110	239	316	359	386
Average no.	Paris Region	0.8	5.7	15	5.7	1.3	4.5
per year	France	2.4	29.3	43	25.7	14.3	13.5

Thus the rapid growth for the Paris Region ceased in 1975-77 and slowed down for France as a whole at that time.

1-26
Delobez's chapter is very informative and readers are referred to it for the detail which cannot be presented here. However, it has to be emphasized that there was a very brief 'Golden Age' from 1972 to 1974 which resulted in an increase in bankruptcy and a change from a beneficial result of opening and developing shopping centres to a negative one. Delobez says 'It became increasingly difficult for small shopkeepers to sell off businesses and retire because their profits were much reduced by competition from the new types of establishment' - these small traders were also well represented politically. Other aspects felt strongly in the Paris Region were multiplication of shopping

12

centres, loss of large areas of land, problems in conserving places of interest, and infrastructure demands of traffic.

1-27

The French government moved from laissez-faire toward repressive policies with the passing of the Royer law on 27 December 1973: Articles 28 to 35 deal with retail planning. What the law involved was, prior to applying for planning permission, the authorisation of a departmental commission of commercial planning (the CDUC, which included retail and industrial representatives) to build a shop of more than 1 500 m^2 in towns with more than 40 000 inhabitants and smaller areas elsewhere. Between 1974 and 1982 the CDUC refused almost half the total number of plans submitted, though the Minister, to whom appeal could be made, reversed some of these refusals so that 71% of submissions were eventually approved.

The Netherlands

1-28

In Holland too, concern was expressed at the number of new shopping centres that were built. Borchert (1985) describes the remedial action that was taken. In 1976 the Physical Planning Act was extended to make retail planning research compulsory at both local and regional levels. Yet, most commentators perceive the amendment as having been too late. Because the effects of the amendment were thought to be inadequate and too expensive for many authorities to be able to handle, Dutch planners put pressure on central government to issue new guidelines on retail development. An official committee made far-reaching recommendations in 1980, but the Minister did nothing, nor did the Minister's successor when the government changed. Eventually a conservative government rejected the proposals in 1983 and in fact suggested that the compulsory research should be simplified.

THIS RESEARCH PROJECT

1-29

The above brief introduction to the retail dilemma suggests there are several issues requiring clarification. They come to a head when considering retail policy in Britain and Germany. As was known at the inception of this research project, Germany had experienced a large number of out-of-centre shopping developments and had made some attempt to control them: was this enough, or would city centres deteriorate further? Britain was in a quite different position, having controlled out-of-centre developments for many years until the laissez-faire policies introduced by the first Thatcher Administration in 1979. What would the effects of this be? The study was established with an hypothesis which was German-oriented, though it was felt that its comprehension would benefit from a clearer understanding of trends in Britain:

> *Very substantial investment in German city centres will not be adequate to counter the competitive pressure from non-city centre (mainly out-of-town) mega shopping centres, and from down-market trends within parts of large and medium-sized city centres.*

As with many hypotheses, in retrospect it would probably have been differently phrased.

1-30

The objective, set up to meet the demands of the hypothesis, was to answer seven key questions:

13

a. How does the extent of outer shopping development in Britain compare with Germany and how far have pressures been resisted in each case?

b. Is the pressure for outer shopping development a phenomenon which cannot be stopped? (Does it cater for everyone's needs?)

c. While German public sector policy toward its city centres is to invest heavily in them, can they continue to resist the pressure for more outer centres, and their competition when built?

d. How far can pedestrianisation and public transport investment maintain the city centre's competitiveness? Are new policies needed?

e. When should an administration act to have most likelihood of success in countering such pressures?

f. What are the broad social (employment, accessibility, residential change, loss of services), economic, environmental and energetic consequences of a laissez-faire attitude toward outer centres? Who pays these costs?

g. Following from the answers to the above questions, are there in fact inalienable reasons for underpinning the city centre's economic viability?

Methodology

1-31

The *Bundesforschungsanstalt für Landeskunde und Raumordnung* in Bonn collaborated with TEST on the study. The BfLR agreed to advise TEST on all German aspects of the study and to provide data from the *Handels- und Gaststättenzählung* (HGZ) surveys; BfLR analyse those data for their own purposes. BfLR also helped select a suitable German student to undertake part of the literature search, preparing substantial abstracts of appropriate works, which in themselves had partly been chosen by BfLR.

1-32

The British literature review was extensive, and a primary input into the data base of major new British shopping centres and stores (other inputs were from the meetings referred to below). The data base was then analysed and extensively used in Chapter 2. Following on from the literature reviews (which helped to structure them) was a range of interviews and attendance at retail conferences in Britain and Germany. This was perhaps the most important source of information. The range of interviews was wide: major retailers; retail associations; research groups and individuals, mainly in universities; commercial research organisations like surveyors, economists, estate agents; and planners in local and higher-level government. Much secondary analysis was undertaken on the HGZ data. The full collection of information was then processed and written up to meet the format of this report.

Selection of Case Study Areas

1-33

It was decided the study should be at national and sub-regional/city levels. First, the United States and Canada were investigated to show the major origins of the 'retail revolution', and their effects. Then various European nations, predominantly Great Britain and the Federal Republic of Germany, were studied. Case studies were undertaken in subregions and cities. Much thought was given to where the most appropriate subregions/ cities might be; in the end the choice was as much influenced by the intrinsic interest of a location, or data availability, as anything else. Some degree of comparison was maintained between the two countries, however. Not in the order in which they appear in this book (because that order is alphabetical), Wolverhampton, part of the West Midlands sub-region, is paired with Dortmund, part of the Ruhrgebiet: echoes of a manufacturing industrial past which has partly disappeared; South Hampshire - including two major cities, Portsmouth and Southampton, and a number of district councils, is paired with the Köln-Bonn sub-region (two important cities again with several adjacent Kreise). And York is paired with Regensburg - two historic cities, largely untouched in the second world war, with a vital tourist trade, and relatively free-standing. Some additional comparisons are made between Regensburg and München, both in the same Land of Bayern, of quite different populations but with special policies that set them apart from most other German cities.

Report Structure

1-34
Following this Chapter 1, there are two pairs of four chapters, and two concluding chapters. Each pair concerns a nation and three case studies - so Great Britain (the Chapter following this one) is followed by Chapters 3-5 on South Hampshire, Wolverhampton and York respectively. The West German Chapter 6 is followed by Chapters 7-9 on Dortmund, Köln and Regensburg-München respectively. Chapter 10 pulls together, comparatively, the findings of the earlier chapters, while Chapter 11 considers the outcomes of various possible futures.

REFERENCES

Borchert, Johan (1985) Dutch Retail Planning Reversed **The Planner** 71,5 May
Conservation Foundation (1987) **State of the Environment: A View Toward the Nineties** Washington
Cox, Roger (1978) **Retailing** Plymouth MacDonald & Evans
Delobez, Annie (1985) The Development of Shopping Centres in the Paris Region in JA Dawson and J Dennis Lord (eds) **Shopping Centre Development: Policies and Prospects** London Croom Helm
Dent, Borden D (1985) Atlanta and the Regional Shopping Mall: the Absence of Public Policy in JA Dawson and J Dennis Lord (eds) **Shopping Centre Development: Policies and Prospects** London Croom Helm
Hallsworth, Alan (1988) **Regional Shopping Centres: some lessons from Canada** London TEST
HM Government (1985) **Lifting the Burden** Command 9571 London HMSO
Lord, J Dennis (1988) **Retail Decentralisation and CBD Decline in American Cities** Working Paper 8802 Institute for Retail Studies, University of Stirling
Morrill, Richard (1987) The Structure of Shopping in a Metropolis in **Urban Geography** 8,2 March-April pp97-128
MPC Associates (1976) **Hypermarket Expansion in Europe 1973-1976** Worcester
Orski, C Kenneth (1987) 'Managing' Suburban Traffic Congestion: A Strategy for Urban Mobility in **Transportation Quarterly** 41,4 pp457-476
Schwartz, Gail Garfield (1984) **Where's Main Street, USA?** Westport Connecticut Eno Foundation
Shaw, Gareth (1985) Shopping Centre Developments in Toronto in JA Dawson and J Dennis Lord (eds) **Shopping Centre Development: Policies & Prospects** London Croom Helm
Thomas, PG (1972) **Modern Retailing Techniques** London MacDonald & Evans
Thomson, JM (1978) **Great Cities and Their Traffic** Harmondsworth Penguin
Unit for Retail Planning Information (URPI)(1982) **List of Hypermarkets and Superstores** Reading
US Department of Commerce (1986) **Statistical Abstract of the United States 1987**
Wilkens, WH (ed)(1967) **Modern Retailing: evolution and revolution in the West European distributive trades** London Business Publications Ltd

GREAT BRITAIN

POPULATION :	AREA :
1975 54.7 million 1980 54.8 million 1985 54.8 million	244 100 km^2

POPULATION DENSITY :	PER CAPITA GROSS DOMESTIC PRODUCT
1975 230 persons per km^2 1980 230 persons per km^2 1985 232 persons per km^2	1975 3 080 ECU 1980 6 728 ECU 1985 10 521 ECU (in current prices) (1985 1 ECU = £0.58)

EMPLOYMENT :	UNEMPLOYMENT :
1975 25.5 million 1980 24.4 million 1985 24.0 million	1975 3.4 1980 6.9 1985 12.0 (% of civilian workforce)

CAR OWNERSHIP

1975	260
1980	277
1984	320

(per thousand population)

PASSENGER TRAFFIC BY MODE

	Cars	Buses	Rail
1975	300	55	35
1980	433	42	32
1985	430	42	36

(billion passenger kilometres)

FINAL CONSUMPTION BY HOUSEHOLDS, PER HEAD IN ECU 1985 (% of total)

Convenience Goods	1200 (19.2)	Health	86	(1.4)
Clothing/Footwear	447 (7.1)	Transport/		
Rent/Fuel/Power	1271 (20.3)	Communication	1028	(16.4)
Household Goods/		Education/Recr	588	(9.4)
Furniture	422 (6.7)	Misc Goods &		
		Services	1209	(19.3)

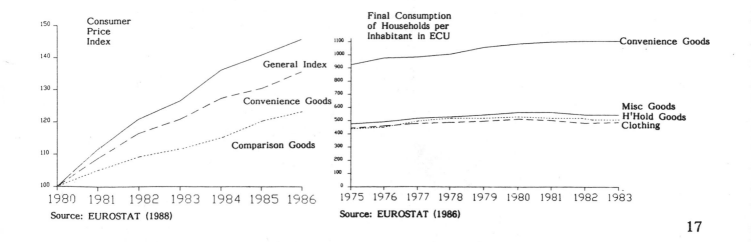

Source: EUROSTAT (1988)

Source: EUROSTAT (1986)

Chapter 2 : Great Britain
Chapter Structure

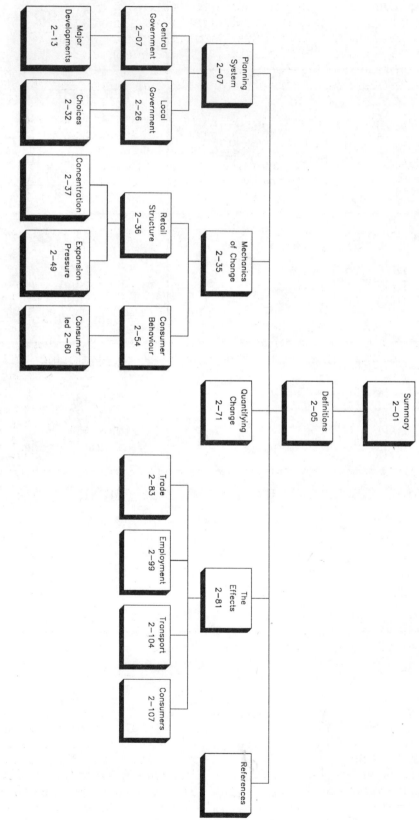

- Summary 2-01
- Definitions 2-05
- Quantifying Change 2-71

- Planning System 2-07
  - Central Government 2-07
    - Major Developments 2-13
  - Local Government 2-26
    - Choices 2-32

- Mechanics of Change 2-35
  - Retail Structure 2-36
    - Concentration 2-37
    - Expansion Pressure 2-49
  - Consumer Behaviour 2-54
    - Consumer led 2-60

- The Effects 2-81
  - Trade 2-83
  - Employment 2-99
  - Transport 2-104
  - Consumers 2-107

- References

Note : numbers refer to paragraphs

2 BRITAIN

SUMMARY

2-01

After defining a number of terms and shop classifications used throughout the
British section, this chapter outlines some of the changes that have affected
retail planning.   Changes in Central Government policies are considered first,
and it is shown that there has been an increasing adherence to market principles.   On a number of occasions it has been stated that the planning system
should facilitate development wherever possible, and this has had the effect of
shifting the burden of proof from the developer to the local planning authority.   The rôle of quantified analysis of the effects of a retail proposal has
been weakened.   Strong political support in rural areas has meant that the current Government is less keen to see development in the open countryside, specially in Green Belt areas.   These changes have altered the context within which
local planning authorities operate.   Many remain committed to established theo-
ries of the shopping hierarchy, together with the concentration of retailing in
town centres that they entail.   While some local authorities have thus seen
retailing as a social as well as an economic issue, others (usually those with
little existing town-centre retailing) have been keen to embrace the Government's 'free-market' principles, and have allowed out-of-centre development.

2-02

The structure of the retailing sector has also undergone substantial change in
the last decade.   The most significant trend is the concentration of ownership
expressed in fewer but larger firms.   The growth of major retail empires has
resulted from economies of scale, and expansion by merger, takeover or organic
growth.   Economies of scale, and increases in operating efficiency have led to
high profit levels, which in turn have been used to fund further expansion
rather than being passed on to the consumer in terms of lower prices.   Often
firms have expanded out-of-centre because of the availability of space, and the
ability to employ efficient methods.   Once one retailer has gone out-of-centre,
and enjoys lower operating costs, competitors must follow or lose trade.   High
levels of profit have made the retail sector an attractive sector for investment by both developers and retailers, and developers have been quick to 'cash
in' on trends toward out-of-centre retailing.   Many large out-of-centre retail
proposals and developments are now developer- rather than retailer- led.   Many
of these changes have been aided by shifts in consumer behaviour.   Higher car
ownership, rising incomes, specially among the more affluent, increasing
amounts of leisure time and trends towards greater equality of the sexes have
all changed the established patterns of shopping.

2-03

The effect of all these changes has been an unprecedented pressure for retail
development.   In many town centres, landowners, developers and local authorities have all been keen to redevelop, refurbish and improve shopping facilities, partly in response to rising consumer expenditure, but also because out-
of-centre development threatens to divert trade from unattractive centres.
While recent development activity in town centres has been high, in terms of
the future, the volume of proposed out-of-centre schemes dwarfs that proposed
in town centres.   While only a small amount of this floorspace will be realised, it is clear that interest has shifted strongly toward more profitable
out-of-centre schemes.   The off-centre retail developments that already exist
have been shown to have effects on traditional shopping centres.   While in some
cases (eg Newcastle, Wolverhampton, Southampton) new developments nearby have
prompted town centre improvement, in many cases (eg Nine Elms superstore, Brent
Cross Shopping Centre) the effect has been to erode the trade of existing

shops. This in turn has had an effect on employment. Far from actually creating employment as many out-of-centre retailers and developers claim, such stores may actually decrease employment as turnover per employee rises. Added to that is the fact that employment in new retail developments is often highly polarised in terms of skill and sex, and there is little chance for career advancement.

2-04
Out-of-centre developments cater primarily for those who are able to use cars; their dispersed locations make them difficult adequately to serve using public transport. As well as reducing access for those without cars, the trend towards out-of-centre shopping thus encourages higher levels of car use, longer trips, and therefore higher traffic levels. While, internally at least, new forms of retailing such as superstores offer those consumers able to reach them a wide range of goods, externally the choice may be reduced as the number of retailers in an area falls, and the trend toward monopoly increases. The negative effects of all these trends are often concentrated among the most disadvantaged types of consumer.

DEFINITIONS

2-05
A number of standard definitions are commonly used throughout the literature. For the sake of clarity, these are set out below.

1. SUPERSTORES are large, self-service outlets, selling predominantly convenience goods. They are often developed in out-of-centre locations, and tend to be highly oriented toward the car user. They have large amounts of surface level car parking, and are invariably one storey buildings. Some superstore developments have been built in or near existing town centres, while others have been included as the basis of district shopping centres, although their catchments extend far beyond the limits of the area in question. Such stores usually have a net floorspace of least 2500 m^2 . Foodstores smaller than this are usually refered to as supermarkets.

2. RETAIL WAREHOUSES originally evolved from the wholesale 'cash and carry' type of operation. Initially furniture, carpet and DIY retailers adopted this format, often selling from converted factories, garages or even cinemas, frequently on industrial estates. Gradually however, such retailers have developed their own type of premises and now often locate on major urban radial routes. The range of retailers using retail warehouses has grown, and now includes companies such as Habitat and Marks & Spencer as well as longer established retail warehouse operators such as MFI, Texas Homecare or Allied Carpets. Retail warehouses usually have a net floorspace of at least 2500 m^2, and are increasingly being developed close to one another in groups, or in specially designed 'retail parks', often sharing parking facilities.

3. HYPERMARKETS tend to be a hybrid of retail warehouse and superstore type developments. Floorspace is divided between grocery and durable goods. The first British out-of-centre development was a Carrefour hypermarket in Caerphilly, South Wales. More recent such stores include the Tesco at Neasden in north London, and a series of joint ventures such that of Sainsbury and British Home Stores (operating as SavaCentre) where two retailers share the same selling space in one building. Hypermarkets usually have a minimum net floorspace of 5000 m^2.

4. REGIONAL SHOPPING CENTRES are purpose-built centres with a range of outlets comparable to those found in town centres. They may be located in town centres, or, as is increasingly being proposed, out-of-centre, in

suburban or semi-rural locations. They are sometimes referred to as 'Mega Centres'. Regional Shopping Centres are defined as purpose built centres which total more than 50 000 m^2 (net). Existing examples include Brent Cross Shopping Centre in North London, and the MetroCentre in Gateshead.

2-06

In addition, two terms are frequently used to classify type of good. **Convenience** goods generally comprise food, drink, tobacco, and other consumables. **Comparison** goods, also known as durable goods, are other types of product which are bought less frequently than convenience goods, and include clothes, footwear, jewellery, domestic hardware, books and records, electrical goods, furniture and carpets. A distinction between these types of good is made because of the different shopping patterns that each creates.

THE PLANNING SYSTEM

THE ROLE OF CENTRAL GOVERNMENT

2-07

The last decade has seen a realignment of many Central Government policies in Britain. The emphasis on 'free market' principles has been reinforced, and an 'enterprise culture' encouraged by the removal of many constraints and disincentives. Policies relating to retail development have been included in this reorientation. The Department of the Environment has been keen to stress that the planning system should not inhibit competition, and that local authorities should adequately demonstrate why a development should not take place. *Laissez faire* principles have been tempered only by issues such as the Green Belt, where the Government has been under pressure to restrain development, or where the traffic effects of a development are particularly bad.

2-08

As early as 1977, Development Control Policy Notes (DCPN) 13 and 14, which related to large stores and retail warehouses, indicated that it was not the rôle of planning to prevent or stimulate competition among retailers. However, the Notes did add that the effects of a development on the established shopping pattern should be carefully measured, and the benefits or disbenefits calculated for the community as a whole. It was also pointed out that the effects of a large retail development could extend far beyond a given local authority boundary: in such cases, local authorities should jointly consider the implications and merits of a proposal.

2-09

These Notes gradually became less important as a series of circulars and statements were issued to clarify the Government's policy. Circular 22/80 initiated the shift in favour of 'free market' development. It stated that local authorities should always 'grant planning permission ... unless there are clear cut reasons for refusal'. However Circular 22/84, a memorandum on local and structure plans, appeared to recognise the harmful effects that large developments could have. It stated that planning policies should be related to the needs of vulnerable groups such as ethnic minorities and the elderly, and suggested that shopping policies should consider 'the need for convenient access to adequate shopping facilities for all sections of the population, the requirements of the retailing industry, the effects on existing shopping centres, and the relieving of traffic congestion.' It went on to say that local authorities should be aware of the effects of a development on the continuing viability of town centres.

2-10

The *laissez faire* principles of Circular 22/80 have been reinforced in subsequent advice. Circular 14/85 repeated that there is 'always a presumption in favour of allowing applications for development ... unless that development would cause demonstrable harm to interests of acknowledged importance.' The meaning of 'acknowledged importance' is left open to question. The circular relegates statutory development plans to the position of 'one, but only one' of the considerations relating to a planning proposal. Even less importance is attached to development plans if they do not deal with new forms of development or the promotion of new employment.

2-11

A Parliamentary Written Answer of 5 July 1985 further elaborated the Government's emerging policies. Again it was stressed that the planning system should not inhibit competition, stating that 'the public needs a wide range of shopping facilities and the benefits from the competition between them.' While local authorities should take into account other recent and proposed developments in the locality, it was argued that only rarely would cumulative impact become a significant issue, and only when the viability of a centre **as a whole** was threatened.

2-12

Although local authorities' control over development has been weakened by Government Circulars, the Secretary of State has always reserved his right to make the final decision on any large development. The requirement that the Department of the Environment should be informed of any departure from approved structure plan policies has been complemented by Circular 21/86 which states that local authorities should refer to the Department of the Environment applications which include gross retail floorspace of 250 000 ft^2 (23 325 m^2) or more, where the authority wishes to grant consent. In addition, the Secretary of State has issued a number of Article 10 Directions (in Greater Manchester and the West Midlands for example) which prevent local authorities from granting planning permission for a given development. Thus while local authority planning controls have been weakened, the Government has retained what could be described as a safety net which it can use to control large developments if it so wishes - either to permit or refuse. However, some observers have criticised the apparently arbitrary way that the Department of the Environment calls in proposals. Thus despite pleas from surrounding Boroughs, LPAC and LSPU, the application to increase the size of Brent Cross shopping centre by over 40% was not called-in, and was subsequently granted permission by the London Borough of Barnet (LSPU 1987a).

Planning Guidance on Major Retail Developments

2-13

In September 1987, the Department of the Environment issued its draft Planning Guidance on Major Retail Development. The Guidance, which superseded DCPNs 13 and 14, reiterated the Parliamentary Answer of 5 July 1985, but also stressed a number of other important points. The note was formally issued in January 1988. The guidance stated that detailed calculation of retail impact is not usually necessary since the effects of development can be judged on the scale of the proposal and the character of nearby town centres. This statement increased the statistical vacuum created by the cancellation of the 1981 Census of Distribution by reducing the importance of quantitative analysis as a means of determining an application. Many observers have recognised the uncertainties that are created by the lack of reliable data, and have called for policies based on an accurate assessment of the impact of different forms of retail development (see Hillier Parker 1988, described below). Cole (Planning 747 4 December 1987 page 5) criticised the 'cursory approach' that was being engendered, arguing that it would increase conflicts of opinion, together with the potential margins of error. A report by Reynolds (cited in Planning [1987]) summarised the views of a wide range of retailers, consultants and academics. There was almost unanimous agreement that the lack of retail information was making it almost impossible accurately to assess the likely impact of a new shopping development.

2-14

While the Guidance welcomed town centre development and refurbishment, specially where it used derelict land and created new employment, it has been criticised for not expressing a stronger commitment that would foster town centre confidence and investment (see for example Hampson 1988, Davies 1988). Reacting to pressure from rural constituencies, the Guidance also pledged the Government's commitment to maintaining the Green Belt. As well as refusing to allow retail development here, it suggested it should not be permitted in open countryside either. In 'exceptional' circumstances, such developments would be permitted where they resulted in reclamation of derelict land and other environmental improvements.

2-15

The Association of Metropolitan Authorities (Planning 751 15 January 1988 page 5) criticised the Guidance for failing to provide a consistent indication of Government Policy. In particular the AMA argued that it will be 'difficult to judge how much weight the department intends should be accorded to the many conflicting statements contained in the guidance note.' It suggested that the guidance should have made some reference to the need for cross-boundary impact assessment, and the rôle of unitary development and structure plans in providing a context for decision making. The Association of District Councils also criticised the ambiguity of some aspects of the note, and complained that it rested on the assumption that changes in retailing are wholly beneficial. the London Planning Advisory Committee (LPAC 1988) suggested that the terms vitality and viability should be defined, arguing that trade impacts as low as 10% could create uncertainty, leading to disinvestment and major store closure.

2-16

Hillier Parker (Planning 1988c) questioned the Government's commitment to retailing as a means of urban regeneration. 'Even in the Government's **Action for Cities** programme which the Prime Minister has claimed is a comprehensive approach to inner cities, retail development is not identified as a way of assisting this programme. Retailing ... is the most dynamic sector of the economy and its benefits should be harnessed for deprived areas.' LPAC (1988) argued that town centre regeneration has a major rôle to play in arresting inner-city decline. Davies (1988) suggested that the Department of Trade and Industry and the Department of the Environment were pursuing conflicting policies, one aiming to regenerate the inner city, the other to free the retail market from planning constraints.

2-17

A survey of 14 major retail groups (Hillier Parker 1988) reflected concern about the lack of guidance from Central Government. In particular, the survey showed that there is a need for basic research to determine the levels of out-of-centre retailing that can be accommodated without seriously damaging town centres. One retailer, the John Lewis Partnership, argued that a set of criteria should be established against which out-of-centre developments could be evaluated. It is significant that many retailers felt that they were not the initiators of the out-of-centre movement, but that the lack of guidance was partly to blame because of the uncertainties it created. The Director of Research and Expansion (an uncompromising title) at John Lewis Partnership argued that 'retail planning is too important to be left to retailers', arguing that what might be in the best interests of the retailer might not be in the best interests of town centres (Hampson 1988).

2-18

Indicative of the concern about the lack of retail planning guidance has been the response of the 'Oxford Group', a group of retailers, developers and investors who meet regularly under the auspices of the Oxford Institute of Retail Management (Davies 1988). The Group argue that there is a need for clarification regarding retail planning's rôle in shaping the future retail environment. Will decentralisation continue apace, or will a more balanced process be encouraged with new investment in town centres? The Group also question the Government's inner city programme's application for city centres.

2-19

Davies (1986) argued that Britain lacked an overall policy of land-use controls designed to 'deal consistently and rationally with the entire spectrum of retail trades.' He cited a jumble of policies relating to retailing from a number of different Government departments, the Department of the Environment being among the least prominent. Davies suggested that the crisis in retail planning had been caused by a change of **attitudes** on the part of Government, but not a change in the **planning framework** which had to implement its wishes. In other words, the Government had relaxed the climate for developers and retailers while the implementation mechanisms of structure and local plans were (and are) still geared to strict enforcement of the retail hierarchy.

2-20

PMA, a property research and information company, argued that there was unanimous agreement among retailers, investors and developers that there was a need for clear policy guidance at national, regional and subregional level (Planning 1987 Vol 745 20 November 1987 p7). PMA's call was echoed by the National Economic Development Office (1988) who argued that such a framework of guidelines was essential if a correct balance between in- and out-of-centre retailing was to be achieved. At a national level, the Planning Inspectorate would be issued with a clear set of strategic criteria with which they could evaluate proposals. Local authorities needed to combine forces to assess current and demanded levels of shopping provision, while counties should coordinate demand for new floorspace in their area. LPAC (1988) warned that by the beginning of the 1990s there could be an oversupply of retail floorspace in London. This would affect the performance of the less dynamic existing centres, especially in Inner and East London.

2-21

Analysis of planning appeals is not necessarily a good indicator of the relative strengths of developers and local authorities. While more appeals might be expected to be successful as Central Government policies become more *laissez faire*, in fact this may not be so as local authorities adjust their decisions to the realities of the political climate, and as developers choose their sites more carefully. Thus many local authorities give consent for developments they might otherwise have refused, knowing that if they lose any subsequent planning appeal they face having costs awarded against them, and will have little influence over the final details of a schemes. By cooperating, they may at least secure some form of planning gain. Pragmatic local decision making can therefore reduce the number of applications going to appeal. On the other hand, developers increasingly concentrate on those sites which are most likely to gain consent outright, or which are likely easily to gain permission at appeal. The avoidance of controversial sites (such as those in Green Belts) may increase the appeal success rate irrespective of Government Policy. Thus Lee Donaldson and Sons (1988) suggest that the ratio of superstore appeals being approved to those being refused increased from 1:3 in 1985 to 1:1 in 1988, partly reflecting developers' careful choice of sites and partly because of the shift in the burden of proof to the local authority.

2-22

An analysis of planning appeal decisions was undertaken as part of the RTPI's retailing study (1988). It was found that the Secretary of State, as the DoE guidance might suggest, generally decides in favour of development. Occasionally the Secretary of State has dismissed an appeal on the grounds that it conflicted with an aim of a local plan. While lower levels of trading impact were not grounds for dismissal, the loss of an anchor retailer in a larger centre was often regarded as significant. The RTPI found that some decisions indicated that the DoE regarded superstore development as a source of new employment. The RTPI disputed this (as do TEST below). One of the most common reasons for appeal dismissal appeared to be traffic problems.

2-23

Against trends which would indicate a reduction in local authority control and a freeing of the market, local planning authorities recently welcomed the dismissal at appeal of the Centre 21 proposals near Leicester. A total of six out-of-centre retail proposals were turned down by the Environment Secretary on the grounds of the impact that they would have on the vitality and viability of the town centre, and because they conflicted with approved Structure Plan policies (Planning 1988b). Even more recently, proposals for a 100 000 m^2 regional shopping centre to complement the existing 50 000 m^2 retail warehouse at Cribbs Causeway near Bristol were dismissed at public inquiry because of the potential impact on city centre retailing (Cheeseright 1988). Many local authorities will see these decisions as supporting their opposition to out-of-centre retailing, while indicating what the Government means by vitality and viability.

2-24

The Government has also influenced the nature of retail development by its designation of Enterprise Zones with their relaxed planning control. Thomas and Bromley (1987) argued that while many district authorities wanted to protect existing retail centres by limiting the permitted retail floorspace in an Enterprise Zone, often the Secretary of State, believing that industrial development was unlikely, modified the floorspace limits to allow relatively generous retail development. Retailers and developers have reacted to the creation of Enterprise Zones in a number of different ways. In the Gateshead Enterprise Zone, an integrated retail warehouse park quickly developed into a regional shopping centre with associated leisure facilities. In Dudley, the Merry Hill retail warehouse scheme is currently being joined by a regional shopping centre (which required normal planning consent). In Swansea Enterprise Zone at least 20 retail warehouses have developed in a largely unco-ordinated way, many with their own car parks and beyond walking distance of each other.

2-25

The Department of the Environment recently began to issue guidance (see for example Department of the Environment n.d.) for metropolitan district councils drawing up Unitary Development Plans following abolition of the Metropolitan County Councils in 1986. While much of the advice echoed that already given in the Planning Guidance on Major Retail Developments, it did emphasise that town centres remain the focus of retail provision, and that other developments should not threaten their viability. It was also stressed that retailing could play a major rôle in achieving urban regeneration.

2-25

In summary, it may be seen that Government policy and guidance have created an uncertain climate for local decision making:

* impact analysis has been made less significant by the cancellation of the 1981 Census of Distribution (the most recent such census being in 1971), and the reduced importance now attached to quantitative analysis.
* Local authorities have been advised to encourage town centre retail development, but have had control over new out-of-centre development reduced. They can now only sustain a refusal on a limited range of grounds, many of which are not shopping related.
* The burden of proof has moved from the developer to the local authority, while their ability to obtain such proof has been reduced.
* Although local control has been reduced, Central Government has reserved its right to determine whether large retail developments take place or not.
* Lack of guidance is illustrated by the importance attached to the outcome of particular appeals, and their use as a form of precedent.

THE ROLE OF LOCAL GOVERNMENT

2-26

There are two main levels of local authorities in England and Wales. The higher tier is the County Council, whose responsibility is to prepare Structure Plans setting strategic planning policies for the whole of its area, its residential and commercial interests. Each county is divided into a number of districts which prepare local plans covering particular areas such as town centres. The situation has been complicated by the 1985 Local Government Act which abolished Metropolitan County Councils. Metropolitan districts will prepare Unitary Development Plans, adding strategic issues to local issues. Development plans, be they structure, local or unitary development plans are used as a basis for the processing of applications for planning permission.

2-27

Local authorities inevitably act within the context set by the Department of the Environment. Policy changes described above have challenged some long held beliefs, and local authorities have to choose between accepting the new 'free market' and maintaining the status quo, each with their own consequences. The result has been ill-coordinated: some local authorities with substantial town centres resist all forms of non-central development, while others, with less of an interest in town centre protection have welcomed large new development (see for example Eastleigh in South Hampshire, Sandwell in the West Midlands, and Selby in North Yorkshire, described in Chapters 3, 4 and 5 respectively) as a means of gaining a slice of the retail cake. Competition between local authorities lessens the rôle of planning and gives developers an added advantage. The size of many recent retail proposals means that local authorities are having to make decisions about developments which have strategic implications (LSPU 1987a). Many authorities lack the expertise and resources adequately to deal with such applications, specially when the resources available to development companies are considered.

2-28

Gibbs (1985) showed how planners' attitudes toward new forms of retailing changed over time (see also Sumner & Davies 1978). In the early 1970s, the first hypermarkets and superstores were appearing in the UK, and were met with outright opposition from local authorities. This reaction was partly because this type of retailing was new, but also because it did not sit within, and indeed threatened the existence of, the shopping hierarchy. Gibbs described structure plan policies which often contained a presumption against out-of-

26

centre development, and which were subsequently modified by the Secretary of State to read 'generally not allowed.'

2-29
When respected High Street retailers such as Sainsbury and WH Smith began to experiment with superstore and retail warehouse formats, so the concept of out-of-centre retailing became less transitory, and was accepted as a permanent feature of the retail scene. At the same time, Gibbs argued, planners realised that the impact of such shopping developments had not been as great as had been anticipated. She also suggested that, given the reality that such development was going to occur, local authorities have been prepared to compromise in order to gain as much from it as possible. Thus superstore development has been used as a means of reclaiming derelict land, has been justified on employment creation grounds, and has been used to form the anchor for so-called district shopping centres. With the lack of strategic planning, local authorities have often accepted or even encouraged development in order to preempt neighbouring districts. However, while local authorities have been prepared to compromise, they have tried to fit development within the existing retail hierarchy. Thus superstores have often been directed to sites in or adjoining existing town or district centres, retail warehouses enouraged to locate on the edge of existing shopping areas, or viewed as entirely new centres **within** the hierarchy.

2-30
Local authority plans have traditionally catered for a hierarchy of shopping facilities based on Central Place Theory. This strategy reflected both the natural form of urban areas, and the structure of the retail industry. Burt et al (1983) argued that retailing gravitated toward Central Place Theory because of the high share taken by small, independent companies, the fact that few national chains existed, and the fact that all sectors of business were relatively buoyant. However, as the structure of the retailing industry has undergone radical change, pressures have grown for locational patterns which no longer reflect Central Place Theory. Local authorities have been caught in a dilemma, having to decide whether retailing is primarily an economic or a social issue. The common response has been adherence to the original shopping hierarchy, and the reluctant accommodation of new forms of retailing where they are otherwise unavoidable.

2-31
Burt et al criticised planners for reacting to change rather than planning for it. Schiller (1986) argued that three discernible 'waves' of retail decentralisation meant that central place theory is no longer applicable. Instead of a town centre sitting at the top of a hierarchy, he argued that a differentiation of function had occurred with out-of-centre retail warehouses and superstores playing a separate and complementary rôle.

Choices for Local Authorities?

2-32
King (1987) amply described the lack of choice facing local authorities. He argued that authorities faced three options when attempting to maintain the retail hierarchy.

1 The decline of smaller centres could be accepted and shop premises rationalised into non-retail uses. At the same time, the town centre's economic base would have to be widened by increasing the amount of office or industrial space to make it less dependent on shopping.

2 Maintain full commitment to the existing hierarchy. King argued that the result of this strategy was inevitable decline of both local centres, and the town centre (a decline that might be described by Government as

negligent and as justifying further reductions in local authority control).

3   The final option was the continued attraction of retail development to the city centre in an attempt to retain the custom of the more affluent. In the medium term, he argued, such a strategy would lead to an over-provision of retail space, and the town centre would suffer decline as it competed with the advantages enjoyed by out-of-centre development.

2-33

King pragmatically concluded that the individual local authority does not have the means to prevent the change that the Government has encouraged. With continued out-of-centre development, local authorities have to accept decline, and plan so that it can be managed, and its worst effects minimised.

2-34

Those local authorities who have resisted pressure for out-of-centre retailing have faced the prospect of losing cases at appeal, and have seen their own town centre trade being drawn to new out-of-centre developments in surrounding districts. In such a situation, many local authorities have adopted a policy of 'damage limitation' by allowing a limited amount of such development to take place in carefully selected locations, where effects on existing trade will be minimised. The end result is that few if any local authorities are able to withstand pressure for out-of-centre development.

MECHANICS OF CHANGE

2-35

Changes in the attitudes of Central Government, and the subsequent growing weakness and fractionalism of local Government have altered the context within which retailing has to operate. Controls which ensured the continuation of the retail hierarchy have now been weakened, and the market is now able to react to fundamental changes in the structure of the retail sector, changes in the demands of the consumer, and changes in urban transport. None of these changes is mutually exclusive. Retailing is organic: it is part cause and part effect of all these factors. The market is now increasingly free to realise the changes that have occurred during the past two decades. In doing so, it has the potential to destroy the urban morphology that it has been instrumental in creating during the last two millenia. Although the shopping hierarchy has been enshrined as a foundation of social and retail planning, Central Place Theory is in fact a model of the market as it operated until relatively recently. Now that market conditions have changed, we face a choice between following current market trends and losing the heritage and equal access afforded by town centres, or maintaining town centres and all they represent.

CHANGING RETAIL STRUCTURE

2-36

Table 2-1 summarises retail change between 1961 and 1984. The clearest pattern evident from this table is the lack of comparability between different years. Frequent reclassification of shop type means that time series analysis is virtually impossible. Whether this is a deliberate tactic designed to deter comparisons is uncertain, but the end result is an aggravation of the shortcomings of retail statistics already described. Given these reservations, a number of observations can be made from Table 2-1. The first is the fall in the number of outlets. Overall there was a 36% decrease in their number between 1961 and 1984. This trend was most marked among grocery retailers where the decrease was as high as 60% up to 1976. A fall in the number of outlets has been paralled by an increase in retail turnover. In real terms, turnover increased by over a third between 1961 and 1984. The most rapid drop in the number of outlets, and

Table 2-1 : Number and Turnover of Retail Outlets, 1961 – 1984 and % change (1984 prices)

Type of Trade	Number of Outlets (X10³) 1961	1966	1976	1984	Turnover £10⁹ 1961 Current	1961 Real	1966 Current	1966 Real	1976 Current	1976 Real	1984 Current	1984 Real
Groceries & Provision Dealers	143.0	123.4	60.0		2.355	16.350	2.908	16.890	7.586	16.990		
Food Retailers				106.8							31.360	31.360
Other Food Retailers	113.8	104.4			1.728	11.990	2.081	12.091				
Other Food Retailers & Off Licences			66.0						4.064	9.103		
Drink, Confectionery & Tobacco				57.3							8.686	8.686
Confectioners, News-Agent, Tobacconists	69.5	63.3	44.0		0.798	5.542	1.046	6.094	2.515	5.634		
Clothing & Footwear	86.4	83.2			1.367	9.487	1.741	10.115				
Footwear, Clothing & General Textiles			61.0						3.869	8.666		
Clothing, Footwear & Leather Goods				56.0							7.476	7.476
Household Goods	66.0	69.8	50.0		0.987	6.854	1.327	7.710	4.007	8.976		
Furniture & Other Household Goods				57.1							12.000	12.000
Other Non-Food	54.5	57.5	57.0	48.0	0.668	4.639	0.988	5.740	3.656	8.189	6.869	6.869
Mixed Retail				10.9							14.787	14.787
Other Businesses with Retail Activities			38.0						2.592	5.806		
Hire and Repair				6.9							1.163	1.163
General Stores	3.5	2.8			0.930	6.458	1.041	6.048				
Dept Stores, Other Gen Stores, & Mail Order			24.0						7.068	15.832		
Total	539.7	504.4	400.0	343.2	8.833	61.340	11.132	64.677	35.358	79.201	82.342	82.342
% Annual Change		-1.3	-2.1	-1.8			5.2	1.1	21.8	2.2	16.6	0.5
Turnover per outlet in real terms (£X10³)	192.6	217.3	335.6	406.6								

Sources : Central Office of Information 1973(p244), 1979(p237), 1987(p267)

the fastest growth of retail turnover both occurred between 1966 and 1976. An inference from Table 2-1 might be that concentration was occurring in the retail sector as numerous smaller stores were replaced by fewer larger ones, in turn reflecting the decline of the independent retailer and the concomitant growth of the multiple. These issues are explored in more detail in the next section.

Concentration of Ownership and Economies of Scale

2-37

One of the most significant trends within the retail sector is that of concentration of ownership. Davies (1984) showed that in the decade between 1961 and 1971, the total number of shops declined by approximately 13%, and that in the 1970s, while the number of outlets fell by almost a third, the number of firms which had only one outlet fell by 40%. Davies argues that the most severe period of reduction in the number of outlets is now past, and that the 1980s have been characterised by rationalisation and store closure among the multiple retailers who are continually moving toward larger operating units. Broadbridge & Dawson (1988) highlighted the decline in the number of retail firms since 1961. By 1984 they found there had been a 35% reduction in the number of retail firms, rising to a decline of 53% in the number of single outlet grocery firms. They found that, between 1982 and 1986, the number of retail firms decreased by 6.9%. Table 2-2 amply illustrates these trends by summarizing data regarding Tesco's retail operations. The net result therefore is a concentration in ownership, and an increase in average store size.

Table 2-2 : Summary of Tesco's retail operation, 1977-1986

Year	Number of Stores	Av. Net Area[1] of New Stores	Av Net Area[1] of All Stores	Total Net Area[1]	Employees[2]	Turnover (£M)[3]	Turnover per Empl(£)	Profit (before tax) (£M)
1977	722	1052	672	484 800	28 413	1122.1	39 491	48.3
1978	673	2621	746	503 800	30 841	1399.0	45 361	42.0
1979	571	2070	924	527 100	35 302	1610.4	45 620	50.5
1980	552	1649	1045	579 400	39 862	1720.4	43 159	41.0
1981	554	2160	1148	638 200	38 809	1820.7	46 913	35.6
1982	544	2056	1231	672 000	40 421	1795.0	44 407	38.4
1983	489	2852	1418	692 800	40 377	1946.5	48 208	45.7
1984	461	2611	1492	686 900	40 363	2101.5	52 066	54.6
1985	441	3425	1567	691 800	42 020	2310.3	54 981	62.6
1986	395	3321	1773	699 900	43 447	2449.4	56 376	89.7

Notes : Turnover and Profit are in 1981 prices
   [1] all floorspace is in m^2
   [2] full time equivalent
   [3] net of VAT
Source : Tesco Plc 1986

2-38

Economies of scale have thus encouraged a small number of retailers to dominate each sub-sector. It has been estimated (Jefferys 1954), that at the turn of the century independent retailers accounted for 80% of the grocery market. However, by the late 1980s, the five largest supermarket chains (J Sainsbury, Tesco, Dee Corporation, Argyll and Asda) together accounted for 52% of all grocery sales (The Times 26 October 1987), and J Sainsbury and Tesco alone for just under a third (Broadbridge & Dawson 1988). Within the DIY and hardware sector, 10 000 goods shops and 3000 hardware stores closed between 1982 and 1984, while Texas Homecare opened branches at the rate of one every ten days, and in 1986 the turnover of DIY retailers grew by over 20% (Parkes 1987c). In 1987, it was estimated that Sainsbury's held 9.7% of the grocery market, while Marks & Spencer held 16% of the clothing market and 5% of the footwear market (Money Observer 1987).

2-39
Companies may expand operations by growing organically, or by takeovers. In recent years, high 'monopolistic' profits have made retailing an attractive area for investment from outside; at the same time, these profits have given companies the means to expand quite rapidly. In the grocery sector, Asda have undertaken a programme of store openings which has taken them from simply regional to national coverage. Tesco provide an example of a company expanding its representation by takeover. One area where the company was underrepresented was Yorkshire, where a number of regional supermarket chains held a substantial share of the market. Rather than attempt to infiltrate this market by a series of store openings which would have to compete with existing, and successful stores, Tesco decided to make a takeover bid for Hillards. This would increase Tesco's market penetration in the area from 3.5% to nearer 10%. Despite strong opposition from Hillards, and the fact that the company had proved itself to be successful, profitable and innovative in its own right, the takeover eventually succeeded, and 101 years of independence ended (Brasier 1987, Pegano 1987a, Parkes 1987b). The Argyll Group have employed a similar tactic to expand and improve its image in one move. By taking over the British chain of Safeway supermarkets, it was able to convert its existing Presto stores to the up-market Safeway format (McRae 1987).

2-40
Concentration of ownership may be less visible. A common tactic is for a company to own a range of different types of outlet within one or more subsectors, allowing them to spread risk, to reach a range of different consumer types, and to expand out of what might be saturated areas. Thus the Burton Group comprises Burton, Debenhams, Principles, Top Shop, Top Man, Evans, Dorothy Perkins and Champion Sport. The Sears retail empire includes Selfridges, Wallis, Fosters, Hornes, Freemans Mail Order, Millets, Olympus Sport, Mappin and Webb, William Hill, Dolcis, Freeman Hardy Willis, Trueform, Saxone and Curtis. WH Smith, operating in a 'mature' section of the market has expanded into a range of specialist shops selling books records and stationery, as well as into DIY. WH Smith's expansion was achieved both by organic growth and diversification, but also by taking over companies such as Our Price records and Paperchase (Cox 1986). Woolworths, whose traditional retail operation has declined, has successfully expanded into DIY (B&Q) and chemists (Superdrug). Marks & Spencer has diversified into home furnishing, and is undertaking a programme of satellite store openings (Parkes 1987a).

2-41
Several retail companies, faced with saturation of the home market, have attempted to satisfy the need to grow by expanding abroad. Marks & Spencer have operated stores in continental Europe for many years. More recently J Sainsbury has taken over the US chain of Shaw's supermarkets (Pegano 1987b). Gateway (formerly the Dee Corporation), the third largest grocery retailer in the UK, has begun similar operations in Spain, together with sports retailing in the US. Dixons too are expanding into the United States with the opening of a small chain of electrical goods superstores (Parkes 1987a).

2-42
The growing internationalism of retailing is by no means confined to British companies expanding abroad. While Woolworth, Carrefour and Safeway were originally offshoots of overseas companies, recent foreign additions include

Benetton, Toys R Us, Tandy, Seven Eleven and Wickes. Additionally, ownership of longstanding companies may be transferred into overseas hands, the classic example being Al Fayed's takeover of the House of Fraser (including Harrods) (Mitton 1987).

Table 2-3 : Concentration of Retail Multiples in Northumberland Street, Newcastle, 1980-1986

Shop Type	1980		1986	
	No	%	No	%
Independents (<3 branches)	15	28	3	6
Service Outlets	3	6	11	20
Multiple Retailer Outlets	36	67	40	74
of which:				
retailers with 5 units in street	1		2	
4	1		0	
3	1		2	
2	1		3	
total in 'multiple multiples'	14	26	22	41
Total number of outlets	54	100	54	100

Source : Howard and Davies (1988 p10)

2-43

Howard and Davies (1988) showed how the concentration of ownership was manifest in Northumberland Street, one of Newcastle's principal shopping streets. While there was frequent turnover of shop units, ownership had become highly concentrated, and 'turnover' often represented no more than a switch to a related company with common ownership. Between 1980 and 1986, they noted that apparent turnover of shop units had been relatively high but in reality, the concentration of ownership had grown. The survey results are set out in Table 2-3.

2-44

Concentration of retail ownership has been the key to pressures for out-of-centre development. Economies of scale have accrued from the centralisation of administration and distribution, but pressures for larger, and more efficient, stores have grown simultaneously. Such a process has been particularly evident in the grocery sub-sector, and Table 2-4 shows the proportion of supermarkets of different sizes in 1980 and 1986.

Table 2-4 : Supermarket Sizes in Multiple Firms (%)

Size of Supermarket (ft^2)	1980	1986
< 2000	30.4	15.0
2000 - 9999	50.9	53.9
10 000 - 24 999	14.3	22.0
> 25 000	4.3	8.9

Note 1 ft^2 = 0.933 m^2

Source : Institute of Grocery Distribution 1987

2-45

Similar pressures have been experienced in the comparison goods sector, and retail warehouses have emerged as a means of lowering overheads and increasing efficiency. Both are justified by retailers in terms of popularity and choice for the consumer.

2-46

Despite the better use of space that modern stock handling methods allow, traditional town centres usually have little room for stores to expand to the profit maximising size they require. In addition, land prices are too high to allow the extensive form of operations which will optimise internal efficiency. The consequence is that retailers look to non-central sites for further growth. Again, it should be noted that store expansion and the move out-of-centre are **enabled** by changes in Government policy, discussed above, and by changes in transport and in consumer behaviour, which are described below.

2-47

Broadbridge & Dawson (1988) suggested that concentration will continue within the retail sector until each sub-sector is dominated by between five and ten retailers totalling a 70-80% market share. They estimated that by the mid-1990s, 50% of retail sales will be controlled by the 60 or so largest companies. While continued concentration of ownership represents a move towards monopoly and away from so-called perfect competition, a limited number of sizeable operators actually **increases** competition, unless some form of agreement or cartel is arranged. The effect is that once one retailer has moved toward the more (internally) efficient, and therefore more profitable, operation of an out-of-centre store, competitors must follow or lose part of their market share. In essence, there is strong competition among retailers to achieve the near monopolistic local trading position that superstore development can create (Plowden 1988).

2-48

The tendency toward monopoly, internal and external economies of scale, and the introduction of new forms of operation have therefore made retailing a very profitable sector. In the year up to the end of January 1987, Wickes, the out-of-centre DIY retailer increased its profits by 73%, Woolworth Holdings increased profits by 40%, and John Lewis Partnership by 28% (Cox 1987b). Sainsbury's half-time profits (in current prices) up to November 1986 increased by a third over those of the previous year (Cox 1987a).

Pressure for Expansion

2-49

High profits enable retail companies to embark on store expansion schemes while attracting the attention of outside investors and developers. McIntosh (1987) argued that the retail sector's attractiveness to investors was a result of sustained high rental growth of prime quality retail property. Thus while retail rentals grew by 157% between June 1977 and December 1984, office and industrial rentals increased by only 117% and 72% respectively. (To put these figures into some kind of context, over the same period, the retail price index rose by 95%.)

2-50

So while new forms of retail development were originally spawned by retailers who sought increased efficiency and profits, more recently the other interests have also seen the potential for profit, and have joined the fray. With low land and development costs, but the potential for high return, out-of-centre sites offer the best potential for such investment. An ironic effect of this is that some retailers are now aware that the quantity of off-centre retailing, specially in the form of regional shopping centres, threatens the continued prosperity of their in-centre outlets. Hampson argued that there is not enough investment available to sustain a large increase in floorspace together with an improvement in existing space. He questioned heavy investment out-of-centre which threatened investment in-centre and the continued existence of facilities such as theatres, post offices and independent shops (The Planner 1987). Hampson (1988) has also argued that the retail sector's preoccupation with increasingly available floorspace does not necessarily reflect market trends. He suggested that increased consumer spending represents not so much an increase in the quantity of goods sold, but an increase in quality and value. He described the experience of some John Lewis Stores where turnover has increased but the number of customers has actually fallen. Hallsworth (1988) suggested that this preoccupation with floorspace expansion is often a result of a corporate need to maintain sustained growth rather than a result of consumer demand.

2-51
Additionally, many retailers are forced to develop out-of-centre to prevent the loss of their market share to competitors who have already made the move (in this respect, parallels may be drawn with weakened local authorities who cannot do otherwise than go along with the 'market' - see above). Thus Habitat, who opened 11 out-of-centre stores in 1987 and 1988 may be attempting to preempt the threat posed by IKEA, the Swedish furniture retailer, who operate throughout Europe from non-central locations and who have recently opened their first British store on London's North Circular road (Cox 1988).

2-52
Many observers argue that while in-town developments and redevelopments are largely led by retailers who benefit from the consumer boom and their internal efficiency, out of centre developments are developer-led (see for example Estates Times 1988, Hillier Parker 1988). The rising popularity of the retail sector as a target for investment can be seen in Table 2-5.

Table 2-5 : Institutional Property Purchases by Sector (% of all purchases)

	Retail	Office	Industry
1971-75	27	54	15
1976-80	21	55	24
1981	30	43	26
1982	41	50	10
1983	35	50	15
1984	55	37	8
1985	57	33	10
1986	48	39	10

Note : Data represent purchases by 36 institutions representing half of all
    those with property holdings of over £100 million.
Source : Investment Property Databank, described in Howard and Davies 1988.

2-53
It is significant that many of the developers and investors involved in out-of-centre developments are fairly recent entrants to the retail field. Table 2-6 shows the top ten in- or out-of-centre retail developers. Hillier Parker (1986) argued that a new breed of developer was emerging who concentrated solely on out-of-centre developments.

Table 2-6 : Top Ten Retail Developers (schemes with planning consent or under construction during March 1986)

Rank	All Schemes	Town Centre	Out-of-Centre
1	Cameron Hall	J.Laing	Cameron Hall
2	Stadium Dev.s	Norwich Union	Stadium Developments
3	Richardson	Town & City	Richardson
4	J.Laing	Charterhall	Chesterfield
5	Norwich Union	Standard Life	Pearson
6	Town & City	Heron	Realmoak
7	Charterhall	Capital & Counties	New Ideal
8	Standard Life	Wimpey	G.A.Estates
9	Heron	NEDA	Ladbroke
10	Wimpey	Shearwater	Sava Centre

Note : Developers ranked by total floorspace for which consent has been granted
Source : Hillier Parker 1986

They found that only 3% of retail developers were involved in both in- and out-of-centre developments. With their Lakeside Shopping development at Thurrock, Capital and Counties are the first long-established developer to move from town centre development to out-of-centre schemes (Chartered Surveyor Weekly 1988). Institutions with investment in existing town centres are naturally more reluctant to promote development which may undermine their trade. Indeed, the threat of competition from new forms of retailing has often stimulated town centre landlords to refurbish or redevelop their town centre assets so they become more attractive to shoppers and retailers. Such moves parallel the varied attempts of local authorities to improve town centres, whether by environmental improvement or otherwise.

2-54
The rise of speciality retailing runs against the trend toward increasing size and out-of-centre development, and as such it offers some hope for town centres whose trade is sapped from outside. Speciality shopping is a fairly recent introduction from the United States (the reconstruction of Washington's Union Station shows this well), and is oriented to leisure shopping. Shop units are small, and typically fit into a 'heritage' location such as Covent Garden or the medieval streets of York. While units are small, the retailers themselves are often national chains or franchises. As we shall see below, where there is an attractive, preferably historic location, such as is found in York, speciality retailing can go some way to fill the void left by the decentralisation of convenience, and latterly comparison, retailing. It is however highly dependent on tourism and relatively high disposable incomes, and does not provide a viable alternative for those unable to visit out-of-centre shopping centres. Recent proposals for speciality shopping schemes include the redevelopment of the undercroft of St Pancras Station, the Little Germany area of Bradford, and parts of Oldham and West Bromwich town centres.

CHANGING CONSUMER BEHAVIOUR

2-55
Many of the structural changes in retailing that are described above are the result of changing consumer behaviour. Retail changes in turn influence patterns of consumer behaviour. The result is a mutually dependent cycle of change in which it is difficult to isolate cause and effect. For instance, while new retail formats encourage new types of shopping behaviour, they also

create new demands from the consumer.

2-56
In discussing Scottish retail trends, Dawson & Broadbridge (1988) attempted to classify the types of change that have influenced consumer behaviour throughout the UK. The kinds of change taking place can be summarised:

1   Changes which have their origin outside the retail sector e.g. the direct and indirect effects of Government policy, and the effects of actions of financial institutions and the economy

2   Changes which have their origin within the retail sector:
    - 'top down' or retailer led changes, e.g. advertising or pricing campaigns or the introduction of new retail formats
    - 'bottom up' or consumer led changes:
        * changes in societal patterns of behaviour
        * changes in group patterns of behaviour
        * changes in individual patterns of behaviour

2-57
Changes in Government policies can have direct and indirect effects on consumption. Thus levels of income tax or VAT will have a direct bearing on how much people are able to spend. Policies such as the sale of council homes to tenants may restrict households' ability to buy other goods, although they could result in increased spending on DIY goods.

2-58
Controls over trading-hours can affect the way people consume and the way that retailing provision changes. If Sunday trading laws are relaxed, it seems likely that out-of-centre shopping would benefit more than in-town centres because of the higher occurrence of car based trips at the weekend, when cars and drivers are more available, and family trips are more frequent (Burke & Shackleton 1986). Currently, generally relaxed enforcement of Sunday trading laws has resulted in many retail warehouses opening for business seven days a week (see for example The Guardian, 28 July 1987 p8). One Payless DIY store in Yeovil has been served with over 100 prosecutions for Sunday trading, reportedly costing the company £70 000 in fines (Clements 1987).

2-59
Central Government, as in recent years, may influence the operations of the financial sector, thereby determining the amount of credit that is available within the economy. The relaxation of credit controls in 1982 has led to what has been termed a credit 'boom' with the amount of outstanding credit increasing by about 12% in real terms a year (Howard & Davies 1988). The combination of tax cuts, rising incomes, and freely available credit recently led to an 'overheating' of the economy, and the creation of record balance of payment deficits (see for example Milner & John 1988). The Chancellor of the Exchequer responded by raising interest rates in an attempt to reduce disposable income, and slow the growth of the economy. While controlled economic growth may be a prudent course to follow, many retailers and developers have planned and expanded on the basis of continued growth of consumer spending. If spending does level-off, or if it should actually fall at some time in the future, it is likely that the retail sector would undergo a process of rationalisation, with less efficient 'dead wood' being stripped away. It is significant that, in retailers' terms at least, the most efficient retail outlets are those large, purpose built units, most often in out-of-centre locations. The knock-on effects of changes in Government policies on consumer behaviour are therefore quite profound.

2-60

Dawson & Broadbridge discriminate between 'top down' changes caused by retail companies, and 'bottom up' changes which originate with the consumer. They argue that 'top down' changes include the effects of advertising, pricing strategies and variations in service and quality. Other such changes include the introduction of new retail formats and store designs. Many of these have been discussed in earlier sections and need no further elaboration here.

'Bottom up' or consumer led changes

These influences embrace a wide range of individual, group and societal changes, which will be reviewed in paras 2-61 to 2-70 below.

Changes in societal patterns of behaviour

2-61

Changes in society alter the context within which individuals operate. Some of these processes have been operating for several decades, while others are relatively recent. Rising personal mobility for many, together with continued deterioration of urban environments have encouraged the counter-urbanisation process to continue. Except for relatively small groups of gentrifiers, there is still a trend of migration from large cities to surrounding smaller towns and the nearby countryside. Such a trend has obvious implications for the location of retail provision, together with the types of goods demanded, and the nature of people's shopping trips.

Table 2-7 : Consumer Expenditure at 1980 prices, £ million

Year	Food, Drink & Tobacco	Clothing & Shoes	Household Goods	Durable & Recreation Goods	Books Newspapers & Magazines	Chemist & Health Goods
1974	36 804	8 244	8 143	6 639	1 999	2 896
1975	36 346	8 354	7 961	6 589	1 892	2 735
1976	36 428	8 406	8 193	6 786	1 831	2 661
1977	35 972	8 529	7 804	6 945	1 822	2 605
1978	37 413	9 333	8 461	7 456	1 840	2 694
1979	38 235	9 996	9 005	7 784	1 856	2 782
1980	37 649	9 863	8 549	7 474	1 856	2 695
1981	36 758	9 797	8 482	7 771	1 805	2 712
1982	36 085	10 141	8 684	8 270	1 748	2 760
1983	36 832	10 823	9 287	8 697	1 697	2 839
1984	36 666	11 416	9 551	9 239	1 674	2 940
% Change 74-84	-0.37	+38.47	+17.29	+39.16	-16.26	+1.52

Source : Central Statistical Office 1986

2-62

The RTPI (1988) calculated that, in real terms, between 1963 and 1986, spending on convenience goods had increased by 14.6% but that spending on comparison goods had grown by 132.9%. Per capita, these growth rates were 8.3% and 119.9% respectively. The relative stability of spending on convenience goods is clear, while in contrast, comparison expenditure has grown enormously.

2-63

Increasing acceptance of new technology, and the rôle of electronics in particular, affects lifestyles together with the kind of goods demanded.   As people
adapt to the advent of 'telecommuting' (using computer workstations located in
their homes), the availability of new electronic goods (video recorders, micro-
wave ovens, compact discs and personal computers for example) new markets, and
thus sources of demand, are created.   Table 2-7 shows, in real terms, changes
in consumer spending on each different group of product between 1974 and 1984.
While spending on food and drink remained almost static, that on durable and
recreation goods increased by nearly 40%.

2-64

Huws (1988) showed the profound impact that many of these new products have on
people's lives, arguing that many new technology-based 'labour saving' products
actually increase a household's investment and labour inputs into its consumption.   While in the past people visited cinemas on a regular basis, that
experience has largely been replaced by the TV and video, which require a high
level of individual investment.   Similarly, the widespread use of washing
machines in the home has required household capital investment, and has reduced
the reliance on outside services or facilities.   Similar processes have
occurred in DIY, transport, and many other areas.   Huws argued the result has
been a substantial increase in consumers' (unpaid) input into the products they
consume.   Equally importantly, the effect has been to individualise consumption, and contain it within the home.   The view that society is becoming more
geared to the needs of the individual is also suggested by Dawson and Broadbridge.   They argue that people feel less responsible for the rest of society,
and that this attitude is supported by both the Government and media.   The
result is a changed set of priorities, values and expectations in which
personal achievement is the determining factor.

2-65

Other important changes in society include the revaluation of time.   With more
active lives, convenience and speed become priorities, so time-saving products
are demanded, and convenient and well designed retail stores are preferred.
Consumption patterns are also affected by demographic changes.   Most important
are the reduction in average household size, and the stabilisation and ageing
of the population.   Higher levels of household formation lead to higher demands
for common household goods, while an ageing population means a fall in demand
for children's goods, and reorientation of the market to the needs of middle
aged and elderly consumers.

Changes in group patterns of behaviour

2-66

One of the most significant changes in recent decades has been the gradual
blurring of rôle stereotyping within the household.   With more women gaining
their independence and following their own careers, the traditional allocation
of household work, including shopping, to women is beginning to break down.
This has meant greater male participation in activities such as shopping, and a
shift of such activities into times outside working hours, be they evenings or
weekends.   Many grocery chains have recognised these changes, and now remain
open till 19.00 or 20.00 on weekdays. The reallocation of rôles is still in its
early days however; the majority of women still remain responsible for basic
household shopping, while many women who have been able to continue their
careers are still expected to fulfil their traditional shopping functions too.
A secondary effect of growing equality is the increasing number of households
with more than one income.   This has implications for shopping patterns, and
the type of goods demanded.

Table 2-8 : Indices of Change 1973-1984

Year	Great Britain Population (000s)	Average Household Size	Av. Hshld Disposable Income	Car Ownership (per 1000 pop)
1974	54 684	2.834	6 699	245.0
1975	54 676	2.812	6 363	247.2
1976	54 665	2.748	6 143	252.3
1977	54 636	2.763	6 054	
1978	54 621	2.717	6 139	252.6
1979	54 675	2.702	6 038	261.7
1980	54 756	2.714	6 332	269.8
1981	54 815	2.729	6 635	272.6
1982	54 768	2.695	6 355	279.4
1983	54 804	2.658	6 034	283.6
1984	54 910			292.3

Source : Central Statistical Office (1986)

2-67
Dawson and Broadbridge argue that two fairly recent, but connected, trends are of growing significance for retailing. The first is the small but expanding segment of the population who have very high incomes and consequently very high purchasing power. This appears to run contrary to the data in Table 2-8 which suggest that average income in real terms has actually fallen. The second is the tendency for inner-city areas of large urban settlements to be subject to gentrification as affluent city workers move into relatively cheap residential areas. This creates a new catchment population with new demands close to the centre of the city where decline brought by competition from out-of-centre retailing may be most marked.

Changes in individual patterns of behaviour

2-68
Dawson and Broadbridge outlined a number of factors that have affected the context of individual behaviour:

*   people are more and more concerned to achieve personal satisfaction
*   people are less concerned with the needs of society as a whole
*   the media have contributed to a 'broadening of perceptual horizons'
*   the recent (and expected future) increase in leisure time resulting from shorter working hours, earlier retirement and longer holidays
*   developments such as 'telecommuting', flexitime and job sharing, mean that the timing of activities such as shopping is less rigidly defined
*   increases in leisure time for many people allow them to pursue a wider range of activities and pastimes, many of which involve consumption of goods in one form or another.

2-69
One of the most profound influences on personal behaviour has been the increase in real and perceived mobility that has resulted from car ownership. Table 2-8 showed that between 1974 and 1984, ownership in Great Britain increased from 245 to 292 cars per 1000 population. The growing proportion of households with more than one car (from 9% in 1973 to 17% in 1983 [Central Statistical Office 1986]), and the increase in people, particularly women, with driving licences means that shopping trips by car are becoming more and more common. The switch

FIG 2-9 TOTAL FLOORSPACE OPENED IN SCHEMES 1965-1987
Source: Chartered Surveyor Weekly 28 April 1988
(Town Centre Retail Supplement)

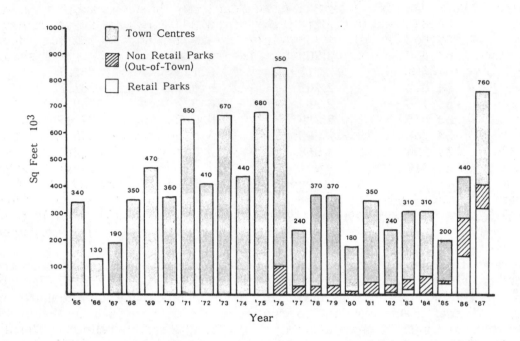

FIG 2-10a **SHOPPING CENTRE DEVELOPMENT: UNDER CONSTRUCTION AND WITH CONSENT**
Source: Hillier Parker Research

FIG 2-10b **SHOPPING CENTRE DEVELOPMENT: PROPOSED**
Source: Hillier Parker Research

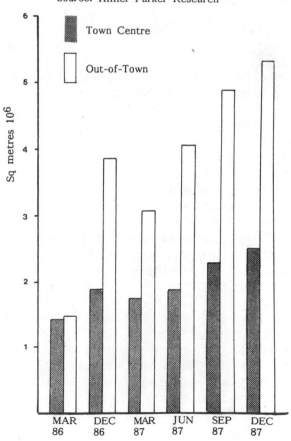

from public to private transport has led to growing levels of road congestion in urban areas. Once people have cars they are usually reluctant to travel by any other means. Faced with a choice between the congested town centre and an out-of-centre shopping development, many consumers opt for the latter. As well as influencing the geography of retailing provision, the use of cars has an impact on the frequency and nature of shopping trips (together with where people choose to live). While on the one hand use of a car allows a large amount of shopping to be carried, resulting in less frequent grocery trips, on the other hand the availability of a car has been found to increase the frequency of durable shopping trips (Howard and Davies). When a family owns a car, it is as cheap for all the family to go along as for just one member, so family trips become more common, and the distinction between shopping and leisure begins to blur.

2-70
Finally, individuals' shopping habits are influenced by the concept of 'consumerism'. Over recent decades people have become more knowledgeable about the goods they are purchasing, and have become more voluble in expressing their demands. The most obvious example of this trend is the growing concern with health and fitness. Consumers have become aware of the effects of unhealthy diets and of the kinds of additives that have gone into common foods. The arrival of additive-free foods, together with comprehensive labelling of ingredients, vitamins and minerals all stand as testimony to the consumer's new-found power.

QUANTIFYING CHANGE

2-71
The effect of changing Government policies, changes within the retail sector, and in patterns of consumer behaviour, have already had a significant effect on the geography of British retailing. Figure 2-9 shows the historical growth of out-of-centre retail development. And although Figure 2-10a shows that shopping developments with planning consent or under construction in town centres still outweigh those in off-centre locations (in terms of m^2), the gap has been narrowing, and Figure 2-10b shows that out-of-centre proposals are running ahead of those in-town.

2-72
In order accurately to assess the number and characteristics of new retail developments in Britain, TEST established a computer database with a range of information relating to each scheme, be it planned, under construction or already in existence. In particular, the database distinguishes schemes by their location (town centre, suburban/district centre, elsewhere within urban areas or out-of-town) and by their type (purpose built shopping centre, retail warehouse or superstore/hypermarket). Other data held relate to their net and gross floorspace, the number of parking spaces, their year of opening, the mixture of retail and non-retail uses, detailed information regarding shopping types, and their national location. Data have been derived from a wide range of basic sources and have been updated with regular reviews of the property press. All out-of-centre retail developments up to June 1987 are included, together with those noted in the property press up to June 1988. Information on recent town centre schemes has also been included. The results are presented in Tables 2-11 to 2-15. The database does not claim to be a precise record of recent retail development, but it does give a good indication of the scale and direction of change. In addition, it should be noted that the subsequent analysis only relates to developments in England, and that complete information on each scheme was not always available, so calculations are made on the basis of varying totals.

41

Table 2-11 : Shop Type by Location (%)
Italic type = vertical percentages, normal type = horizontal percentages

Shop Type	Town	LOCATION Urban, & Out-of- Centre	Out-of- Centre	District Centre	Town TOTAL
Purpose Built	14.9	14.6	9.6	60.7	100.0
Shopping Centre	*49.0*	*3.6*	*26.9*	*86.3*	*18.6*
Retail Warehouse	4.6	92.6	0.0	1.9	100.0
	41.8	*63.3*	*6.1*	*7.5*	*51.0*
Superstore/	1.7	81.0	14.6	2.6	100.0
hypermarket	*9.2*	*33.0*	*66.9*	*6.2*	*30.4*
TOTAL	5.7	74.6	6.7	13.1	100.0
	100.0	*100.0*	*100.0*	*100.0*	*100.0*

2-73

Table 2-11 shows the relative numbers of shopping schemes by type and location. While most purpose built shopping centres (managed shopping centres comprising groups of mainly comparison goods retailers) exist, or have been proposed in town centres, the great majority of both retail warehouses and superstores are located outside existing shopping areas, but within the urban area. Almost half of the out-of-town developments or proposals are purpose built shopping centres while 63% of urban, but out-of-centre, schemes are for retail warehouses. An equivalent proportion of schemes in district or suburban centres are superstores. Most recent town centre developments take the form of purpose built shopping centres.

Table 2-12 : Average Gross Retail Floorspace by Shop Type and by Location (m^2)

Shop Type	Town	LOCATION Urban, & Out-of- Centre	Out-of- Centre	District Centre	Town TOTAL
Purpose Built					
Shopping Centre	33 266	69 308	22 379	18 316	29 936
Retail Warehouse	16 716	8 627	10 530	12 319	8 997
Superstore/					
hypermarket	5 496	5 017	4 472	5 781	4 963
TOTAL	23 540	9 003	8 034	16 620	10 323

2-74

Table 2-12 shows the average gross retail floorspace according to shop type and location. Overall, purpose built shopping centres are the largest schemes, averaging out at just under 30 000 m^2. Interestingly, the largest purpose built shopping centres are located within the urban area - and include examples such as the MetroCentre, Brent Cross shopping centre and proposals for regional shopping centres at Sandwell and Manchester. The large average size of retail warehouses reflects the trend away from stand-alone units and toward retail warehouse parks. Average supersore size stands at just under 5 000 m^2, and varies little between different locations.

Table 2-13 : Average Number of Car Parking Spaces, by Shop Type and Location

Shop Type	LOCATION				
	Out-of-Town	Urban, & Out-of-Centre	District Centre	Town Centre	TOTAL
Purpose Built Shopping Centre	5725	4098	890	857	1940
Retail Warehouse	1316	210	766	110	230
Superstore/ hypermarket	382	333	423	498	456
TOTAL	2928	376	478	819	476

2-75

Table 2-13 shows how strongly modern retail developments are oriented toward car users. Out-of-town purpose built centres (regional shopping centres) and retail warehouse parks have particularly large amounts of car parking. Superstores' parking provision, however, tends to increase as they become integrated into existing shopping facilities.

Table 2-14 : Existing Retail Warehouses and Superstores, (1988) Number and % by Region

Region	RETAIL WAREHOUSES			SUPERSTORES		
	No.	%	Pop per Store (000)[2]	No.	%	Pop per Store (000)[2]
Northern	29	4.5	106.6	39	7.3	79.3
Yorkshire/Humberside	61	9.4	80.4	66	12.3	74.3
North West[1]	30	4.6	172.5	28	5.2	184.9
West Midlands[1]	46	7.1	55.0	36	6.7	70.2
East Anglia	23	3.5	84.3	27	5.0	71.8
South East[1]	136	20.9	76.1	116	21.7	89.3
South West	85	13.1	52.5	52	9.7	85.8
East Midlands	58	8.9	66.8	55	10.3	70.4
Inner London	15	2.3	)	20	3.7	)
Outer London	97	14.9	) 60.3	26	4.9	)146.9
Merseyside	11	1.7	135.5	9	1.7	165.7
West Midlands	27	4.2	98.0	26	4.9	101.8
Greater Manchester	31	4.8	83.5	34	6.4	76.1
TOTAL	649	100.0	72.3	534	100.0	87.93

Note : 1 excludes Metropolitan Areas
2 1984 mid year estimates (Central Statistical Office 1986)

2-76

Table 2-14 analyses the development of retail warehouse schemes and superstores by region. In each case the population per store is calculated, revealing sizeable differences between regions. Thus while the South West comes out with only 52 000 people per retail warehouse (or group of retail warehouses), in the North West there are over three times as many people per store. Similar contrasts exist in the distribution of superstores. One store per 70 000 in the

West Midlands contrasts with 184 000 in the North West. Table 2-15 looks at the development of purpose built shopping schemes, in and out of established town centres since 1985. Distinction is also made between those which already exist or which are under construction, and those which have been granted permission, are applications, or which have not yet been submitted. A high level of recent activity in town centres compares with comparatively low levels of planned and future development. The clustering of schemes in and around large urban areas is also evident.

Table 2-15 : Recent, Future & Planned Purpose Built Shopping Centres by Region (1988)

	IN EXISTING SHOPPING CENTRES				OUTSIDE EXISTING SHOPPING CENTRES			
	A	B	C	D	A	B	C	D
Northern	4	2	2	1	1	0	0	1
Yorkshire/Humberside	8	7	3	3	4	2	5	2
North West[1]	4	1	3	1	0	1	1	0
West Midlands[1]	10	0	4	1	1	0	1	0
East Anglia	2	3	1	1	0	0	0	0
South East[1]	21	13	13	6	4	4	17	2
South West	11	4	3	4	1	4	6	4
East Midlands	3	5	0	3	0	1	2	1
Inner London	4	5	3	1	0	1	0	0
Outer London	4	7	4	3	0	1	2	0
Merseyside	1	0	1	0	0	1	0	0
West Midlands	7	4	1	1	2	1	1	3
Greater Manchester	2	0	0	2	0	0	7	0
TOTAL	81	51	38	27	13	16	42	13

Note : 1 excludes Metropolitan Areas
        A = Centres in existence and under construction
        B = Centres with full or outline planning consent
        C = Centres whose applications for consent are under consideration or at appeal
D = Centres where an application for consent has not been submitted, or where status is uncertain

2-77
The importance of town centre purpose built shopping centres should not be underestimated. Although there is currently strong interest in out-of-centre developments, in 1981 Britain had over 130 centrally located shopping centres of more than 15 000 m^2 gross retail floorspace (Falk 1983). Table 2-15 shows that a substantial number of new schemes have been completed or proposed in town centres in recent years, and these include the Coppergate Centre in York and the Cascades Centre in Portsmouth are examples from our case studies. As we have seen, recent town centre shopping developments are primarily a response to retailers' demands for additional shopping floorspace. Several studies (see for example Hillier Parker 1988 - discussed above) indicate that most retailers actually want to stay in town centres, but are often forced out by lack of room to expand together with competition from other retailers who are already represented in off-centre locations. Developers and landowners have not been slow to react to these demands, specially since out-of-centre retailing has become such a threat to existing investment.

2-78

The threat of out-of-centre shopping development has also encouraged local authorities to adopt more positive and accommodating attitudes toward town centre shopping schemes (Seidle 1988). Town centre shopping development commonly takes two forms; comprehensive redevelopment of town centre sites, or refurbishment of exisiting shopping centres. Refurbishment of dated 1960s and 1970s developments is becoming increasingly common, and in 1987, approximately 100 of the 600 such developments were undergoing refurbishment, or had already been refurbished (Vines 1988). The Mander Centre in Wolverhampton is an example of a shopping centre which has undergone recent improvement. Refurbishment of an existing shopping centre can range from the redesign of shop-fronts to a thorough reconstruction of a complex which could include the expansion of the total floorspace, and the creation of larger stores. In some cases, open air centres and even streets are being enclosed (a trend also to be found in Germany) in an attempt to make them more attractive to shoppers, and closer to the 'qualities' offered by out-of-centre developments.

2-79

It should be noted that many of the shopping centres built outside traditional shopping areas, and analysed in Table 2-15, are of a size smaller than the 50 000 m^2 gross retail floorspace which classifies a development as a regional shopping centre. As yet, only two such centres are operating - the Brent Cross centre in north London, and the MetroCentre in Gateshead, although more are underconstruction (eg Merry Hill in the West Midlands). Hillier Parker (Planning 20 May 1988 p8) found that the number of regional shopping schemes decreased in the year up to March 1988. Proposals for centres larger than 500 000 ft^2 (46 650 m^2) fell from 43 to 32. They argued that the reduction was in some case due to the downscaling of schemes (eg MetroTees proposal changed from a regional shopping centre to a retail warehouse park), together with the with-drawal of schemes where nearby proposals had been granted consent (eg the withdrawal of the Parkgate, Rotherham scheme following the approval of the Meadowhall proposal in the Lower Don Valley). Of the 32 schemes still in the running, 6 had been granted permission or were under construction, while half of the remainder were on greenbelt or greenfield sites which were affected by Government guidelines.

2-80

It is worth briefly examining some of the characteristics of the MetroCentre. It was originally conceived by Cameron Hall, its developers, as a large retail warehouse park. The development, located within the Gateshead Enterprise Zone which freed it from conventional planning controls and allowed it to benefit from financial incentives, quickly attracted the interest of Marks & Spencer, and subsequently a wide range of high street retailers. The result of this retailer interest was that the MetroCentre scheme grew from being a large retail warehouse park, to being a full-scale out-of-centre regional shopping development. The centre opened in a number of phases between 1986 and 1988. It comprises a total of 150 000 m^2 gross retail floorspace together with exten-sive leisure facilities, a bus station, and an eventual total of 10 000 parking spaces. The latter feature is reflected in the centre's modal split. Howard & Davies (1987a,b) found that almost 80% of shoppers using the MetroCentre travelled there by car, compared with 38% in nearby Newcastle city centre. Although public transport only accounts for about 20% of visitors, long dis-tance coach trips to the centre are becoming popular (on one December day 235 coaches arrived at the MetroCentre from places as far afield as Northampton [Ingham 1988]), and package rail trips from London are being suggested.

2-81

Relatively little is known about the effects of out-of-centre shopping developments. This is probably because the effects have not been as immediate and
dramatic as many observers previously thought. Both Schiller (1986) and Gibbs
(1985) argued that local authorities consistently opposed each 'wave', or
generation, of out-of-centre retailing. While this opposition might have been
justified in terms of the expected impact on existing shopping, and uncertainties regarding new types of development, given the often limited impact of such
developments, in the longer term it has undermined local authorities' ability
to influence retail policy. Planners are thus thought of as crying wolf too
often. However, it could be argued that it is precisely now, when the growth
of consumer spending is likely to come under control, and when town centres are
threatened with competition from the new wave of regional shopping centres,
that local authorities' fears should be heeded. If consumer spending were to
stabilise or decrease, and the type of shops available in town centres were
replicated in car oriented out-of-centre developments, the impact on existing
shopping facilities could be profound.

2-82

This section brings together a range of evidence to assess the impact of
existing forms of out-of-centre retail development on trade, employment and
access.

TRADE

2-83

SEEDS (1987) argued that new forms of retail development are affecting the
trade of existing shops in two main ways. First there are the effects of
companies' internal expansion strategies. Some firms are undergoing expansion
programmes which involve a smaller number of substantially larger stores than
in the past. Thus while the number of Tesco stores fell from 722 in 1977 to 395
in 1986, their average size more than tripled in the same period (Tesco Plc
1986). Such strategies necessitate the closure of smaller outlets, often affecting the trade of surrounding stores which relied on a multiple to act as an
anchor for trade. SEEDS argued that many small but profitable stores are closed
simply because their profits per employee are not considered high enough, or
because they do not fit into a company's evolving structure. An area which
exemplifies these trends is Kentish Town Road in north London which has lost a
small branch of Marks & Spencer and will shortly lose its Sainsbury supermarket
as it is replaced by a superstore in Camden Town to the south.

2-84

The second way that trade is affected is through the impact of new developments
- superstores, retail warehouses or regional shopping centres - on existing
patterns of shopping. Where a new element of retail provision is introduced,
unless it attracts completely new spending, it is likely that its gain in trade
will be other retailers' loss. As we have seen above, this is likely to be
particularly true in the convenience goods market which has experienced relatively static levels of consumer spending during the past decade. There are
numerous examples where out-of-centre retailing has affected the trade of
existing shopping facilities: some are described below.

2-85

The Carrefour hypermarket in Caerphilly, which opened in 1972, had a gross
floorspace of 10 000 m^2, of which just over half was selling space. There was
parking provision for 1 000 cars at surface level in front of the store. A
study in 1974 (Donaldson & Sons 1975), two years after the store opened,
assessed its impact on the local shopping hierarchy. While it was argued that

decline of convenience outlets in the store's immediate catchment had not been large (a fall from 321 to 276), the effects on Caerphilly town centre had been more pronounced. Between May 1972 and September 1974, the number of convenience outlets there declined from 20 to 12, a 40% fall. It was estimated that in current terms, spending in the centre had fallen by 20%, the decline in real terms being even greater. Thus as early as 1975, the trade effects of large out of centre, and car based, shopping developments were known.

2-86

A study by the Departments of Environment and Transport (1977) attempted to assess the impact of another hypermarket. Carrefour in Eastleigh, Hampshire opened in 1974 and totalled 9 500 m^2 gross floorspace (4 700 m^2 net). This store was in a true out-of-town location, and attracted a high proportion of infrequent, one stop shopping trips. The study found that Chandlers Ford, the shopping centre closest to the hypermarket, had lost two supermarkets since Carrefour had opened. However a causal link between the new store's opening and their closure was not strongly identified. Additionally, Chandlers Ford's remaining supermarket subsequently underwent expansion. Eastleigh district shopping centre lost five small food shops, though this was thought to be partly the result of a new Tesco supermarket which opened there.

2-87

The Tesco superstore that opened in Finchley Central in 1978 provides an interesting comparison with the relatively free-standing Carrefour in Eastleigh. A study by the Greater London Council (GLC 1979) gauged the Tesco store's trading impact. In constrast to the hypermarket's trading characteristics, the store attracted a high proportion of frequent (more than once a week), relatively low-spend shopping trips. The GLC found that Tesco's largest trading impact was felt within Finchley Central itself, and the number of convenience stores in its catchment had fallen from 48 to 44, though again, a concrete link between these closures and the new store's opening was difficult to establish.

2-88

Evely (1980) described the conclusions of two studies of the effects of an Asda superstore which opened in Coatbridge town centre in 1976. Again, the central location resulted in relatively frequent visits (while more than 60% of visits were made by local residents, more than 50% of these customers shopped there more than once a week) and a localised impact. Whereas the new Asda took 17% of the Coatbridge convenience goods market, reduced the average amount spent in other shops, and halved the number of people using existing outlets within the centre, the impact on nearby Airdrie town centre and other shopping centres was less than had been expected. Thus while trade loss in neighbourhood centres in Coatbridge was as high as 30% for convenience goods, in Airdrie town centre it was only about 5%. It was argued that by accommodating the new Asda in Coatbridge's existing town centre, continued accessibility was assured, while it acted as an anchor for a number of other shops which located nearby.

2-89

An impact study by the London Borough of Havering (1984) assessed a 5 000 m^2 gross floorspace (2 400 m^2 net) superstore in Hornchurch town centre. Again, this location meant that visits to the store were relatively frequent, and were often combined with visits to other stores in the centre. The study found that the most significant trade diversion was from nearby Romford, from which 32% of the store's spending had been diverted. Only 13% of trade was diverted from Hornchurch town centre outlets. The study found that almost half the new store's trade had been drawn from existing Sainsbury outlets, particularly a store in Upminster which closed in 1985.

As part of a survey of residents' shopping patterns, the Royal Borough of Kensington and Chelsea (1984) undertook a study of the trading characteristics of a 5000 m^2 gross floorspace (2500 m^2 net) Sainsbury superstore on Cromwell Road in West London. A survey of residents found that 15% of respondents in the Borough used the store on a regular basis. Of respondents who used the store (a third of all respondent residents), half visited it at least once a week. It was found that North End Road in Fulham suffered the biggest trade impact following the Sainsbury store opening. 19% of shoppers at the Cromwell Road store had previously shopped in North End Road, and the London Borough of Hammersmith and Fulham estimated that between 1980 and 1985, the road suffered a 9% decline in its trade, mostly as a result of the new Sainsbury store, but also because of competition from Hammersmith town centre. Of Royal Borough of Kensington and Chelsea residents who used the Cromwell Road Sainsbury, 25% had previously used convenience goods shops in Kings Road, 11% Gloucester Road, and 10% Kensington High Street.

Table 2-16 : Impact of Nine Elms Sainsbury Superstore on Competing Centres

	Annual Turnover 'lost' to Nine Elms store (£M)	Estimate of 'lost' turnover as a % of convenience turnover within centres	
		a	b
Major Centres			
Brixton	4.17	9.7	11.6
Kings Road	3.01	11.2	13.4
Wandsworth TC	2.70	6.3	7.6
Rye Lane, Peckham	1.37	1.9	2.3
Streatham High Rd	1.26	1.4	1.4
Walworth Road	1.05	8.4	10.0
Clapham Junction	0.91	8.0	9.7
Balham	0.88	3.9	4.7
Tooting	0.53	6.8	8.2
District and Neighbourhood Centres			
Stockwell	2.59	20.8	24.9
Victoria Street	3.15	18.3	22.0
Wandsworth Road	2.10	27.4	32.8
South Lambeth Rd	1.05	16.6	19.9
Wilcox Road	0.60	18.3	20.0
Clapham High St	0.53	1.7	2.0
Battersea	0.49	8.2	9.8

Notes : a assumes £600 convenience turnover per ft^2 sales space
b assumes £500 convenience turnover per ft^2 sales space
Source : London Boroughs of Hammersmith & Fulham and Lambeth (1986)

2-91
A study by the London Borough of Hammersmith and Fulham and the London Borough of Lambeth (1986) measured the impact of an inner city superstore in an out-of-centre location. The Sainsbury superstore opened at Nine Elms in 1982. It has a gross floorspace of 5 500 m^2, and a net floorspace of 3 400 m^2. The store is oriented towards car users; only two bus services pass directly outside the store, while underground facilities are some distance away at Vauxhall. The study found that only 7% of users visited the store more than once a week - it clearly attracts one-stop shopping trips. For surrounding shopping centres and district centres, the annual amount of turnover lost to the new store was

calculated. Amounts ranged from £0.49 million in Battersea to £4.17 million in Brixton. The results of these calculations, together with their implications for each centre's convenience trade are shown in Table 2-16. The table shows that while the biggest trade diversion came from Brixton, Wandsworth Road experienced the largest relative decline, losing between 20 and 25% of its convenience goods turnover. Shop closures in surrounding shopping centres were limited however, and the study concluded that while some outlets had fallen vacant, or had changed to other shop uses, many convenience outlets were simply operating at lower turnover levels than previously.

2-92
A report by the London Borough of Brent (1986) brought together the results of two surveys which assessed the impact of a large out-of-centre Tesco hypermarket at Neasden, North London. LB Brent carried out a survey of a supermarket in nearby Blackbird Hill, while the Greater London Council (GLC) conducted a survey of shoppers using the new hypermarket. The new Tesco store was the biggest of its kind in London, with a gross floorspace of 9 300 m^2 and a net floorspace of 5 600 m^2. The store is heavily oriented towards car users; it is located on a large site next to the North Circular Road, and has sufficient parking for 1 000 vehicles. In addition to selling Tesco's usual range of convenience items, the store sells a wide range of comparison goods and has a range of other facilities, including a chemist, café, bank facilities and a petrol station.

2-93
The LB Brent 'before and after' study of the Safeway supermarket in Blackbird Hill indicated that, following the opening of the Neasden hypermarket, it lost 11% of its customers, but 26% of its turnover. Losses were highest on Saturdays. This represents the diversion of more affluent, car-borne shoppers to the new store. LB Brent estimated that this decline represented a fall of £50 000 in takings each week. Findings from the GLC survey of shoppers broadly confirmed this level of diversion from Blackbird Hill. Other results from the GLC survey indicated that estimated levels of trade diversion that had been considered at the 1981 Planning Inquiry were substantial underestimates, and that the Inspector had allowed the appeal on the basis of inaccurate information. Thus while the GLC survey suggested that Tesco's annual convenience turnover amounted to £29.27 million, at the Public Inquiry Tesco's consultants had estimated it would lie within the range of £16.24 to £19.9 million. As expected, the survey found that the highest trade diversion came from existing large stores in Park Royal and in Brent Cross. However, there were also significant trade diversions from established shopping centres in the Borough, particularly Wembley, Blackbird Hill, Kilburn and Kingsbury. It noted that the decline in these centres' trade was extra to that resulting from the earlier opening of large stores at Park Royal and in the Brent Cross Shopping Centre.

2-94
The development of Brent Cross, a major self-contained shopping centre, in north London in 1977 affected the trade of surrounding areas. Although Donaldson & Sons (1977) argued that the centre drew most of its trade from London's West End, and presented little competition for local centres, SEEDS (1987) show that attempts to redevelop Harlesden town centre were being hampered by it. The London Borough of Brent attempted to halt Harlesden's decline by redeveloping much of the centre around a new Marks & Spencer store. The scheme depended on attracting another large multiple to complement Marks & Spencer, but this is being undermined by Brent Cross's presence about 3km away. Matters have been made even worse by the London Borough of Barnet's decision to grant planning consent for a 42% increase in the size of Brent Cross.

2-95
SEEDS (1987) also indicate the trading impact that retail warehouses can have,

despite claims that they represent an entirely new section of the market. The Wembley area, in north west London, has one of the highest concentrations of retail warehouses in the country. The effect of such concentration has been marked in Wembley town centre particularly among furniture and DIY retailers. Up to four town centre furniture retailers have closed in recent years. The large number of retail warehouses has created even more wasteful competition among out-of-centre retailers, with some upgrading or relocating two or three times, simply to maintain market share. In a situation where competition among retail warehouse companies is so stiff, less efficient town centre retailers stand little hope of competing effectively.

2-96

The trading impact of the MetroCentre on nearby Newcastle city centre appears to be less than expected. This has in part been due to improvements within Newcastle city centre that were stimulated by the arrival of new competition. With a wide consumer catchment, and a preponderance of family trips, it is likely that the MetroCentre has attracted and created a different kind of shopping trip from that common in Newcastle. Howard & Davies (1988) conclude that the biggest effect of the MetroCentre may be to accelerate the speed of changes in the retail sector as a whole. A survey by Gateshead Metropolitan Borough Council (Planning 20 May 1988 p9) suggested that the MetroCentre had little impact on the Borough's durable shopping, although it did concede that the effects on Newcastle city centre would be higher, undermining trade and limiting the scope for new development.

2-97

It is often small, independent retailers who have suffered most from new forms of retailing. The response of small retailers to the squeeze created by large multiples together with near monopolistic wholesalers has been varied. Some have attempted to specialise, notably by extending opening hours, and moving towards delicatessen type products. However, even here they have to compete with national, or international multiples such as Cullens, or 7-Eleven. Other retailers have grouped together to form retail federations such as Spar and Mace. Such groupings help cut overheads, give corporate identity, and spread the costs of advertising. Some small retailers have simply continued trading with declining levels of turnover and profit. Many family businesses may continue trading after they cease to be profitable, simply because the whole family is geared towards the business. Other shops just close.

2-98

As well as having implications for the traders themselves, the decline of small shops is of significance for society generally. Most district centres comprise independent shops, and when these are forced to close they can have a profound effect on access to shops for the less mobile. While most impact studies have concentrated on effects on town centres, the decline of local centres may have an equal or even greater bearing on people's accessibility to shops. Decline of family businesss can also have a marked effect on particular groups within society. Many members of ethnic minorities have found that retailing is an area where they can be relatively free from the widespread discrimination which exists throughout the wider labour market. Many Asian families in particular have established independent retail companies. As the small shop sector comes under pressure from larger retailers, so the opportunities for this group become more limited.

EMPLOYMENT

2-99

Out-of-centre retail developments are often promoted in terms of their ability to create employment in areas where unemployment is high, and local authorities often see this as a positive side of such schemes (Moore 1987, Sparks 1983a,b).

50

It is true that such developments, be they superstores or retail warehouses do result in immediate job creation, and may often seem an attractive alternative to reserving the site for industrial uses which show little sign of appearing. The issue of job creation was a key issue at the public inquiry for Tesco's 'flagship' store at Neasden in north London (Moore 1987). However, when the total number of jobs created by a development is set against the number lost as the trade of smaller shops decline, the issue becomes far less clear cut.

2-100

If we take the grocery sector as an example, it is not hard to see that super-store development actually results in a net loss of jobs. We have seen above (Table 2-7) that the grocery sector, unlike the comparison goods sector, has experienced a slight decline in consumer spending in recent years (-0.37% between 1974 and 1984). To all intents and purposes therefore, consumer spending on convenience goods may be regarded as static. However, when this is set alongside the performance of Tesco (in Table 2-2 above), one of the top grocery retailers, claims about the employment generating effects of superstore development seem fallacious. Thus a real increase in turnover of 118% between 1977 and 1986 was sustained by an increase in employment of only 53%. Such performance reflects the extensive and efficient methods of retailing that can be employed in large superstores. Since the market shares of each of the largest convenience retailers is growing, while the total market is static, we can assume that their gains are the losses of small retailers. Economies of scale mean that turnover per employee is higher in Tesco stores than among the small retailers who have lost trade. The result then, is a loss of employment as trade is diverted from relatively inefficient stores to highly efficient superstores. SEEDS (1987) quote a study that estimated that a superstore led to a net loss of 100 jobs in its catchment. It should be noted that these job losses would be spread over a number of years, as retailers adjusted to their new trade levels by closure, redundancy or by reorienting the business.

2-101

A study by Portsmouth City Council attempted to determine accurately the net employment creation of retail warehouse parks (Planning 1988a). Given rising spending on comparison goods, it was recognised that some employment would be a response to this new expenditure, but that many 'new' jobs would be the result of the shift of trade away from existing shops. By calculating the growth of comparison turnover, and comparing it with the expected turnover of new developments, it was possible to calculate how many new jobs would result, and how many would be relocated jobs. The city council concluded that in a retail warehouse park development with a total employment of 200, only 50 or 80 of these jobs would be new jobs, the rest would represent trade (and therefore employment) transferred from existing businesses. Frequent claims, made in proposals and at appeals, about the benefits of retail warehouse over other types of development were therefore often overstated.

2-102

The development of superstores and retail warehouses is also having an effect on the types of employment available. Mechanisation together with economies of scale have resulted in a polarisation of skills within retailing. The majority of workers are now semi-skilled, filling shelves and operating checkouts, while a small minority are skilled management staff. With this comes a polarisation of sex with most semi-skilled staff being female, and most managers male. Unlike in traditionally structured retailing firms, there is now little or no opportunity for people's careers to progress from these low skill and low pay jobs towards management. Instead, managers now tend to be well qualified graduates, well versed in business theory. Table 2-17 shows the average employment structure in a sample of 175 superstores. Polarisation of skill and sex is immediately obvious.

Table 2-17 : The average employment structure of a sample of 175 superstores

| Employment | Full Time | | Part Time | | Casual | | Total | | Total |
	Female	Male	Female	Male	Female	Male	Female	Male	M & F
Managers	3	16	0	0	0	0	3	16	19
Supervis.	10	4	4	0	0	0	14	4	18
Prof/Tech	1	0	0	0	0	0	1	0	1
Sales	33	16	131	21	5	1	169	38	207
Clerical	5	0	3	0	0	0	8	0	8
Trainees	0	1	0	0	0	0	0	1	1
Ancillary	4	15	5	6	0	0	9	21	30
TOTAL	56	52	143	27	5	1	204	80	284

Source : Dawson et al (1986)

2-103
While highlightling the unequal distribution of employment between the sexes, the above table also indicates the important rôle that part-time employment plays in modern retailing. Percy & Lamb (1988) argue that part time employment, while making a firm able to react to business variations, leads to uncertain working hours and few benefits such as overtime or tea breaks for employees. They suggest that wage rates for part-time workers in retailing are below average for the sector, which in itself is the second lowest paid group in the country. SEEDS (1987) argue that the types of jobs created by a superstore do not help reduce primarily male unemployment created by the decline of manufacturing. It was noted that while sales assistants are recruited locally, managerial and technical staff are not. SEEDS suggest that the development of superstores and retail warehouses, together with their extensive surface car parking, uses up land that at some later date might have been used for more productive manufacturing development which would provide a more suitable source of employment.

TRANSPORT

2-104
The development of out-of-centre forms of retailing is having a profound effect on patterns of transport within British urban areas. Whereas most town centres developed as a focus of public transport networks, out-of-centre retailing is a response to growing levels of car ownership, and people's ability to free themselves from the natural constraints on movement that a declining public transport network imposes. While these new forms of shopping are, in part, a response to growing car ownership and use, they in turn encourage car use, and discourage public transport use, hastening its decline.

2-105
Table 2-18 brings together data from a wide number of sources to show the difference in the modes of transport used for in- and out-of-centre shopping facilities. The difference in modal split between in- and out-of-centre shopping facilities is most noticeable where data for similar catchments are available. Thus while an average of 18% of shoppers in Kensington High Street travelled by car, 60% of residents of the Royal Borough of Kensington and Chelsea who used the Sainsbury in Cromwell Road travelled to it by car. Similarly, while only 27% of Newcastle city centre shoppers had travelled by car, almost 80% of people using the MetroCentre on the other side of the River Tyne had travelled by car.

Table 2-18 : Shopping Modal Splits, %

	Car etc	Walk (50m+)	Public Transport	Other	Source
TRADITIONAL SHOPPING CENTRES					
Birmingham 1983					City of
City Centre					Birmingham 1986
Convenience	19	13	67		
Comparison	34	3	58		
Erdington					
Convenience	35	26	36		
Comparison	52	16	19		
Leicester 1984					Hurdle 1986
City Centre	35	17	48	1	
Wakefield 1985					City of
City Centre					Wakefield 1987
Convenience	45	10	44	1	
Bromley 1987					TEST 1987
Tuesday	41	19	39	1	
Saturday	58	13	29	0	
East Ham 1987					TEST 1987
Tuesday	15	45	37	3	
Saturday	22	35	43	0	
Kensington High Street 1987					TEST 1987
Tuesday	14	34	48	3	
Saturday	22	25	49	4	
Newcastle City Centre 1987[1]	27	?	63	9	Davies & Howard 1988
SUPERSTORES, RETAIL WAREHOUSES AND REGIONAL SHOPPING CENTRES					
MetroCentre Gateshead 1987[1]	79	?	16	5	Davies & Howard 1988
Brent Cross, Barnet 1977	70	9	19	2	Donaldsons 1977
Carrefour, Eastleigh 1977	91	5	16	2	DoE & DTp 1977
Tesco, Finchley Cent. 1979	49	35	16	1	GLC 1979
Asda, Coatbridge c1977	50	20	25	5	Evely 1980
Homebase, Croydon[2]	99	0	1	0	) Roberts
Texas, Park Royal[2]	92	6	2	0	) & Wenden
Wickes, Harrow[2]	80	13	7	0	) 1984
Sainsbury, Cromwell Road[3]	60	36	3	1	RBK&C 1984
Sainsbury, Hornchurch 1984	71	17	11	1	LB Havering 1984
B&Q, Havant 1986	96	1	1	2	Hallsworth 1986
Sainsbury, Nine Elms 1986	57	24	14	5	LBH&F & LBL 1986
Asda, Portsmouth 1981	69	16	13	2	Hallsworth 1981

Note : 1 'Other' includes walkers
2 Car includes taxi and motorcycle, walk includes cycle
3 Borough residents only - all users may include a higher proportion of car users.

2-106
The combination of the trade impact of new non-central shopping schemes and their orientation toward car users leaves non-car users at a disadvantage. Those without access to private transport are left with declining shopping facilities, and little or no means of reaching the new ones. If non-car users are able to reach an out-of-centre shopping development by public transport,

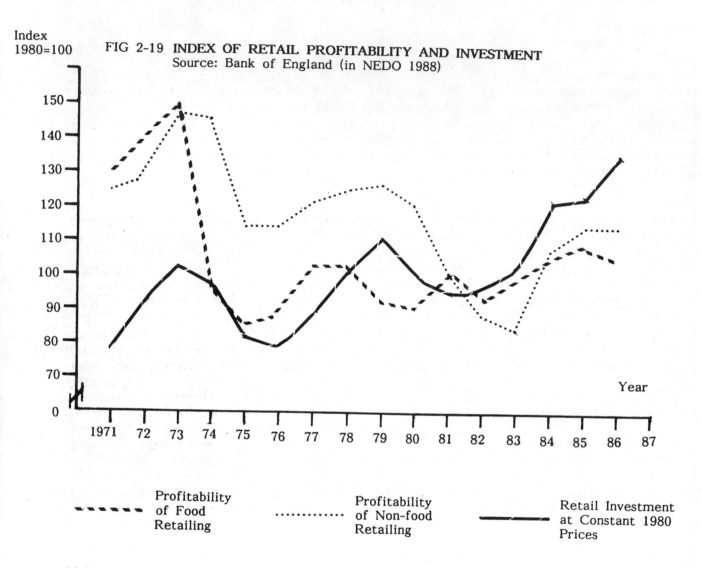

Index
1980=100

FIG 2-19 **INDEX OF RETAIL PROFITABILITY AND INVESTMENT**
Source: Bank of England (in NEDO 1988)

Year

- - - - - Profitability
of Food
Retailing

·············· Profitability
of Non-food
Retailing

━━━━━ Retail Investment
at Constant 1980
Prices

Note
Profitability of Publically Quoted Companies
Profitability is shown as rates of return on capital employed lagged by one
year

54

they will lack the physical ability to carry the quantities of goods commonly purchased by car users. The choice facing such people will be between easier trips to nearby, but declining facilities, or difficult and lengthy trips to distant superstores or shopping centres. It should be noted that the elderly, sick and deprived are least likely to be car owners, and thus more likely to face this choice. If new forms of retail development are to take place then, it would seem logical to steer them into locations in or close to existing centres where they can be reached by everybody.

CONSUMERS

2-107
For many consumers, new forms of retail development, such as superstores, retail warehouses and regional shopping centres are undoubtedly attractive. More affluent households generally own at least one car, and are thus able to enjoy the convenience that car-based retail locations can offer. Superstores and retail warehouses provide wide ranges of goods under one roof, while out-of-centre regional shopping centres such as the MetroCentre offer a wide range of national name multiple retailers in an enclosed and modern complex.

2-108
However, even the benefits of such developments for car users are called into question when they are put into the context of a growing concentration of ownership together with the movement towards spatial monopoly. These trends are particularly evident in the grocery sector where five operators dominate, and where one superstore captures the market for a large area surrounding it. With one retailer dominating an area a local monopoly may be established, with little competition to keep prices low. It might be argued that few of the efficiency gains of superstore operation have been passed onto the consumer in the form of lower prices (there being little difference in the prices charged in a conventional high street supermarket and those in superstores), and that the main operators thus benefit from high profit levels capable of supporting ambitious expansion programmes. High profit margins are reflected in substantial expansion programmes rather than in lower prices for the consumer. With only five companies dominating the sector, it seems there is little incentive to introduce more competitive pricing schemes. The conclusion must be that development out-of-centre is the basis of expansion programmes which are sustained on the high profit margins. Figure 2-19 illustrates the link between retail profitability and investment by retailers. Fluctuating levels of profitability and investment indicate that investment reflects profit margins, though with a time lag of about one year.

2-109
Dawson & Broadbridge (1988) argued that although the first British superstores and hypermarkets adopted competitive, if not aggressive pricing policies, more recently they have 'traded up' and profit margins have grown. A consequence of this increase in profit margins is that there is potential for a discount grocery operation to develop, although this would quickly come under pressure from existing large retailers. The existence of artificially high prices is therefore the result of the grocery sector's move toward monopoly, and seems to be more in the interest of retailers than consumers.

2-110
While the more affluent car owning consumers stand to benefit from greater convenience, if not from lower prices, new forms of retail development may reduce the range of choice for some groups of people. The RTPI (1988) outlined a number of such (overlapping) groups:

* People on low income
* People living in areas badly served by public transport
* Those without access to a car for their shopping trips
* Those with caring responsibilities (most often women), be they for the young, the old or for disabled people.
* The elderly
* Disabled and those with mobility problems
* The young
* Ethnic minorities

2-111

The RTPI pointed out that in some cases superstores might benefit the disabled, but that often the less mobile, those without access to a car, and the poor would be dependent on local and neighbourhood shops and unable to benefit from the advantages of a distant superstore. These local shopping facilities are likely to decline in turn as their more affluent customers switch to super-stores. The disadvantaged would thus be caught in a cycle of decline. When assessing the effects of a number of non-central shopping centres in and around Greater Manchester, Roger Tym & Partners (1986) argued that few of the propos-als would benefit the residents of deprived inner-city areas, indeed they might even reduce the range of shops within existing centres.

2-112

The RTPI argued that ethnic groups, while making a major contribution to retailing in Britain, are rarely served by national retail multiples. Studies of Asian-run shops show how retailing is a sector where people can work without much of the racial discrimination that is common throughout the rest of the employment market, yet these retailers are being squeezed by competition from large retailers and the near monopoly commanded by wholesalers (SEEDS). Thus such shops, which are important in terms of support for ethnic minorities are under threat. In addition, problems of poverty and low car ownership are disproportionately concentrated among members of ethnic groups.

2-113

Despite moves toward greater equality of the sexes, women are still frequently responsible for shopping. At the same time, fewer women than men possess driving licences, and still fewer have access to cars for regular shopping trips. While some households may compromise by undertaking weekly or less frequent shopping trips on a Saturday, women often depend on public transport to get to and from the shops. Given their generally non-central, car based locations, superstores and other new forms of retailing may be out of reach of many women. If they are able to get to one on foot or by public transport, it is likely that they will have to carry their shopping for much greater distances than previously.

REFERENCES

Brasier, M (1987) Tesco Bids £151M for Hillards Supermarkets in **The Guardian** 11 March p28

Broadbridge, A M and J A Dawson (1988) **The Growing Concentration of Market Power in Retailing** Institute for Retail Studies, University of Stirling

Burke, Terry and J R Shackleton (1986) **The Likely Impact of the Deregulation of Sunday Trading on Consumption and Employment** Polytechnic of Central London Faculty of Social Sciences and Business Studies   Research Working Paper 27

Burt, S, JA Dawson & L Sparks (1983) Structure Plans and Retailing Policies in **The Planner** Vol 69 No 1 January/February

Central Office of Information (1973,1979,1987) **Britain 1973/1979/1987 : An Official Handbook** London HMSO

Central Statistical Office (1986) **Annual Abstract of Statistics** HMSO London

Chartered Surveyor Weekly (1988) **Riding into in-town centres with Capco** Town Centre Retail Supplement 28 April p26

Cheeseright, Paul (1988) Bristol retail complex rejected on fears for city centre shops in **Financial Times** 21 September

City of Birmingham (1986) **Birmingham Shopping Survey First Report**

City of Wakefield (1987) **Printout of Shopping Survey** Unpublished data

Clements, Dr Michael A (1987) Sunday Trading : is partial deregulation the answer? in **Retail & Distribution Management** March/April Vol.15 No.2 pp14-16.

Cox, R (1986) John Lewis Partnerships Maintains Excellent Progress in **Retail and Distribution Management** November/December pp66-68
- (1987a) Will confident Sainsbury be overtaken by energetic Tesco? in **Retail and Distribution Management** January/Febraury pp62-64
- (1987b) The onward and upward progress of Woolworth in **Retail and Distribution Management** May/June 1987 pp66-68
- (1988) Another outstanding performance from Sainsbury in **Retail and Distribution Management** September/October pp58-60

Davies, Ross L (1984) **Retail and Commercial Planning** London Croom Helm
- (1986) Retail Planning In Disarray in **The Planner** Vol 72 No 7 July
- (1988) The High Street in Britain : Choices for the Future in Hass-Klau, Carmen (ed) **New life for city centres** London The Anglo-German Foundation

Dawson, John A, A M Finally and L Sparks (1986) **Anatomy of Job Growth : Employment in British Superstores** Institute for Retail Studies University of Stirling Working Paper 8601

Dawson, John A and Adelina M Broadbridge (1988) **Retailing in Scotland 2005** Institute for Retail Studies, University of Stirling

Departments of the Environment and Transport (1977) **The Eastleigh Carrefour hypermarket after three years**

Department of the Environment (1987) **Draft Planning Policy Guidance: Major Retail Development**
- (1988) **Planning Policy Guidance: Major Retail Development**
- (n.d) **Strategic Planning Guidance for the West Midlands** Birmingham

Donaldson & Sons (1975) **Caerphilly Hypermarket Study Year Two**
- (1977) **Brent Cross Study**

Estates Times (1988) **In-town Shopping** 29 April

Evely, Richard (1980) The Impact of New Developments : The Coatbridge Study in PTRC **Retailing** (Proceedings of Summer Annual Meeting)

Falk, B (1983) **Europäische Shopping-Center-Untersuchung - Deutschland-Überblick** Urach, Baden-Württemberg Institut für Gewerbezentren

Gibbs, Anne (1985) Planners and Retail Innovation in **The Planner** Vol 71 No 5 May

Goad (1986) **Directory of Out-of-Centre Retailing**

Greater London Council (1979) **The Impact of a Superstore : Tesco Finchley Central**

Hallsworth, Alan G (n.d.) **Trading Patterns, Asda, Waterlooville** Department of Geography Portsmouth Polytechnic

- (1986) **Trading Patterns : B&Q Havant** Department of Geography Portsmouth Polytechnic

Hampson, Stuart (1988) Planning a Future of Quality Shops in **Town and Country Planning** Vol 57 No 9 September

Hass-Klau, Carmen (ed)(1988) **New Life for City Centres : Planning, transport and conservation in British and German Cities** London The Anglo-German Foundation

Hillier Parker (1986) **Shopping Schemes in the Pipeline** June
- (1988) **Call for Action**

Howard, Elizabeth B, and Ross L Davies (1987a) **Retail Change on Tyneside : Third Consumer Survey in the Metro Centre** Oxford Institute of Retail Management Research Paper A14, Templeton College Oxford
- (1987b) **Retail Change on Tyneside : Pedestrian Surveys in Newcastle and the Metro Centre** Oxford Institute of Retail Management Research Paper A13, Templeton College Oxford
- (1988) **Change in the Retail Environment** Harlow, Essex Longman

Hurdle, David (1986) **Shopping Trips to Town Centres. GLTS Analysis Report No 15 TS Note 172** Greater London Council

Huws, Ursula (1988) Consuming Fashions in **New Statesman and Society** 19 August pp31-34

Ingham, John (1988) A social experiment in shopping in **Chartered Surveyor Weekly** 31 March pp44-45

Institute of Grocery Distribution (1987) **Food Retailing Review** IGD Watford

Jeffreys, J B (1954) **Retail Trading in Britain 1850 - 1950** Cambridge University Press

King, William (1987) The Future Rôles of Town Centres in **The Planner** Vol 73 No 4 April

Kirby, Dr David (1987) **Personal Communication** St David's University College Lampeter

Lee Donaldson Associates (1986,1988) **Shopping Centre Appeals Review**

London Borough of Brent (1986) **Tesco, Neasden : a study of the retail impact**

London Boroughs of Hammersmith & Fulham and Lambeth (1986) **Sainsbury's at Nine Elms : a study of an inner city superstore**

London Borough of Havering (1984) **Hornchurch Sainsbury : a superstore survey**

London Planning Advisory Committee (1988) **Strategic Planning Advice for London : policies for the 1990s** LPAC

London Research Centre (1986) **Retail Warehouses in London** Review and Studies Series Number 30

London Strategic Policy Unit (1987a) **Superstores and Their Impact : A Coherent Approach** London LSPU
- (1987a) **Shopping in Sheds : Retail Warehouses - an Inner London Perspective** London LSPU

McIntosh A P J (1987) The Future for Retail Property Investment in PTRC **Retailing out-of-town : the Issues and Implications** (Proceedings of Summer Annual Meeting)

McRae, H (1987) There is no hey presto way of getting your local food store into the up-market area in **The Guardian** 13 August p18

Milner, Mark, and Daniel John (1988) Hey big spenders - it looks like the party's over in **The Guardian** 27 August p11

Mitton, Alan E (1987) Foreign Retail Companies Operating in the UK in **Retail and Distribution Management** January/February pp29-31

Money Observer (1988) **Battle of the Giants: M&S v J.Sainsbury** August pp4-7

Moore, Stuart (1987) **Personal Communication** Tesco Stores PLC

National Economic Development Office (1988) **The Future of the High Street** London NEDO Books

Parkes, C (1987a) Restless and Growth Hungry in **Financial Times** Special Supplement 10 June pI
- (1987b) Majors fight for sheer bulk in **Financial Times** Special Supplement 10 June pIII
- (1987c) A whole family affair in **Financial Times** Special Supplement

10 June pIV

Pegano, M (1987a) Shocked Hillards attack greed of Prudential in **The Guardian**
16 May

- (1987b) Sainsbury takes control of US chain in £115M deal in **The Guardian** 20 June

Percival, Graham (1987) **Personal Communication** Surrey County Council

Percy, Steve and Harriet Lamb (1988) Stuck in the basement in **New Statesman and Society** 28 October   pp27-28

Planning (1986) **Bradford sets out stall for west end equivalent** No 695
21 November p5

- (1987a) **Camden Considers Station Area Plans** No 730   7 August p6
- (1987b) **Revival of Street** No 732   21 August p2
- (1987c) **Sandwell Approves plans for Disabled** No 733   28 August p5
- (1988a) **Portsmouth proof of retail pudding** No 752   22 January p7
- (1988b) **Leicester Wins on Centre Plan** No 776   8 July p3
- (1988c) **Urban Role Remains Unrecognised** No 776 8 July p3

Plowden, Stephen (1988) Superstores in **The LATA Review** No 66 p8 Winter

Roger Tym and Partners (1986) **Greater Manchester Shopping Study**

Roberts, John and Sarah Wenden (1984) DIY Outlets : In or out of town? **Paper to PTRC Annual Summer Meeting** University of Sussex

Royal Borough of Kensington & Chelsea (1984) **1984 Residents' Shopping Survey**

Royal Town Planning Institute (1988) **Planning for Shopping Into the 21st Century**

Schiller, Russell (1986) Retail Decentralisation - The Coming of the Third Wave in **The Planner** Vol 72 No 7 July

SEEDS (1987) **Trade Winds : the Changing Face of Retailing and Retail Employment in the South East - An Alternative Strategy** The SEEDS Association

Seidle, Amanda (1988) In-town Shopping in   **Estates Times** April 29

Sparks, Leigh (1983a) Employment and Superstores in **The Planner** Vol 69 No 1 January/February p16

- (1983b) A Review of Retail Employment Since 1959 with Specific Focus on Aspects of Superstore Employment in PTRC **Retail Planning and Development** (Proceedings of Summer Annual Meeting)

Sumner, Jennifer and Keri Davies (1978) Hypermarkets and Superstores : What Do The Planning Authorities Really Think? in **Retail Distribution and Management** Vol 6 No 4 July/ August pp8-15

Tesco PLC (1986) **Annual report and Accounts 1986**

TEST (1987) **Big Spenders By Bus** London TEST

The Planner (1987) **Retailer condemns free run of market forces** May Mid Month Supplement p5

Thomas, Colin J and Rosemary D F Bromley (1987) The Growth and Functioning of an Unplanned Retail Park : The Swansea Enterprise Zone in **Regional Studies** Vol 21.4 pp 287-300

Thorpe, Dr D (1987) **Personal Communication** The John Lewis Partnership

Unit for Retail Planning Information (URPI) (1986) **List of Hypermarkets and Superstores** Reading

3 SOUTH HAMPSHIRE

SUMMARY

3-01
South Hampshire illustrates many of the processes that have been outlined in Chapter 2. The policies adopted by Hampshire County Council in its Structure Plans have been tempered by the Government's market principles, changing from measures designed to restrict retail development to town centres to policies which suggest that two retail warehouse parks and one non-central regional shopping centre should be permitted. The adoption of a more flexible approach to out-of-centre retailing has at the same time given the County a more credible stand, and encouraged more development pressure to build up.

3-02
Within South Hampshire, the cities of Southampton and Portsmouth are strongly opposed to out-of-centre retail development, and are keen to improve their own shopping facilities. Both cities have major shopping centres under construction, while Southampton also has a number of major proposals in the pipeline. The threat from off-centre schemes has stimulated environmental improvement, both cities are committed to pedestrianisation, and are even considering glazing over sections of the prime shopping streets to improve shopping conditions. There is also a concern to make the city centres more attractive to car users by increasing the number of parking spaces and even roadbuilding. It is argued that by trying to mimic the car access of out-of-centre developments, cities may be putting their own future at stake by destroying those features which make town centres attractive as places to be.

3-03
While Government policies have ensured a relaxation of County planning policies, and town centres have concentrated on consolidating their retail provision, pressure for out-of-centre retailing has grown. The area has above average income and car ownership rates, and has the east-west M27 running like a spine between the two cities - all factors which have made the area attractive to developers. Around Southampton, in Test Valley and Eastleigh districts, a large number of proposals for retail warehouse parks and larger schemes have come forward, often clustered around motorway junctions. There are proposals for regional shopping centre type schemes at Adanac Park in Eastleigh and on Lord Romsey's estate, while there are suggestions that such a scheme could be built at Whitely. These outer local authorities, while not supporting all such proposals, clearly stand to gain from any trade that might be lured away from established sub-regional centres.

INTRODUCTION AND BACKGROUND

3-04
South Hampshire includes the cities of Southampton and Portsmouth and a number of smaller centres such as Fareham, Gosport and Eastleigh. The area is bounded by the sea along its southern edge, and it goes as far north as the southern outskirts of Winchester. This area is experiencing some of the strongest pressures for non-central retail development found in Britain today. These pressures are clearly exposing the growing weaknesses of the planning system. Urban local authorities are set against non-central shopping, fearing the erosion and possible collapse of their well established town centres, while others, particularly those espousing the 'free-market ethic' and those in expanding peripheral locations, see new forms of retailing as a means of bringing employment and wealth to their district. We have seen that Central

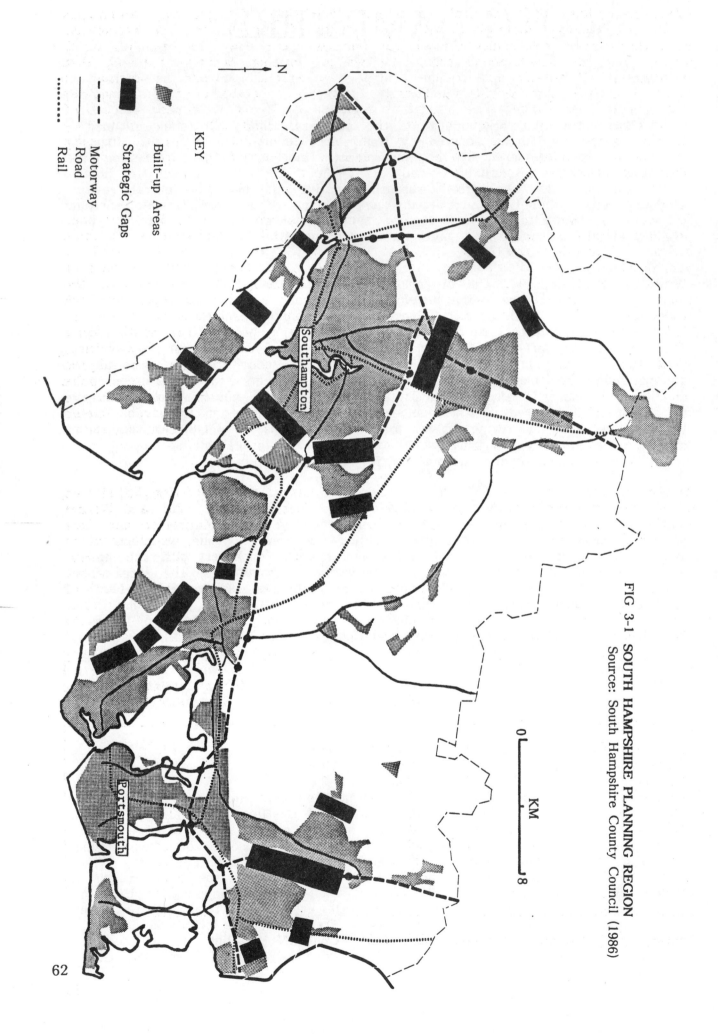

KEY

Built-up Areas

Strategic Gaps

Motorway
Road
Rail

Southampton

Portsmouth

0   KM   8

FIG 3-1 SOUTH HAMPSHIRE PLANNING REGION
Source: South Hampshire County Council (1986)

62

Government has made several statements indicating that planning authorities should not concern themselves with the effects of competition. The result has been that Hampshire County Council has had to move away from policies which stated that all development should be within existing centres, realising that if it set itself totally against non central development it would be accused of being unrealistic and would stand little chance of success at public enquiries and appeals. The County has altered its policies to favour a **limited amount** of out-of-centre retail development, in the hope of channelling and restricting it. The success of this approach has yet to be seen. Meanwhile South Hampshire districts are dealing with this huge issue in an uncoordinated, uninformed and often self interested manner.

3-05

The planning region of South Hampshire, which is shown in Figure 3-1, has been provided with a network of rapid roads such as the M27, which links the main cities. Figure 3-2 illustrates the huge catchments that have been created by the construction of South Hampshire's motorways. Portsmouth and Southampton also have good rail links, with each other, with cities such as Winchester and London, and with the south coast to east and west. Despite its legacy of dock industries and recent pressures for urban growth, South Hampshire is an area of environmental constraint. In the north east of the region lie the South Downs which include Queen Elizabeth Country Park, to the West is the New Forest, while the Solent and English Channel lie to the south. The importance of the environment is reinforced by a series of 'strategic gaps' or mini-green belts between built up areas, also shown in Figure 3-1. These are areas which are often subject to the greatest pressures for development, but which remain essential if further urban expansion is to be controlled to prevent the region from developing into one large conurbation.

3-06

The South Hampshire planning region does not correspond to district boundaries. It includes the whole of Southampton, Eastleigh, Fareham, Portsmouth and Havant districts, together with parts of New Forest, Test Valley, Winchester and East Hampshire Districts. Table 3-3, which displays population and unemployment in these districts, indicates that population has been increasing with the exception of Southampton, Portsmouth and Gosport. These districts also have above average unemployment levels, factors which reinforce the attractiveness of outer areas to developers.

Table 3-3 : South Hampshire Population and Unemployment

| District | Mid-year population (000s) | | | Unemployment (%) |
	1981	1983	1984	September 1985
East Hampshire	91.9	93.6	95.0	6.5
Eastleigh	93.0	96.0	97.6	7.4
Fareham	89.0	90.8	92.6	8.4
Gosport	77.8	77.1	77.2	8.4
Havant	115.7	116.6	117.4	13.0
New Forest	145.5	149.0	151.3	9.0
Portsmouth	191.4	191.6	188.6	15.3
Southampton	209.9	206.3	203.9	15.1
Test Valley	93.7	95.5	97.1	7.1
Winchester	93.0	92.3	92.4	6.9

Source: OCPS Mid-year Population Estimates, SERPLAN 1986

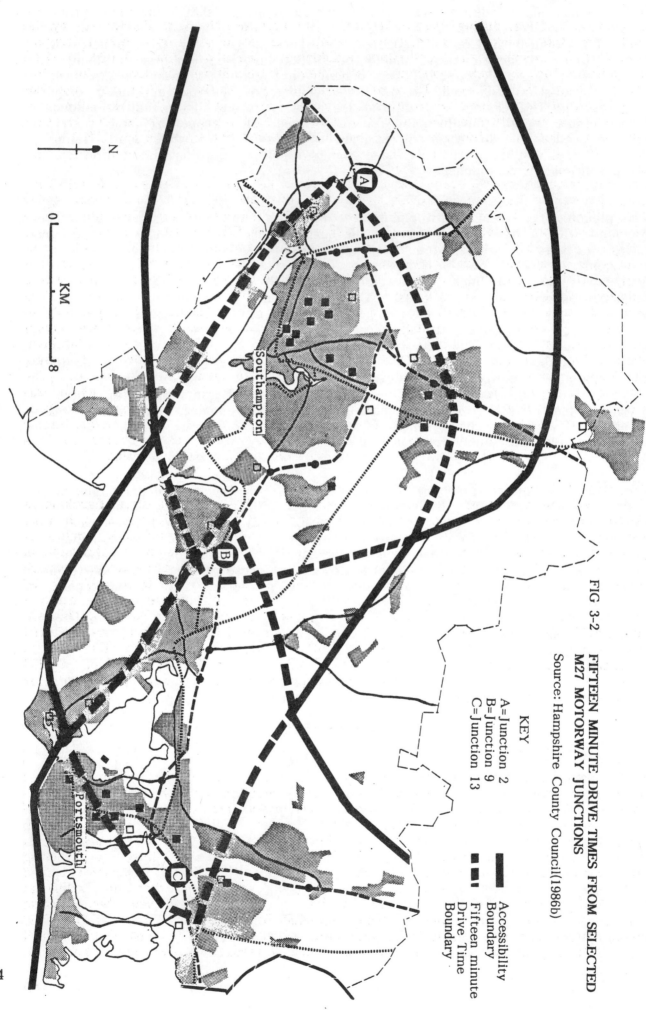

FIG 3-2
FIFTEEN MINUTE DRIVE TIMES FROM SELECTED
M27 MOTORWAY JUNCTIONS

Source: Hampshire County Council(1986b)

KEY

A=Junction 2
B=Junction 9
C=Junction 13

Accessibility
Boundary

Fifteen minute
Drive Time
Boundary

Southampton

Portsmouth

N

0

KM

8

64

3-07

Despite a decline during recent decades, Southampton is still dominated by its dock facilities. Today most traffic takes the form of containerised cargoes rather than luxury ocean liners. Dock employment stood at about 10 000 in 1986. In addition to the dock functions, Southampton is dominated by five major employers - Ford, BAT, Vosper Thorneycroft, Pirelli and Mullard. The city also has a substantial administrative role, with office floorspace totalling 450 000 m^2. Southampton has a catchment of half a million people, and has been able to develop as the region's primary shopping centre (Chartered Surveyor Weekly 1986).

3-08

Portsmouth too has had long associations with the sea, largely as a naval base. Employment at the base, however, has fallen from 25 000 in 1945 to about 2 500 today. Civilian ferry operations have prospered however, mainly at the expense of Southampton. In 1985, Portsmouth handled 1.74 million passengers and 400 000 vehicles. While overall there has been a fall in employment in the docks, new industries have moved into the area. The most important new employer is undoubtedly IBM who have located their UK headquarters at North Harbour. This was a considerable boon for the City, and is viewed in the same terms as gaining Marks & Spencers or John Lewis in a new shopping development! IBM employ 2 000 people in Portsmouth and occupy 100 000 m^2 of office space. Other electronics companies, primarily in the field of defence include names such as Marconi, Plessey and Thorn-EMI (Chartered Surveyor Weekly 1986). Unlike Southampton, Portsmouth does not benefit from a single, well developed shopping centre. The ten original shopping areas were gradually reduced to five, but even this leaves the city with a dispersed pattern of retailing. This aggravates the problems brought about by Portsmouth's location on a peninsula, since it suffers a limited market catchment and a lack of room to expand. These problems combine to leave Portsmouth vulnerable to competition from beyond its boundaries.

3-09

Other centres in the region include Fareham, Eastleigh and Gosport. Fareham is at the centre of an expanding area and has received huge investment in housing and employment. The Solent Business Park near Segensworth typifies a number of proposals which should ensure the continued growth of high income employment in the area. The largest employer in the area is Plessey. Within Eastleigh Borough there are two growth areas - Chandlers Ford and Hedge End. Proposals for the area include a business park. Eastleigh's employment is provided by a mixture of traditional industry (eg British Rail Engineering and Rank Hovis McDougall) and new light industrial and high technology companies. Gosport has suffered high unemployment rates, but is currently trying to build on its tourism potential. Developments are likely to result in the construction of a 600 berth marina at Haslar Lake and the construction of a new hotel complex (Chartered Surveyor Weekly 1986).

PLANNING HISTORY

3-10

South Hampshire has long been an area of planning controversy. This has most often been the result of growth imposed from outside onto a largely conservative area. The 1964 South East Study anticipated growth and the importance attached to decentralisation from London. The study concluded that South Hampshire would be able to absorb an additional 300 000 migrants in addition to its natural rate of increase. A report by Buchanan for the Ministry of Housing and Local Government completed two years later (the **South Hampshire Study**) endorsed the region's potential for growth, and suggested that an additional 1 million people could be absorbed by 1981. The study argued that existing congestion in Southampton and Portsmouth called for major new urban growth, and it suggested that this should take the form of a settlement which would spread from Southampton eastwards for about 24 miles towards the West Sussex border in an 8 mile wide grid of development. Regional plans produced in 1967 and 1970, did not propose growth on the scale envisaged by Buchanan, but nevertheless did support further growth in the area. This was to be encouraged by the construction of motorways and other infrastructure such as sewerage systems.

3-11

These strategies for growth, and the Buchanan Report in particular, helped focus the minds of conservative local authorities in South Hampshire. A number of different models of growth were considered during the formulation of the South Hampshire Structure Plan (submitted in 1973, approved in 1977). The final choice was perhaps the most limited of the available alternatives and suggested that growth would be allowed along the motorway corridor between Southampton and Portsmouth, together with limited expansion of existing towns.

3-12

Examining the development of South Hampshire's Structure Plan shopping policies, Hallsworth (1987) observed an acceptance of future growth in car ownership, of continued suburbanisation and the growth of consumer demand. Planners at this time may have been toying with the concept of decentralised retailing, but a visit to the United States by the County Planning Officer may have put the County off the whole idea. The Draft Plan, published in 1972, argued that suitable conditions for non-central shopping would not exist until the late 1970s or the early 1980s, and at that time local planning authorities would refuse even to consider such development. Soon after the publication of this Draft Plan, however, permission was granted on appeal for a Carrefour hypermarket at Chandlers Ford, Eastleigh. The County simply altered its statement so as to indicate that local authorities would not consider **further** non-central stores. This stance was justified on three grounds; first that the County wanted to concentrate development in existing district centres, second because the effects of large new stores had not been properly examined, and third because such developments would not fit into Structure Plan provisions such as those for transport. This total refusal to consider non-central stores was included at the insistence of elected members, it had no legal status since local authorities are obliged to consider any application made to them. It is not suprising therefore that the Secretary of State modified the Structure Plan so that each application would be considered in the light of its provisions, and any additional information which became available about the effects of such stores.

3-13

The South Hampshire Structure Plan therefore showed a strong commitment among elected members to the maintenance of the existing shopping hierarchy. However, it is unlikely that the main motive for this lay in principles of welfare and fairness. Hallsworth (1987) implies it was largely a result of the heavy postwar investment in both Southampton and Portsmouth city centres, and because of the vested interests of the elected members, many of whom represented small businesses. Non-central development was seen as a threat to the viability of town centre retailing which had been the focus of reconstruction efforts after the war. Small businesses were concentrated in these areas and stood to lose out should custom be lured away by large retail groups located near the wealthier suburbs.

3-14

By 1978 Hampshire County Council were well aware of the threat posed by out-of-centre retailing. One hypermarket had been built (Carrefour at Chandlers Ford), permission having been won on appeal; elsewhere two appeals had been dismissed and the decision on a third was awaited. The political climate was very different from that prevailing today, and the County was able to put forward the strategy it thought best for retailing in the region. This meant confining new retailing development to town centres. The County felt that changes in retailing were occurring so rapidly that the Structure Plan was already outdated. Consequently it published a draft document for public comment titled 'Shopping Policies in South Hampshire'. This was a policy statement that set out the County's approach to retailing development and reiterated its commitment to town centres.

3-15
Hampshire County Council already recognised the growing attractiveness of car-based grocery stores to a large section of the population. While not objecting to them in principle, the County wished to steer such development toward existing town centres (This, they argued, would be dependent on shopping centres expanding their car parking facilities and improving their roads...'If centres are to remain competitive, so that their essential social and community roles can be maintained, the local planning authorities must take steps to implement their policies and to invest in roads and car parks in town centres'). Continued town centre development was seen as advantageous for the following reasons:

* centres are readily accessible to most sectors of the population,
* the concentration of facilities in centres is economical,
* the concentration of facilities in centres which are readily accessible by different means of transport gives flexibility to accommodate economic, social and technological changes which might fundamentally alter the way people travel,
* centres help generate a sense of identity,
* greater benefit for the community can be achieved by guiding commercial development into town centres.

3-16
The County considered that provision should be allowed for car-borne shoppers, but that such development should take place within existing centres. The existing network of superstores at Lord's Hill, Chandlers Ford and Gosport would be supplemented by new stores at Totton, Waterlooville and Park Gate, to ensure that a superstore was within 10 minutes off-peak drive of all built up areas. Retail warehouse developments would normally only be allowed in centres or on their fringes.

3-17
Support for this approach came from the Government in Development Control Policy Note 13 (HMSO 1977), where it was stated that investment in these new shops should help to benefit older urban centres rather than be used to develop sites outside towns. Thus the County was putting forward these directions with the support of central government, a situation very different from that of today.

3-18
In 1978 then, Hampshire County Council's position was clear:

'The County recognises that adequate provision should be made for those who wish to shop in large car based stores. There is no aspect of recent trends in retailing which suggests that shopping development cannot or should not continue to be concentrated in district centres. The County Council therefore considers that provision for large car-based stores should be made in district centres where adequate access and parking can be provided. Consideration should be given to out of centre facilities only where adequate provision cannot be made in district centres.' (Hampshire CC 1978)

3-19
Earlier chapters have shown that retailing has been affected by enormous changes since the late 1970s. These changes have occurred in consumer behaviour, in the structure and operations of the retail sector itself, and probably most

profoundly, in Government policy. The effect of these changes has been to shift developers' and retailers' interests from town centres to out-of-centre retailing. The combination of market changes with the reorientation of Government policy has meant that the balance of power now rests with developers and retailers rather than with local authorities.

3-20

By 1984 Hampshire County Council was able to submit alterations to the South Hampshire Structure Plan. The alterations show a slight movement away from the position held in the past. They were prepared on the premise that the best interests of both shoppers and retailers are served by encouraging the provision of a variety of different types of shopping centre. These included stores easily accessible both to pedestrians and by car. However, the County went on to conclude that its strategy of concentrating additional retail floorspace in existing centres had been successful. The alterations were also drawn up on the basis of reduced estimates of population growth and spending growth, with the result that existing commitments were considered sufficient to last until the early 1990s. The Council therefore concluded there was only very limited scope for further new schemes. All new floorspace was to be developed in existing or proposed centres, and it stated that superstores would not normally be granted permission outside such a location.

3-21

The Alterations provided floorspace guidelines (Table 3-4) which reflected the established hierarchy of centres. First priority was to be given to improving and strengthening the role of Portsmouth and Southampton as sub-regional centres. This would include implementation of the Cascades Centre in Portsmouth and the Western Esplanade scheme in Southampton. Eastleigh and Fareham needed additional floorspace to secure the improvement of facilities, while new and expanded centres would serve the needs of the population moving into new growth areas such as Totton, Fareham Western Wards and Whitely. Other main centres would be encouraged to improve and modernise. It is significant that no guidelines were given for out-of-centre developments. Superstores and discount warehouses were to be encouraged to develop within or on the edge of centres, though where sites were not available permission to develop out of centre might exceptionally be granted. Table 3-4 highlights the failure of the County's 1981-1996 floorspace guidelines to influence the nature of development. By the end of 1985, out-of-centre retailing, which the guidelines had not permitted, exceeded that built in-centre, while the total amount of retail space completed amounted to nearly 40% of that allocated up to 1996.

3-22

By late 1986 planning officers at Hampshire County Council once again felt that it was time to reconsider the Council's strategic policies toward retailing. It was spurred into action by several factors. The market was demanding very large additions to floorspace in certain locations, while previous estimates of the growth of consumer expenditure were proving to be underestimates. The most significant factor however was the free market approach emanating from the Department of the Environment. Recalling its earlier failures when opposing hypermarket development in the 1970s, the County was determined to develop positive but regulating policies which would be viewed as realistic by the Secretary of State and the developers involved. It seemed that any County policy would therefore have to include some measure of non-central development, not because the County necessarily thought this was the best policy for South Hampshire, but simply because if it was to have any influence over the outcome it would have to be regarded as credible and progressive. Central Government had therefore shifted the planning debate from **whether there should be out-of-centre** retailing to **how much and where** this should be.

Table 3-4: Shopping Floorspace Guidelines and Completions 1981-1985 (m^2)

	Structure Plan Guideline 1981-1996	Floorspace Built 1 November 1981- 1 November 1985[2]
East Hants out-of-centre	-	0
Hythe Centre	3 000[1]	1 100
Totton Centre	10 700	6 300
New Forest out-of-centre	-	0
Eastleigh Centre	28 500	3 200
Eastleigh out-of-centre	-	4 200
Romsey Centre	3 000[1]	0
Test Valley out-of-centre	-	0
Southampton Centre	28 000	0
Shirley Centre	3 000[1]	5 300
Lord's Hill Centre	4 750[1]	1 900
Portswood Centre	0	0
Bitterne Centre	6 500	3 100
Woolston Centre	0	0
Southampton out-of-centre	-	4 700
Fareham Centre	25 000	0
Fareham Western Wards Centre	7 200	8 500
Porchester Centre	3 000[1]*	0
Fareham out-of-centre	-	18 300
Gosport Centre	2 500	0
Gosport out-of-centre	-	0
Commercial Road, Portsmouth	37 000	0
Southsea Centre	0	0
North End Centre	0	3 500
Fratton Centre	0	0
Cosham Centre	9 800	2 200
Portsmouth out-of-centre	-	6 900
Havant Centre	12 000	0
Waterlooville Centre	3 000[1]	0
Leigh Park Centre	3 000[1]	0
Havant out-of-centre	-	8 700
Whitely Centre	7 500	0
Winchester out-of-centre	-	0
TOTAL in centres	-	35 100
out-of-centres	-	42 800
TOTAL	197 450	77 900

Notes : 1 Subject to provisions on timing and outstanding commitments at 1 November 1981

2 Floorspace 1981-1985 derived from monitoring of net changes in gross shopping floorspace: changes of more than +/- 1 000 m^2 only

Source: Hampshire County Council 1986a

3-23

Between 1981 and 1985 there was substantial pressure for retail floorspace increases, clearly indicated by a large number of enquiries, applications and appeals for in-centre and out-of-centre schemes. This pressure has been mirrored in the amount of new floorspace actually completed during the period (Table 3-4). Hampshire County Council (1986a) estimated that in 1971 the gross shopping floorspace in South Hampshire stood at 1.075 million m^2. By 1981 this had risen to 1.289 million m^2 of which 55% was located in defined centres, while in 1985 the total stood at 1.367 million m^2. 55% of the increase in floorspace between 1981 and 1985 was located outside defined centres. The shift of interest on the part of retail developers was also evident in the take up of commitments. Table 3-5 shows that commitments in town centres were being taken up at a significantly slower rate than developments in non-central locations. In addition, while commitments in town-centres are quite large and represent several years development, prospects for new floorspace (ie enquiries and applications not yet given permission) have completely dried up, while prospects for non-central development are very substantial. While it should be noted that a large proportion of non-central schemes will not reach fruition, the contrast with in-centre development is stark. The commitments and prospects at July 1986 are shown in Table 3-5.

Table 3-5 : Commitments and prospects for floorspace in South Hampshire July 1986 (m^2)

	Change 1981-85	Commit- ments[1]	Prospects[2]	Total commitments & prospects, 1986
IN CENTRES				
Ordinary shopping	28 900	121 500	0	121 500
Retail warehouses	6 200	4 700	0	4 700
Total in centre	**35 100**	**126 200**	**0**	**126 200**
OUT OF CENTRE				
Ordinary shopping	8 500	15 200	148 700	163 900
Retail warehouses	34 300	57 600	88 300	145 900
Total out of Centre	**42 800**	**72 800**	**237 000**	**309 800**
TOTAL				
Ordinary shopping	37 400	136 700	148 700	285 400
Retail warehouses	40 500	62 300	88 300	150 600
TOTAL	**77 900**	**199 000**	**237 000**	**436 000**

Notes : 1 Includes schemes built from November 1985
2 Planning applications and proposals not yet applications, estimated at July 1986

Source: Hampshire County Council (1986a)

3-24

Having examined the changes which have been affecting retailing, and gauging the extent of pressure for development by monitoring applications, Hampshire County Council set about deciding what its policy stance should be. It argued that pressure for development can be classified into four types of scheme:

* regional centres of up to 100 000 m^2, known as "mega-centres",
* centres of up to 25 000 m^2,
* retail warehouse parks,
* new leisure facilities, either freestanding or in conjunction with one of the above.

3-25
The county undertook a study to determine whether any sites suitable for large retail developments existed in South Hampshire. The study concluded that there was no site suitable for a 100 000 m^2 centre which had both suitable physical/ highway characteristics and an absence of key policy or other constraints. As a result county planners argued that this type of development should be ruled out at present.

3-26
The impact of 25 000 m^2 schemes was also considered. The evaluation concent- rated on the corridor formed by the M27. To the north of Southampton any development would be complex because of its location close to Eastleigh Airport, and it would threaten the Eastleigh-Southampton strategic gap. Impact on Eastleigh town centre could also be a problem. Further east at Hedge End and Bursledon, the motorway passes through strategic gaps where development is constrained. In addition, development here would threaten the urban structure to the east of Southampton. Development at Whitely would be possible given certain highway improvements, although the impact on Fareham town centre would have to be carefully considered. Sites north of Fareham and Portsmouth were ruled out because of landscape and strategic gap policies, while expansion at Waterlooville had already been vetoed by the Secretary of State in his approval of the first South Hampshire Structure Plan.

3-27
Having considered South Hampshire's ability to accommodate various forms of retail development, the County Council proceeded to put forward five scenarios of development as a basis for public consultation.

1. **Concentrate shopping floorspace in existing centres and resist entirely out- of-centre developments as indicated in previous shopping policies.** The County suggested that this approach had become unrealistic given the Secretary of State's decisions at recent appeals. This stance would be regarded as 'out of touch' and the County would be left with no influence over the final outcome.
2. **Encourage new floorspace in existing centres but allow some limited out-of- centre development.** This would have less impact on established centres, but would not meet market demands. It could also lead to a less convenient dispersal of shopping facilities. Such a policy might encourage the spread of retail warehouses.
3. **Allow one or two large developments out-of-centre of up to 25 000 m^2 in addition to current commitments to improve and extend established centres.** The County suggested that it would not be easy to reconcile this kind of development with policies for landscape protection, and the impact on existing town centres would have to be carefully considered. The locations of such developments would have to be closely controlled, and further pressure resisted. The advantage of such a planned approach would be that new development would be in locations where both the retailers and the local planning authority wished to see development.
4. **Allow a 'Mega Centre' of 100 000 m^2.** This would correspond to the total floorspace requirement till the end of the century. Major problems of traffic access and impact on nearby centres would be created. On the other hand, South Hampshire would gain a prestigious new development.

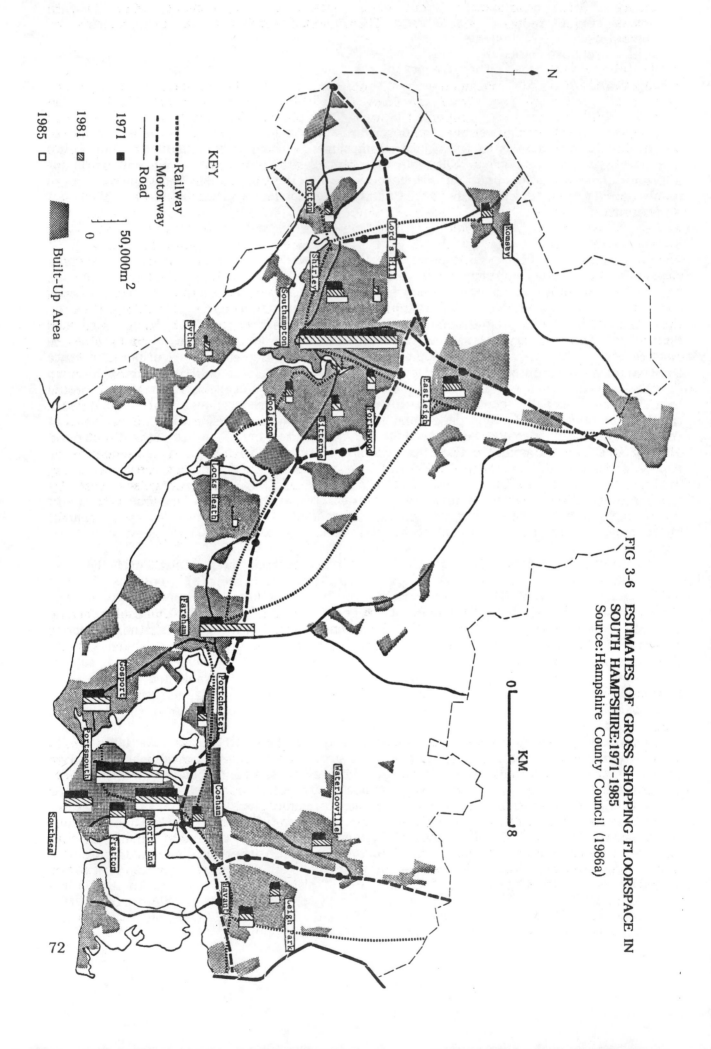

FIG 3-6 **ESTIMATES OF GROSS SHOPPING FLOORSPACE IN SOUTH HAMPSHIRE:1971-1985**
Source:Hampshire County Council (1986a)

KEY

Railway
Motorway
Road

1971 ■
1981 ▨
1985 □

Built-Up Area

50,000m²

0

0 KM 8

N

72

5. **Allow unrestrained development of new retailing where retailers wish to locate.** Most development would occur outside existing centres, which in turn would suffer reduced viability. There would probably be overprovision of floorspace.

3-28

The County Council obtained the reactions of local authorities and other interested parties to the above scenarios (Hampshire County Council 1987b). The majority of respondents supported further emphasis on existing centres, but attitudes toward out-of-centre development were less uniform. For instance, while local authorities such as Fareham and Southampton called for restraint, others like East Hampshire District Council argued that two large out-of-centre schemes should be permitted. Among private individuals, retailers, developers and their agents there were similar mixed attitudes towards non-central retail development. The County Council, while taking these views into account, still had to consider how it should go about creating a policy framework that would appear positive to the Secretary of State and which would be able to stand up at appeal. Inevitably the result was a compromise. On the one hand the County expressed continued emphasis on encouraging development within centres, while on the other it recognised the need to allow a limited amount of decentralised retailing. The final proposal suggested one regional centre totalling between 30 000 and 50 000 m^2 located somewhere halfway along the M27, along with two retail warehouse parks, one at either end of the corridor. The County Planner hinted (Nye 1987) that the new community being developed at Whitely might be a suitable location for the regional centre. This is despite Hampshire County Council's own Local Plan for Whitely (Hampshire County Council 1987a) which stated that 'a site of approximately 6.5 hectares is proposed for a district centre in which floorspace will be limited to no more than 7 500 m^2 gross' (policy DC1). This discrepancy clearly illustrates the speed with which the County has had to alter its position on new forms of retailing. A consequence of the acceptance of the inevitability of out-of-centre retailing has been a string of applications for such development. The County Council recognises that by going along with the market, even only to a limited extent, it has effectively compromised its ability to argue against such development in the future. However, political realities meant there was little alternative open to them.

EXISTING SHOPPING CENTRES AND RETAIL CHANGE IN SOUTH HAMPSHIRE

3-29

Figures 3-6 and 3-7 show the development of retailing in South Hampshire during the last two decades. Figure 3-6 shows the development of traditional centres between 1971 and 1985, Figure 3-7 indicates the location of existing out-of-centre retail warehouses.

Southampton

3-30

Southampton is the principal shopping centre in South Hampshire. The main streets are Above Bar Street, Bargate Street, East Street and part of High Street. The City Council is aware of the threat posed by out-of-centre development, and is therefore strongly promoting the city centre as a location for new retail development, and as a centre for education, administration, culture, entertainment and tourism. Several important town centre schemes are under construction or planned, and the city council is concerned that their success may be undermined by shopping developments outside the main centre. Figure 3-8 shows Southampton, together with the principal out-of-centre proposals current in 1987.

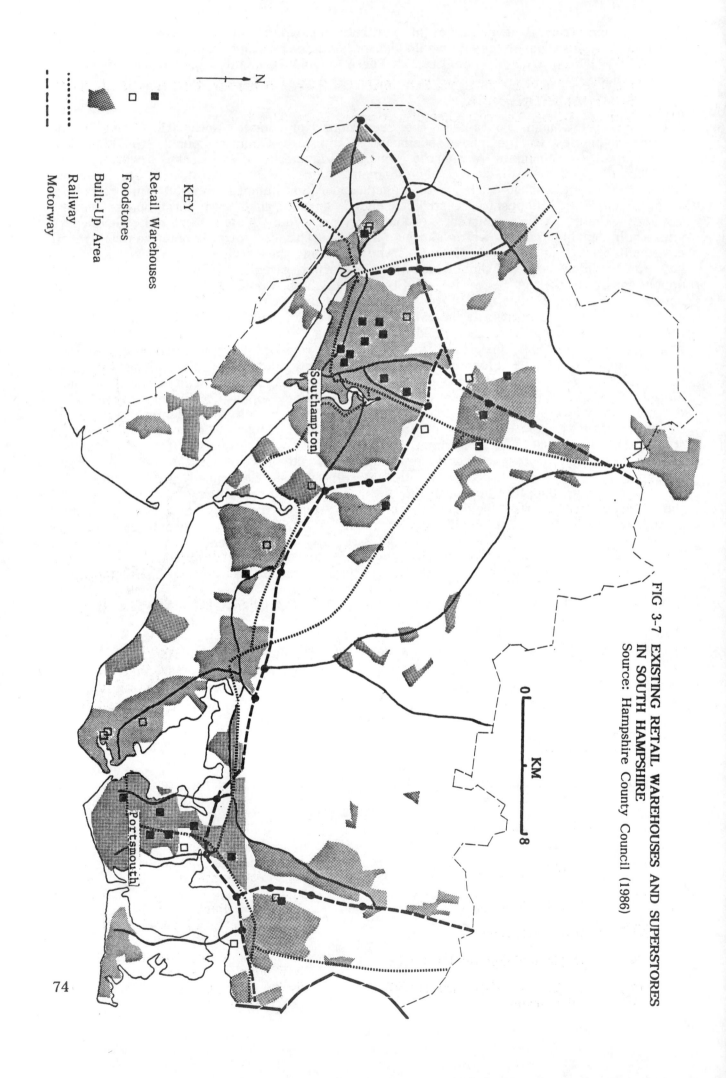

KEY

Retail Warehouses
Foodstores
Built-Up Area
Railway
Motorway

Southampton

Portsmouth

0   KM   8

FIG 3-7 EXISTING RETAIL WAREHOUSES AND SUPERSTORES
IN SOUTH HAMPSHIRE
Source: Hampshire County Council (1986)

74

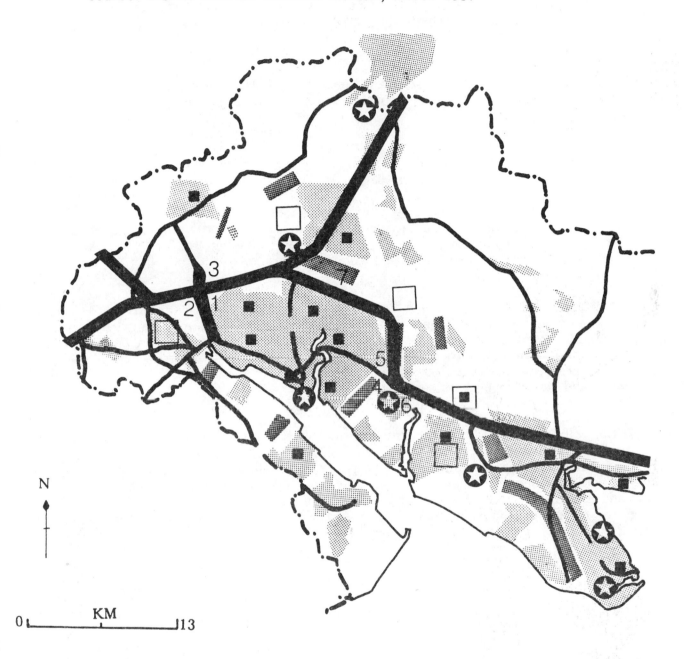

FIG 3-8

CURRENT APPLICATIONS FOR OUT-OF-TOWN SHOPPING CENTRES IN THE SOUTHAMPTON AREA
Source: DCAR District Councils Review; March 1987

N

0 ———— KM ———— 13

KEY

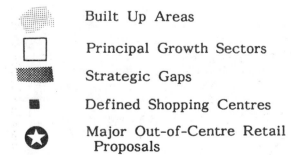

Built Up Areas

Principal Growth Sectors

Strategic Gaps

Defined Shopping Centres

Major Out-of-Centre Retail
Proposals

New Applications

1=Adanac Park
2=Nursling(retail warehouse)
3=Grove Lodge Farm
4=Hamble Lane, Hound(M&S)
5=Windhover Centre
6=The Grange
7=Wide Lane

75

3-31

For many years there have been attempts to secure development on the Western Esplanade to the northwest of the shopping area. Currently under construction is the Marlands Centre. Due for completion in mid-1990, the scheme totals 25 000 m^2 of retailing anchored by a department store, together with 7 000 m^2 of offices. Next to the Marlands centre, Gateway are building a 6 000 m^2 super-store. The project has been delayed on several occasions, but once completed will help stimulate the northern half of the shopping area, and is likely to lead to further pedestrianisation.

3-32

Nearby a 4 000 m^2 Toys R Us retail warehouse recently opened. This area, known as the central sector, is under consideration as a location for further retail warehouse development.

3-33

In the heart of the town centre, the first phase of a new speciality retailing centre is currently under construction. The Bargate Centre, which will comprise 50 or so small units, an atrium and a fast food court, will total 15 000 m^2 gross, although net trading floorspace will be about 8 000 m^2. The scheme will link into the pedestrianised Bargate Street and will include the replacement of an existing Woolworth store with a three level shopping mall. The scheme's second phase has already been granted planning permission.

3-34

A very different speciality centre is proposed at Princess Alexandra Dock. The scheme, known as Ocean Village, centres around a 300 berth marina with a speci-ality shopping centre called 'Canute's Pavilion' alongside. The pavilion inc-ludes 40 small trading units, a food hall, wine bar and restaurant. Proposals for two retail warehouse parks in the docks have recently been refused permission and have gone to appeal.

3-35

Given the current level of interest and activity in the city centre, it is cle-arly in the interests of the City Council to ensure that it remains an attrac-tive and viable shopping location. There is a feeling that out-of-centre devel-opment could seriously undermine many of the current schemes, not to mention older and more marginal areas of the town centre. As a consequence, the City is trying to underline the importance of the town centre in a number of different ways;

- the City Council has proposed to improve shopping facilities in the northern end of the city centre by extending pedestrianisation, and possibly by glazing over the street. Indeed, in July 1987 three development companies and the City Council were drawing up a major scheme for the northern end of Above Bar Street. The development will total some 40 000 m^2 and will house John Lewis's Tyrrell and Green department store as well as Plummers and C&A. The stores will link onto an enclosed shopping mall built on what is now Above Bar Street.(Chartered Surveyor Weekly 1987a).
- in attempts to make the city centre compete on equal terms with non-central schemes, the council has identified a need for an additional 1 400 to 2 300 car parking spaces.
- the city council became so worried about by the threat of out-of-town retailing that the elected members initiated a campaign designed to publicly highlight the disadvantages of such development. The Council employed a public relations company who ran a series of advertisements in the local press (see Figure 3-9). The campaign soon developed as a national campaign, and now aims to organise local authority opposition to non-central retail development, and to lobby government.
- councillors have considered a monorail network with twelve stations as a

SOUTHAMPTON NEEDS AN OUT OF TOWN SHOPPING CENTRE JUST AS MUCH.

When you've spent all your life working hard to build the best possible home for yourself and your family, you would feel pretty devastated if someone else came along and ruined everything you had strived for.

Fortunately — unless you're very unlucky — it won't happen to you. But it IS happening to the towns and cities in which most of us have made our lives.

Cities like Southampton haven't just 'arrived' overnight. The town which has been your home, your shopping centre, your source of business and interest, is the result of unceasing hard work and human endeavour stretching back over the centuries. Today it is successful because people are committed to making it a better, healthier, more attractive place in which to live and work.

Or rather, most people are because sadly, while we and other public and private sector bodies are spending on your behalf millions of pounds to build and maintain a more interesting and invigorating city, a handful of landowners, property developers and major financial institutions have other plans for your city's future.

For hard nosed business reasons they are trying to build vast out of town shopping centres on green field sites all around South Hampshire's main towns and cities. Already, applications have been submitted to build more than 3,500,000 square feet of shopping in your countryside. That's equivalent to well over two complete Southampton city centres or five Fareham's!!

Why? Well, they'll tell you that it's progress, that it's what you and everyone else wants. In truth, it's because they'd rather make millions quickly by throwing up retail warehouses on cheap land in the countryside than invest in the future of our towns and cities through developing the areas that are already there.

Anyone who tries to tell you that out of town retail megacentres won't affect long established shops and stores in city and district shopping centres really is pulling the wool over your eyes.

Not only would these retail parks rapidly kill off our main urban shopping centres, but they'd also

inflict extensive damage on all the other 'in town' attractions we have come to rely on — theatres and galleries, restaurants and leisure facilities, pubs and discos. The proof is already there to see, in the great North American cities which have been ruined by out of town retail schemes. And in Britain, where the "Let's move everyone out of town" planning mentality of the 50s and 60s is still taking its toll.

People belong in our towns and cities. We have created and built our villages, towns and cities because we are an urban society. The countryside serves the cities and towns by providing our food and our environment. It is not for superstores or vast car parks.

How can it make sense to transplant this type and scale of development into the rural belt, when most towns and cities have hundreds of acres of prime development land waiting for investment? Money that would provide new jobs, fresh opportunities and even greater amenities.

Even worse, how can it be right to let the developers of out of town shopping centres destroy the fabric of our urban heritage? Would YOU let them destroy everything you personally have worked for? No — you have worked and contributed to the building of our cities and centres of community life.

Get the facts about out of town shopping centres today, before out of town shopping centres become the undesirable fact of life tomorrow. Write for your free brochure now, to Southampton City Council, Room 318, Civic Centre, Southampton SO9 4XR.

SOUTHAMPTON CITY

Working for you

FIG 3-9 Southampton's Campaign Against Out-of-Centre Retailing

means of attracting shoppers to the city centre and away from prospective out-of-centre stores. (Planning 1987a)

3-36
Southampton City Council is therefore concentrating on enhancing its town centre shopping both to preclude out-of-centre development, and to enable the city to compete effectively should it occur. The city is in a vulnerable position given the proximity of major proposals in the neighbouring districts of Test Valley and Eastleigh. Any development here is beyond Southampton's control and yet could profoundly affect the viability of its town centre shopping. Hence the City Council's efforts to initiate a national campaign.

Portsmouth

3-37
Portsmouth City Council is also concerned about the possible effects of out-of-centre retailing on its shopping facilities. Indeed, Portsmouth has a much less cohesive retail structure than Southampton, and therefore is likely to be more vulnerable to competition from elsewhere. The linear form of most of the shopping areas also detracts from the city's attractiveness as a sub-regional centre. In terms of quality, Portsmouth also tends to lose out; too many of the city's shops are small and operating close to the margin of profitability. The town has very little room for expansion because of the high density of development and the fact that the city is surrounded on three sides by the sea. Portsmouth has a dispersed pattern of centres of which none has gained total dominance. However, large multiples have for many years been queueing up to get premises in the city, although most shopping units are too small for their current style of operations. It would seem that the City Council are justifiably worried about the effects of new forms of retailing.

3-38
Over the last twenty years it has been the City's policy to consolidate the existing five centres comprising Commercial Road, Palmerston Road, North End, Cosham and Fratton. This has been achieved by pedestrianisation, the provision of rear servicing access and the construction of multi-storey car parking. Retail development outside these areas has been discouraged. In the Commercial Road area, the largest of the five centres, additional problems have been posed by the Tricorn Centre. This brutalist concrete shopping precinct has become run down and has several vacant units, partly as a result of its poor design and partly because of its location on the very edge of the shopping area. On a neighbouring site however, work is under way on the Cascades scheme, a new shopping centre on Moores Square between the existing pedestrianised area of Commercial Road and the Tricorn Centre. Phase I will total 30 000 m^2 and will boast an atrium, wall-climbing lifts, a fast food court and an element of speciality shopping, all to be anchored by a BHS store. The scheme is due to open in 1989. An agreement suggests that Phase II of the Cascades Centre will include the renovation and integration of the Tricorn Centre.

3-39
The City Council is keen to exploit improvements that the new Cascades Centre will bring. The aim is to ensure the city centre's competitiveness with non-central shopping development should it occur on a substantial scale. As with Southampton, an apparent solution is to make the accessibility of the centre more like that of non-central developments, which results in a preoccupation with road building and car parking provision. The city estimates that it will be necessary to accommodate an additional 2 000 parking spaces. In addition there are plans to upgrade the pedestrianisation of Commercial Road, perhaps even glazing over the street to create a climatically controlled environment. Another idea being considered is to appoint a town centre management team who would be responsible for all aspects of the centre's day to day running.

FIG 3-10 EXISTING SHOPPING AREAS AND PROPOSED RETAIL WAREHOUSE PARKS IN PORTSMOUTH

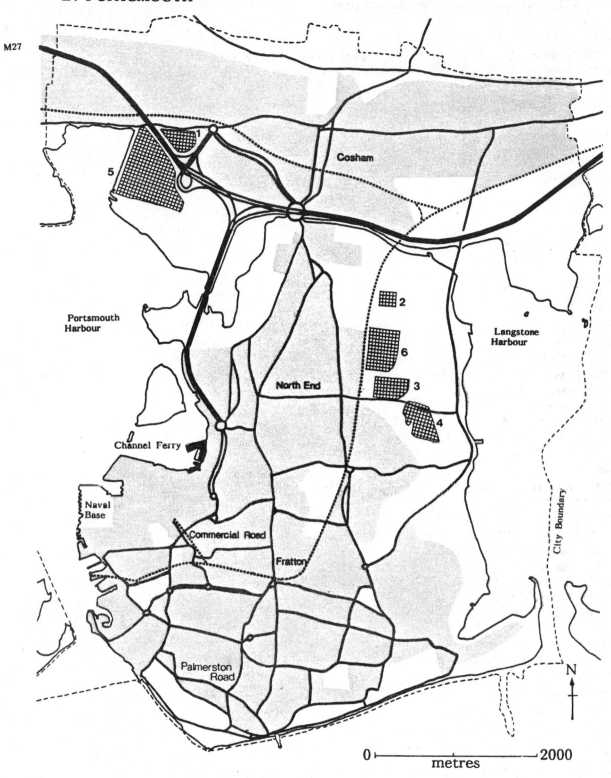

KEY

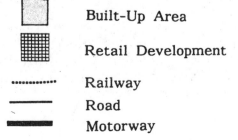

Built-Up Area

Retail Development

.... Railway

——— Road

━━━ Motorway

Developments

1=North Harbour Leisure Gardens
2=Airport Industrial Site Nº2
3=Metal Box Site
4=South Burfields Road Site
5=Port Solent Retail Site
6=Hilsea Gasworks Site

79

3-40

The City also sees advantage in capitalising on its tourism potential. British Ferries have been appointed to create a major tourism development on newly released land in Portsmouth Naval Base. The scheme could include up to 6 000 m^2 of speciality retailing. Other improvements include speciality shopping in Palmerston Road. The shopping street at Cosham may be upgraded and pedestrianised. These improvements could cost Portsmouth City Council £20M over the next ten years.

3-41

The emphasis on upgrading existing shopping facilities in Portsmouth is largely a response to the threat posed by new forms of retailing both within the city and beyond its boundaries. Existing and proposed retail warehouses are shown in Figure 3-10. Recognising the pressure for retail warehouse development, the City decided to try and guide these new stores to locations where their negative impact would be minimized. The Council identified five sites in or near existing shopping centres where such units could be built. The first of these to be completed is a W H Smith 'Do It All' close to Portsmouth's main railway station near Commercial Road. This initiative has already been overtaken by the next wave of retail warehouse development, the retail warehouse park. There were ten applications, totalling 140 000 m^2, for such schemes in the Portsmouth area in the space of twelve months. Unlike single units, these schemes cannot easily be fitted into existing centres, usually requiring greenfield sites or derelict land. The City Council decided to defer a decision on these applications until it had reviewed its policies in the light of the changes affecting retailing.

3-42

The economist Harvey Cole was commissioned to report on the possible impact of different retail warehouse locations, while the Council undertook public consultation the outcome of which reinforced the importance of town centre shopping. As a result of these assessments and consideration of the pressure for development, the City decided to permit a maximum of 20 000 m^2. Having decided on the appropriate level of provision, the council proceeded to consider the applications for retail parks.

3-43

Four applications were retail warehouse parks on council owned allotments near junction 12 of the M27 (Figure 3-10). The council rejected these proposals because they threatened a nearby row of houses and were the subject of much local opposition. The council was able to decide there would be no development here for the simple reason that it owned the land, so any appeal would not be upheld. Powers of land ownership are therefore much stronger than a local authority's planning powers. Central Government's measures to ensure local authorities dispose of their land holdings will negate this form of control.

3-44

Several applications for retail warehouse parks had been received for the area of land off Eastern Road. One scheme for the land vacated by Hilsea Gas Works was refused consent on the grounds that it would result in an unnacceptable loss of industrial land, while a scheme for 8 000 m^2 on the airport site was rejected because the level of development was too dense for such a small site. MFI, however, were given personal planning permission to extend their existing store by 2 400 m^2 to 5 500 m^2 in total. The two remaining applications in this area were for retail warehouse parks on either side of Burrfields Road. The schemes were almost identical, both totalled 18 500 m^2 and consisted of four or five units with a garden centre. However, the proposal on the southern side of Burrfields Road also included a leisure pool and a much sought after ice rink. The land to the north of Burrfields Road was owned by Metal Box, while that to the south was owned by the County and City Councils and was used as informal open space abutting the sea shore.

3-45

The City Planning Officer recommended that the northern site should be developed despite the loss of industrially zoned land. The Planning Committee however, probably attracted by a leisure facilities carrot, decided to grant permission to the southern scheme, given highway improvements and Section 52 controls over the types of retailing. This application was strongly supported by Charles Mos, a city councillor who had hoped to manage the ice rink. However, the County Council, who owned much of the required land, refused to make it available. Such a move would have been in conflict with their policy of securing as much informal open space along South Hampshire's coast as possible. Meanwhile the proposal for the Metal Box site was taken to appeal, and the developer of the southern scheme attempted to assemble enough land that was not owned by the County. Ironically, if the southern development had occurred it would have been between the County's land and the sea. The Metal Box proposal gained consent on appeal, and Wyncote pulled out from the southern site. However, for a time there was a strong possibility that Portsmouth would end up with two retail warehouse parks on neighbouring sites, precisely the uncoordinated kind of development that the City was attempting to avoid. This situation could still arise if appeals on other proposals are won.

3-46

As Harvey Cole's report indicated, it is doubtful that the market in Portsmouth is sufficiently strong to absorb an additional 40 000 m^2 of retailing without substantial effects being felt in existing centres. If two sites were developed, it is unlikely that the City would be able to maintain such strong control over the types of goods sold. Any relaxation of such conditions would bring the retail warehouses into more direct competition with existing facilities. These proposals illustrate both the failure of individual local authorities to deal with strategic proposals in a rational way (the councillors went against their officers' advice, swayed by the attraction of an ice rink, and even personal vested interest), and the inability to sustain the decision at appeal.

3-47

To the north of the city, Port Solent is being developed. This is a mixed scheme consisting of a marina, some waterside homes and a limited amount of specialist and speciality retailing. The City Council recently received an application to expand the retailing element by the addition of 10 000 m^2. The proposal was refused planning consent because the council wished to maintain the development as a local centre for tourists and the yachting fraternity.

3-48

Portsmouth's approach to retailing fits quite neatly into the strategy proposed by the County Council. One retail warehouse park at Burrfields Road could form the park at the eastern end of the M27 corridor. This would suit Portsmouth quite well since it would be fairly close to the existing retail centre yet controls would limit its impact on town centre shops. The park's position would ensure that Portsmouth would benefit from trade from much of south east Hampshire, and from West Sussex too. Less attractive however is the suggestion that a regional centre of 25 000 m^2 might be located at Whitely, since this would compete directly with existing town centres. In reality, Portsmouth is likely to experience greater competition from new developments in Fareham town centre.

Fareham

3-49

Very close to the town of Fareham lies Junction 11 of the M27, ensuring that the centre has easy car based access to and from much of South Hampshire. The District Council is well aware of the fact that such accessibility can work in both directions, so policies have been designed to make the town centre more attractive to shoppers, rather than allowing local spending power to be siphoned off to other retail facilities in the area. There has already been substantial retail development in the centre of Fareham with the first two phases of a town centre shopping mall completed to the north of West Street. The Submitted Alterations to the South Hampshire Structure Plan suggested that Fareham town centre could be expanded by the addition of a further 25 000 m^2 by 1996. It recommended that this floorspace should include a department store and should complement existing shops. The County argued that new retail development should take place in the town centre rather than at the nearby motorway junction.

3-50

Fareham District Council agreed with these guidelines, and placed great emphasis on having the John Lewis Partnership occupy the department store. It was believed this would give the centre status as well as a magnet for other quality retailers. The Council produced the Fareham Town Centre Action Area Local Plan which envisaged comprehensive development to the south of West Street to provide an additional 32 500 m^2 of floorspace. The plans went out to tender, and after a large response from developers, Heron was selected. When the scheme is complete it will bring the town centre's floorspace total up to 100 000 m^2.

3-51

Fareham District Council are very concerned about suggestions from the County Council that a 35 000 m^2 regional centre should be developed at nearby Whitely, as proposed by Arlington Securities. In particular they are worried that the John Lewis Partnership might see Whitely as a more attractive location for a new department store. If Fareham lost John Lewis it is estimated that the town centre scheme could be placed in jeopardy, at the least being delayed for eight or ten years. The Council has made its views clear to the Secretary of State but did not receive a favourable response. They are currently concentrating on securing the support of local MPs who will be able to lobby the DoE. The Council has also joined Southampton's campaign opposing out-of-centre retailing.

3-52

A retail warehouse strip has evolved at Segensworth close to Fareham. Units already trading here include MFI, Queensway, B&Q, Allied Carpets and Halfords. There is currently an application for an hotel, a fast food centre and some retailing, but the council is set against further retail warehouse development. Recent public inquiries have considered appeals for retail warehouse schemes here and at nearby Speedfields Farm.

Other Major Retail Proposals

3-53

Several major retail proposals exist in Test Valley Borough close to the boundary with Southampton. A focus of interest for developers is being close to junction 3 of the M27 at Nursling. Already Taylor Woodrow have won consent to build a 11 500 m^2 retail park on land near the M271 link (Planning 1987b). This planning permission is in accordance with the County's strategy of locating retail parks at either end of the M27 corridor. Occupiers are likely to include Texas Homecare, Harris Queensway, Allied Carpets and Power City (Hampshire County Council 1986). In addition there are outstanding applications for a retail park totalling 20 400 m^2 at Grove Lodge Farm, Upton, and a regional centre totalling 80 000 m^2 of net retailing floorspace with other major leisure, business and residential facilities. This latter scheme, known as Adanac Park is opposed by Hampshire County Council, and were its developers to win their appeal, it would provide major competition for Southampton and Eastleigh town centres. There are also plans for a 20 000 m^2 regional shopping centre on part of Lord Romsey's estate. The development would fund maintenance of the estate, and has therefore received a mixed reception from the county council who value the need for conservation (Planning 1988).

3-54

A second area of pressure is along the M27 corridor in the Borough of East-leigh. Despite contrary advice from its planning officers, Eastleigh Borough Council gave its support to Marks & Spencer's proposal to build an out-of-centre store at Bursledon (Estates Times 1987). The scheme proposes 13 600 m^2 floorspace, parking for 1200 cars, and a link into the nearby Tesco superstore. The application included substantial road improvements and the offer of £1.35M towards a new bypass (Hampshire County Council 1987). Eastleigh Borough Council justified their support on the grounds that the new store would benefit South Hampshire as a whole (Estates Times 1987). Surrounding local authorities, and the County Council did not see the development in quite the same way, arguing that the scheme was an encroachment onto the strategic gap identified in the recently approved Structure Plan Alterations. The Secretary of State heeded these objections and dismissed the appeal. It is significant that Eastleigh had previously refused permission for other schemes using the same argument.

3-55

While Eastleigh Borough Council have refused permission for a number of retail warehouse schemes, they have granted consent to the John Hunt Group to build 8 500 m^2 at Wildern Mill, and to Queen's College Oxford to build 12 000 m^2 nearby. Meanwhile, permission has been granted for an 18 000 m^2 SavaCentre at junction 7 of the M27. In the town of Eastleigh itself, Shearwater Property Holdings are developing a 30 000 m^2 town centre shopping scheme. This scheme will include an 8 000 m^2 superstore and parking for 850 cars.

3-56

There are important development proposals in Bournemouth to the west. Any substantial schemes here could affect shopping in South Hampshire, particularly in Southampton. Chancery Lane Developments have made an application for the refurbishment and extension of the Hampshire Centre. This shopping centre was built in the 1960s and totalled 25 000 m^2. The proposed scheme doubles the size of the centre itself and adds up to 20 000 m^2 of retail warehouses. A second application has already been rejected by Bournemouth Borough Council. Grosvenor Developments proposed a 25 000 m^2 shopping scheme at The Square in the town centre. The application was refused consent because, as a council spokesperson said, the scheme was 'too big, took too much of the gardens and provoked too much reaction to prolong it any further'(Chartered Surveyor Weekly 1987b). It is likely that further proposals will come forward for the site.

3-57

Of all the out-of-centre retail proposals being considered in South Hampshire, it is likely that only three will be given planning permission, in line with stated policies. Most likely is that there will be retail warehouse parks at Nursling and at Portsmouth, and a regional shopping centre at Whitely. Whether the Secretary of State will uphold refusals for other schemes in the light of Hampshire County Council's new positive policies has yet to be seen.

CONCLUSIONS

3-58

This case study has indicated that South Hampshire is currently experiencing huge pressures for retail change. These pressures threaten the future viabil-ity of existing town centres, and the preservation of open countryside around them. In addition, new developments with their extensive land-take preclude other uses such as industry or housing particularly if they are located within the urban area. The development of out-of-centre shopping will reduce the access of less mobile people to retail outlets and will make the rest of the population more dependent on the motor car. Ironically perhaps, the threat of out-of-centre retailing has prompted town centres to improve their facilities in an attempt to preempt and compete with new developments.

3-59
The most significant conclusions of this case study relate to the rôle of the planning system. When supported by Central Government policies, the County's strategy was relatively successful. However as national policies changed, the County had to change too in order to be seen as credible and realistic. At a local level, the strategic issue of major out-of-centre development has brought an uncoordinated response from district councils. Some, who clearly have much to lose, are forthright in their opposition. Others, who may see such developments as a means of stealing the retail thunder of the existing centres, are not so ill-disposed. In addition to this fragmented approach, small district councils are now considering applications for developments whose implications reach well beyond their boundaries, often beyond the County boundary too.

3-60
Thus district councils with limited resources are having to evaluate strategic issues. The safety net provided by the Secretary of State now has larger holes; on many occasions it has been made clear that planning should not restrict competition and that there is always a presumption in favour of development. It has become easy for a local authority to approve an application, but if they refuse it they face the prospect of an appeal and the possibility of costs being awarded against them should they lose. If developers lose at appeal, any costs that are awarded against them are offset against the possible profits that would accrue from such a development. The equation has become unbalanced as developers wield huge resources while local authorities who are supposed to independently assess each application are often working with limited human and financial resources. The most successful means of control in South Hampshire has been municipal land ownership; in Portsmouth several schemes for retail parks were abandoned because the land was owned by the City Council. The use of this measure highlights the weakness of planning as a means of control. The importance of land ownership will decrease as the current Government pursues its policy of reducing the land held by the public sector.

3-61
Until the early 1980s, Hampshire County Council pursued policies designed to concentrate development in existing centres. This approach was broadly supported by the Department of the Environment. With the change of government in 1979 it became clear that policies would have to change. The 'free market' approach of the Department of the Environment meant that the County's policies would no longer be regarded as realistic at appeals. Change was necessary if the County was to have any influence over the final outcome. At the same time pressure for new retail development on out-of-centre sites was building up as developers responded to new government policies and the boom in consumer expenditure. By 1987 the County accepted that there would be out-of-centre development regardless of the policy they pursued. It was clearly in their best interests to recognise this pressure and to develop policies which would channel it and limit its extent. They were aware, however, that by giving approval to a limited amount of out-of-centre retailing they could be opening the flood gates. Thus as far as the County is concerned, the Secretary of State had succeeded in shifting the planning agenda, in line with the Government's **laissez faire** approach. It remains to be seen whether the County's approach will succeed in staving off a complete free-for-all.

3-62
District attitudes towards the issue of out-of-centre retailing vary according to their own particular interests. There is no statutory framework to ensure

84

that each district's decisions correspond to an overall strategy. The result is district policies which often conflict with one another. Southampton is the strongest opponent of out-of-centre retailing. Its position as the sub-regional shopping centre means that it is threatened by proposals close to its boundary in Test Valley, and in Eastleigh. The city has responded to this threat by attempting to improve its own centre. It has also mounted a campaign designed to increase public awareness of the issue and form a lobby of concerned local authorities. Portsmouth too is concerned about the effects of out-of-centre retail development. It has made some concessions however, trying to accommodate retail warehouses, and latterly a retail warehouse park. Now, however, the city is faced with the possibility of two such parks which together would substantially affect the viability of the existing shopping facilities. Fareham Borough Council is also opposed to out-of-centre retailing. It sees the development of a regional centre at Whitley as a substantial threat to the third phase of its own town centre shopping scheme.

3-63

Not surprisingly then, those districts which have existing shopping facilities, and stand to lose out to competition from out-of-centre developments, are opposed to such schemes. Others without substantial retail provision seem less concerned. Thus Test Valley District Council has given permission for a retail park at Nursling, while Eastleigh Borough Council is supporting an application to build a large Marks & Spencer store next to an existing Tesco superstore at Bursledon.

3-64

The threat of out-of-centre retailing, and the apparent willingness of some districts to back such development have been major stimuli for town centres. Observing that people are attracted to non-central stores primarily because of their easy car access, cleanliness, climatic control and security, existing centres are trying to replicate these conditions to make town centres more attractive. Some of the measures, such as pedestrianisation and improved cleanliness, are undoubtedly positive effects of this stimulus. However, both Portsmouth and Southampton have responded by proposing road building and increased numbers of car parking spaces. Surely such an approach threatens any vestiges of character that town centres still possess. It is unlikely that town centres will be able to match many of the real and perceived advantages that out-of-centre retail developments offer car-users. While town centres may be able to increase car access and develop new enclosed shopping malls, they will have difficulty matching both the low land costs which permit extensive operations, and the high level of accessibility for car users. People without cars will have inferior access to these developments since public transport networks have the town centre as a focal point. A more appropriate approach may be for town centres to build on and exploit their character and variety to provide a unique and colourful alternative to ubiquitous marble malls and seas of tarmac and chrome.

REFERENCES

Chartered Surveyor Weekly (1986) **Centrefolio: Southampton/Eastleigh/Havant/
Portsmouth/Fareham/Gosport Vol 16** pp203-223
Chartered Surveyor Weekly (1987a) news item **Vol 20** p11 2 July
Chartered Surveyor Weekly (1987b) Eagle Star's Hampshire Centre **Vol 20** 9 July
Cochrane, William (1987) Planning bids exceed requirement **Financial Times** 29.5
Davies, EJ (1982) **Moores Square Area Redevelopment: Proof of Evidence** GL
Hearn & Partners London
    - (1977) **Proposed Retail Store: Littlepark Havant: an appeal on
behalf of the Portsea Island Mutual Cooperative Society Ltd** GL Hearn &
Partners London
Estates Times (1987) **M&S wins out-of-town support from council** 7 August
Hack, J (1987) **Personal Communication** Hampshire County Council
Hallsworth, AG (1981) **Trading Patterns of a District Superstore: Asda
Waterlooville** Department of Geography Portsmouth Polytechnic
    - (1986) **Trading Patterns: B&Q Havant** Department of Geography Portsmouth
Polytechnic
    - (1987) PHd Thesis Department of Geography Portsmouth Polytechnic
Hallsworth, AG and T Lewington (1986) **Shopping Provision at Anchorage Park
Portsmouth** Portsmouth Polytechnic Portsmouth
Hampshire County Council (1978) **Shopping Policies in South Hampshire**
Winchester Hampshire County Council
    - (1986a) **South Hampshire Shopping Study: Background Paper** Hampshire County
Council
    - (1986b) **Shopping Policies in South Hampshire** Hampshire County Council
    - (1987a) **Whitely Local Plan** Hampshire County Council Winchester
    - (1987b) **Shopping Policies in South Hampshire: Report of the County
Planning Officer and County Surveyor** 16 March Hampshire County Council
    - (1987c) **Shopping Applications in South Hampshire: Report of the County
Planning Officer and County Surveyor** 20 March Hampshire County Council
    - (1987d) **Criteria for Development of Out-of-Centre Shopping: Report of the
County Planning Officer and County Surveyor** 20 March Hampshire County
Council
    - (1987e) **Shopping in South Hampshire: Report and Recommendations of
Shopping Policies Panel** 30 March Hampshire County Council
    - (1987f) **Minutes of the Meeting held 30 March 1987** Hampshire County Council
HMSO (1977) **Development Control Policy Note 13** HMSO London
Johnston, Bryan (1988) Hampshire faces up to third wave in retailing <u>in</u>
Planning Vol 760 18 March pp10-12
Luken, Mark (1987) **Personal Communication** Southampton City Council
Nye, David (1987) **Personal Communication** Fareham District Council
Piper, Cliff (1987) **Personal Communication** Portsmouth City Council
Planning (1987a) **Monorail idea 1** May p28
Planning (1987b) **Warehouse Park Won Vol 730** p24
Planning (1988) **Marks and Spencer fail to bridge gap Vol 782** 19 August p28
Portsmouth City Council (n.d.) **Draft District Plan for the Fratton District
Shopping Centre** Portsmouth City Council
    - (1987a) **Shopping Development Policies: reports of the Director of Develop-
ment and the City Planning Officer**
    - (1987b) **Planning Applications in Respect of Retail Development**
SERPLAN (1986) **Regional Trends in the South East: The South East Regional
Monitor 1985-86** SERPLAN London
Southampton City Council (1987) **Out of town shopping centres - some key
questions** Southampton City Council Southampton
Waley, Simon (1987) **Personal Communication** Hampshire County Council
Whitehead, Alan (1987) Keep our local shopping centres - Southampton launches
its campaign **District Councils Review** March p8

4 WOLVERHAMPTON

SUMMARY

4-01

Wolverhampton is an example of a well established sub-regional shopping centre whose prosperity is threatened by competition from off-centre regional shopping centres. Despite strong support from the local chamber of commerce, Wolverhampton Metropolitan Borough Council have been unable to maintain policies which prevent out-of-centre development. A limited amount of superstore and retail warehouse development has been permitted as close to the town centre as could be accommodated. The council are encouraging town centre refurbishment and are implementing a programme of environmental improvement and traffic management in an attempt to make the centre more attractive to shoppers.

4-02

For a long time Wolverhampton has been second only to Birmingham City Centre as a West Midlands shopping centre. In recent years however, this position has been threatened by incremental retail change in the region, and more recently by the development and proposal of entirely new shopping schemes which individually threaten to parallel the size of Wolverhampton's comparison retailing floorspace. While being quantitatively similar, qualitatively such centres will benefit from a large number of national-name occupiers, which will more than rival Wolverhampton's mix of national and local retailers. These centres will cater specifically for car-borne shoppers, (with attractors such as large amounts of free parking) and will therefore attract the highest spending section of the catchment population.

4-03

The metropolitan district council are, not unreasonably, opposed to out of centre developments, and they have pursued policies which concentrate retailing within an area bounded by the inner ring-road. However, the biggest threats to Wolverhampton's prosperity come from developments beyond the borough's boundaries - specifically in Sandwell and in Dudley - areas which stand to gain from Wolverhampton's decline. With individual districts making ad hoc decisions in an attempt to win as much retailing as possible, the need for some effective strategic control could not be more obvious. Without such control, centres such as Wolverhampton will decline as a large part of their trade is lost to modern centres in car-based locations.

INTRODUCTION AND BACKGROUND

4-04

The Metropolitan Borough of Wolverhampton is located in the northwest of the West Midlands conurbation. Until 1 April 1986 strategic planning in the region was undertaken by West Midlands County Council. While the West Midlands County

Table 4-1 : Population of West Midlands and Wolverhampton

	1961	1971	1981
West Midlands	2 731 892	2 793 288	2 648 939
Wolverhampton	261 552	269 112	254 561

Source: Office of Population Censuses and Surveys (1984)

Structure Plan remains in force, it will be replaced by Unitary Development Plans drawn up by metropolitan districts under guidance from the Department of the Environment. Abolition has therefore meant the removal of a regional tier of strategic planning. The populations of the County and the Borough are shown in Table 4-1. Changes in the town's population have mirrored the experience of most metropolitan areas, with growth tailing off in the 1970s, to be replaced by decline.

4-05
Table 4-2 shows Wolverhampton's employment structure. The proportion of the workforce engaged in manufacturing industry remains higher than the national average, despite the region's economic decline. The borough's unemployment rate is the highest in the West Midlands, and is more than 50% higher than the national average.

Table 4-2 : Employment and Unemployment 1981 (%)

	Agri-culture	Energy	Manu-facture	Constr-uction	Distri-bution	Trans-port	Other Service	Unemployment Rate
GB	2.2	3.1	27.0	7.0	19.2	6.5	34.0	10.1
W Midlands County	0.2	1.4	41.2	6.0	18.2	4.7	27.5	14.5
Wolver-hampton	0.1	1.0	42.6	6.7	18.2	4.3	26.3	16.5

Note : Unemployment calculated as a percentage of economically active people between the ages of 16 and 64 (male) and 16 and 59 (female).
Source : Office of Population Censuses and Surveys (1984)

RETAIL POLICY FRAMEWORK

4-06
The 1980 West Midlands County Structure Plan embodied the County's commitment to town centre retailing. It stated that centres should act as a focus of 'shopping, commercial and social activities for the areas they serve'. Shopping development outside these centres was to be restricted to the replacement of existing floorspace, or that necessary to satisfy local needs. Wolverhampton was to be maintained as the sub-regional shopping centre serving the north western part of the conurbation together with parts of Staffordshire and Shropshire. As such new stores or extensions to existing stores would be encouraged within the centre.

4-07
Department of the Environment (n.d.) guidance for metropolitan districts drawing up Unitary Development Plans reiterated much of the advice contained in Planning Policy Guidance note 6 (see Chapter 2). It stated that town centres should continue to be the main focus of retail provision, and that any out-of-centre proposals should not threaten their continued viability. The guidance suggested that retailing can make a substantial contribution to urban regeneration.

4-08
The Written Statement for the Wolverhampton Town Centre Local Plan, published in 1987, reiterated the need to keep new retail development within the existing town centre. The only major exceptions were where new retailing necessary to

the continuation of Wolverhampton's subregional rôle could not be absorbed within the town centre. Specifically, this meant that the local plan made provision for one new superstore on a site north of the Molineux Football Ground, while a wedge of land running north from the ring road was being reserved for large non-food based stores.

4-09

Wolverhampton's Town Centre Local Plan also set out an environmental improvement and traffic management plan that aimed substantially to improve the pedestrian environment while maintaining good access for public transport. Proposals for the town centre are shown in Figure 4-3. The existing pedestrianised Dudley Street is being complemented by a growing network of traffic-calmed streets. Meanwhile, bus access will be maintained by the designation of bus and pedestrian streets. The centre already benefits from well integrated bus and rail stations. Many of the improvements have already been implemented or are under construction, under the capital programme, the Inner Area Programme and use of conservation area mechanisms. Plans for a light rail system linking Wolverhampton town centre with other centres in the region are being enthusiastically supported by the council. If all the proposals are realised, Wolverhampton will have one of the most extensive traffic-calmed town centres in Britain. Experience from many European cities (TEST 1988) shows that the result of improving shoppers' environment by restricting car access can have positive economic effects, and help a centre repel competition from out-of-centre developments.

Retail Composition

4-10

Birmingham City Centre has long been the preeminent shopping centre in the West Midlands. The 1980 West Midlands Structure Plan identified Wolverhampton and Coventry (in the south east of the conurbation) as the two sub-regional shopping centres. Other town centres in the region include Walsall, Dudley, Solihull, West Bromwich, Sutton Coldfield and Stourbridge. In addition, there are some 17 district centres together with numerous local and neighbourhood centres.

4-11

Wolverhampton's rôle as the region's second shopping centre was reinforced in the 1960s and early 1970s by the development of two purpose-built shopping centres in the heart of the town. The Mander and Wulfrun Centres substantially added to the town's stock of shops and its total floorspace. Despite these two centres, the town's primary area is the pedestrianised Dudley Street. As well as longstanding retailers such as British Home Stores, C&A, Littlewoods, Marks and Spencer (recently extended) and Woolworths, Dudley Street has more recently attracted some of the new generation of multiples including Next, Benetton, Laura Ashley and Olympus Sport. Wolverhampton has three department stores, Beatties (15 900 m^2 net) which acts as an important magnet to draw shoppers into the town, Owen Owen (2 200 m^2 net) and Rackhams (2 300 m^2).

4-12

Table 4-4 brings together information from a number of different sources to give an indication of the changes in Wolverhampton's retail composition that have occurred over the last two decades. Like most other traditional shopping centres, the town has experienced a decline in the number of convenience goods shops. On the other hand, it would appear that the growth in the number of comparison outlets has more than compensated for this. There is insufficient information accurately to assess vacancy rates, although the 9% of floorspace that was vacant in 1986 may indicate some slackness in the market. Turnover has increased in real terms, growing by a quarter between 1971 and 1986.

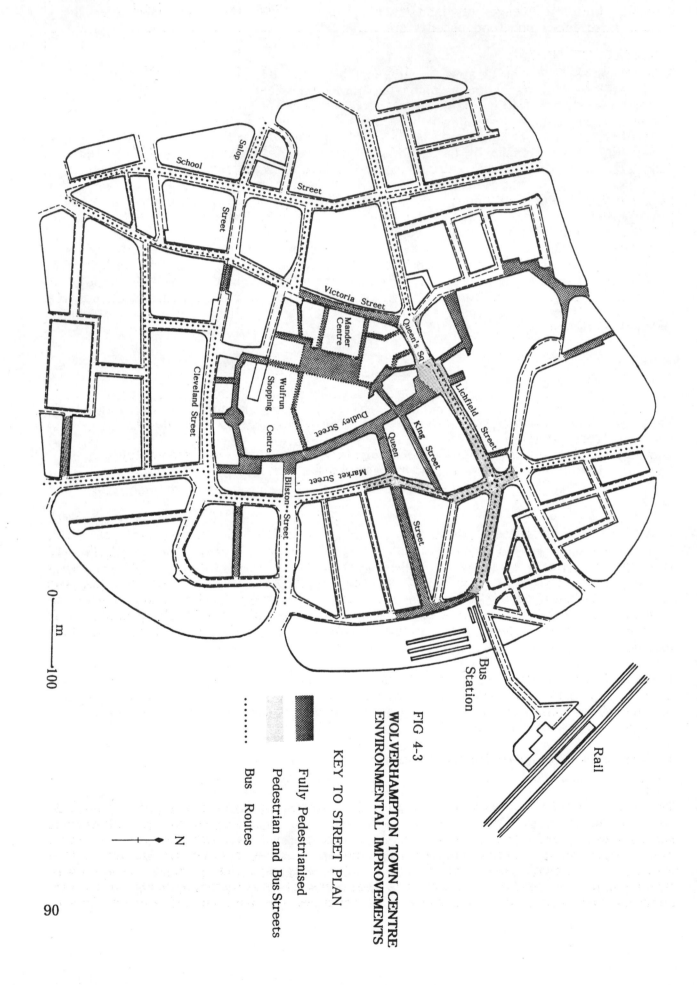

FIG 4-3
WOLVERHAMPTON TOWN CENTRE
ENVIRONMENTAL IMPROVEMENTS

KEY TO STREET PLAN

Fully Pedestrianised

Pedestrian and Bus Streets

Bus Routes

90

Table 4-4 : Retail Outlets in Wolverhampton

	1971	1977	1986	1987
NUMBER OF UNITS				
Convenience	136	130	112	N/A
Comparison	412	444	462	N/A
Services	N/A	189	157	N/A
Misc	N/A	N/A	117	N/A
Vacant	N/A	52 (6%)	N/A	N/A
TOTAL		**815**	**848**	**817**
FLOORSPACE (000s m^2)				
Convenience	8.4	7.8	7.8	7.8
Comparison	85.6	90.8	95.0	92.0
Services	N/A	12.3		8.8
Vacant	N/A (3%)	4.5 (4%)		19.6 (9%)
TOTAL		**115.4**	**119.6**	**119.6**
TURNOVER (£M 1984 prices)				
Convenience	39.4		42.4	
Comparison	118.2		155.2	
TOTAL	**157.7**		**197.6**	

Note :   1986 turnover is an estimate based on Drivers Jonas (1987) and
Jones (1987)

Sources: Drivers Jonas (1987), Goad (1986), Jones (1987) and Wolverhampton
Metropolitan Borough Council (unpublished data)

4-13

On face value, Wolverhampton would appear to be trading relatively well. However, several trends, not least the development of out-of-centre retailing, threaten to destabilise what is essentially a rather weak centre.   Edward Erdman and Co (1986) described Wolverhampton's vulnerability.   While rental levels, until 1979, grew only slightly slower than in most other centres, the relative decline since has been dramatic.   Standard shop unit rentals in Walsall and Dudley have actually exceeded those prevailing in Wolverhampton.   A number of factors have contributed to Wolverhampton's instability, and they include:

1   The effects of 1960s retail developments
2   The growth of competing town centres
3   The competition from superstores and retail warehouses in surrounding areas
4   The prospect of massive out-of-centre developments

1   The Effects of 1960s Retail Developments

4-14

The 1960s and early 1970s were a period of retail growth in Wolverhampton.   In common with many other areas, new trends in retailing such as self-service supermarkets, and the introduction of comprehensive redevelopment schemes, meant that many district centres experienced relative decline as Wolverhampton grew.   The town's new found vigour also increased its competitiveness with Birmingham city centre.   As we have seen, new shopping developments in Wolverhampton were based on two purpose built schemes, the Wulfrun and Mander Centres totalling approximately 56 000 m² (the latter being developed by Manders Property Ltd - part of the Wolverhampton based paint manufacturers and an important local influence). While both Centres had supermarkets as anchors (Sainsbury [since moved to a superstore] in the Wulfrun Centre and Tesco in the Mander Centre) most of their shops sell comparison goods.

4-15

Although the development of two large shopping centres reflected and inspired 1960s confidence in Wolverhampton, the long-term effects have been less positive. The most profound effect has been a relative over-supply of small shop units in the town. While there is some evidence that a few large multiple retailers would welcome large stores on Dudley Street (CSW 1986), the glut of smaller premises has led to a relatively high vacancy rate, relatively low rental levels, and a tendency for certain parts of the town centre, particularly in the Worcester Street, Salop Street and School Street area, to undertrade.

4-16

A second problem has been the lack of incentive to renovate or refurbish the two shopping centres. Both the Wulfrun and Mander Centres are partly open-air, and have car parking on a level above the stores. Over the years the centres have both become dated and worn, and it is only since there has been a threat from out-of-centre retailing that the landlords have embarked on refurbishment programmes. Recent improvements in the Mander Centre include the installation of a sliding roof over the previously open-air sections, the paving of floor surfaces with marble, the addition of new eating facilities and the inevitable introduction of wall climbing lifts linking the shopping levels with the roof-top carpark. The effect of the refurbishment has been to reduce vacancy rates throughout the town centre particularly in the nearby Victoria Street and Queen's Square where a strong demand for premises has emerged (Estates Gazette June 11 1988 p121 and Lillywhite 1988). Proposals to refurbish the Wulfrun Centre are also being drawn up.

4-17

However, one advantage resulting from the high level of 1960s investment has been the strong interest that now exists in maintaining the rôle of the town centre. The Mander Holdings Plc is a potent local influence, and its concern to protect its town centre investment from out-of-centre competition has been strongly voiced by the town's Chamber of Commerce (one of the few local chambers in Britain which seems to have been able to influence decision-making). Wolverhampton MBC have recognised this threat from new non-central development and, as is shown below, have developed policies which emphasise the rôle of the town centre.

2 The Growth of Competing Town Centres

4-18

While Wolverhampton leapt ahead of neighbouring town centres in the 1960s, in recent decades the latter centres have consolidated their retailing, and now act as stronger competitors. Competition has been further strengthened by the development of Telford new town to the north west, together with the continued success of Birmingham City Centre to the south.

4-19

Although a study in 1976 (WMCC 1976) found that in some wards of Walsall, Sandwell and Dudley, Wolverhampton was the most frequently named centre for main clothing purchases, in recent years the gap between Woverhanpton and its smaller competitors has been closing. Towns such as Dudley, West Bromwich and Walsall have consolidated their retailing, often with new shopping developments, attracting many of the larger retailers who were previously only represented in Wolverhampton. One result has been the convergence of rental levels found in the town and in other, smaller centres.

Birmingham

4-20

While Wolverhampton's retail sector has weathered a period of stagnation following the expansionist 1960s, Birmingham City Centre has experienced renewed interest among retailers and developers. Despite the competitive threat posed by the plethora of out-of-centre applications, Birmingham has been able to attract substantial retail investment. In 1986, the New Street Centre (above the station of the same name) was refurbished at a cost of £2 million, and renamed the Pallasades. In 1987, the old Co-op department store in the High Street was replaced by a four level, climatically controlled shopping centre called the Pavilions. The centre cost £60 million, provides 23 300 m^2 of floorspace and comprises four major stores and 38 smaller units.

4-21

Recently completed is a mixed office and retail development called City Plaza. The retail element comprises 4 600 m^2 spread over three levels. Currently under construction is a shopping development built on the site of the former Debenhams in Bull Street. The centre, to be known as The Academy, will total 8 400 m^2 and will link into the recently restored Great Western Arcade. The scheme is due to open by December 1989 and will comprise an 1 800 m^2 anchor store together with 41 shops on four levels.

4-22

The largest, and most recent scheme is the proposed redevelopment of the Bull Ring centre together with the Rotunda office block. London and Edinburgh Trust plan to build a new centre with approximately 116 000 m^2 of retail floorspace, replacing an existing 56 000 m^2. The scheme will include a major department store on three levels, two other large stores on two levels, 175 smaller units, a range of restaurants together with parking for 3500 cars (Estates Gazette 11 June 1988).

4-23

In addition to these developments, the City Council is developing a major convention centre, and has plans to improve the environment of the city centre which may include the extension of pedestrianisation. Inevitably, some of this interest in improving the attraction of Birmingham City Centre reflects efforts by landlords and the city council to preempt any out-of-centre developments. Councillor Chapman, the chair of the city's planning committee suggested that 'our minds have been concentrated by out-of-town shopping stores and the effect these are likely to have on the city centre' (quoted in Estates Gazette 11 June 1988 p113). However, it is undeniable that the centre is currently benefitting from the confidence of shoppers and developers alike.

4-24

As well as experiencing growing competition form longstanding shopping centres, Wolverhampton has also suffered from the development of Telford new town about 25 km to the north-west. Although Wolverhampton's immediate catchment is less than affluent, traditionally it benefitted from more wealthy trade from Staffordshire and Shropshire. Telford, with its modern shopping facilities, free car parking, and easy access by road has lured some higher spending and car-based shoppers away from Wolverhampton.

4-25

To conclude this section, it is clear that, even without substantial out-of-centre development, Wolverhampton is a retailing centre under siege from all sides. Smaller neighbours have consolidated their facilities, and have attracted retailers who previously were found in Wolverhampton. To the south west, Birmingham city centre is enjoying an upsurge in its retail fortunes, while to the north west Telford has become a major magnet for the more affluent residents of Staffordshire and Shropshire who previously relied on Wolverhampton.

3 Competition from Superstores and Retail Warehouses in Surrounding Areas

4-26

Despite the development of policies which aim to reinforce the preeminent rôle of the town centre, in the absence of strategic planning controls, Wolverhampton has faced a dilemma. Surrounding boroughs (frequently having less at stake) have often been less restrictive, and Wolverhampton is increasingly finding that much of its trade is being drawn to new retail warehouses and superstores outside the borough. If the council adopted a dogmatic approach and maintained a ban on such developments within the borough it is likely that even more substantial amounts of trade would be lost to surrounding boroughs. In addition, it is unlikely that such a policy would survive the appeal system. Faced with the prospects of the outflow of trade and the development of such stores following appeal, many otherwise resolute local authorities have to bow to the will of the market and allow some form of development. In Wolverhampton's case, retail warehouse and superstore development have been carefully steered into locations where they will do the least damage to existing shopping, and where they may even attract additional trade into the town centre.

4-27

A number of retail warehouses have been constructed on the margins of the town centre, just outside the ring road. Occupiers include companies such as B&Q, MFI, Texas Homecare and Queensway. The Town Centre Local Plan (see above) has set aside land for large non-food store development to the north of the ring road, while a four unit retail warehouse park opened in the area in 1987 with retailers such as Queensway and Fads (Lillywhite 1988).

4-28

Greater debate has been generated by the demand for superstore development in the borough. Until very recently there were only four foodstores larger than 9 300 m^2, and none of these exceeded 18 600 m^2. The largest supermarket was a Safeway at Pendeford in the north west of the borough. Both Sainsbury and Tesco were represented in the town centre, and there was an International on Warstones Road. This fairly low level of provision contrasted with areas surrounding Wolverhampton. Jones (1987) indicated that there were up to 20 superstores and hypermarkets drawing trade out of the borough. These range from a 6 900 m^2 hypermarket at Merry Hill in Dudley, to smaller stores located in town centres such as Walsall and Willenhall. Most of these stores are located to the south east and east of Wolverhampton, and draw trade primarily from Wednesfield, Bilston and Ettingshall areas of the Borough. Market research by Intermarket Research Ltd (described by Jones 1987) suggested that 25% of households used stores outside the borough for their main convenience shopping.

4-29

In an attempt to modernise convenience shopping facilities in the town, and so retain greater amounts of convenience spending within the borough, the local authority supported a proposal by Sainsbury to build a new superstore in the south east of the town centre, next to the ring road. Wolverhampton MBC argued that an important factor was the additional trade that could be generated for comparison outlets in the town centre who would benefit from higher numbers of passers-by. Manders Property recognised this 'knock-on' effect, and supported the decision despite the fact that the trade of the Tesco store in the Mander Centre would be affected. The willingness of the local authority to allow the development probably reflected their inability to prevent it as much as the 'benefits' of locating it on the fringe of the town centre where both private and public transport users could reach it without entering the centre proper. The Sainsbury store, which totals 2400 m^2 net (5700 m^2 gross) and has 470 parking spaces, opened early in 1988.

4-30

Two further applications for superstores followed the Sainsbury consent. One proposal was for a Gateway store at Bushbury about one mile north of the town centre, the other for an Asda on land adjoining the Molineux Football Ground, just to the north of the ring road. The Gateway store was refused planning consent and taken to appeal, while the Asda proposal which was supported by Wolverhampton MBC was called-in by the Department of the Environment as a departure from the approved structure plan. Both applications were considered at a Public Inquiry in June 1987. Wolverhampton MBC were represented by Bernard Thorpe and Partners (Jones 1987), who argued that the combined effect of both stores' development would be significant impact on the trade of the Tesco Store in the Mander Centre. However, the effect of Tesco closing would not have significantly affected the viability of the town centre as a whole as defined by a Department of the Environment Circular. If only one store were developed, it was argued that the Tesco store would still be operating at above Tesco PLC's group average. On balance Wolverhampton MBC's representative concluded that the Asda proposal would create more passing trade for other shops, and would be most accessible whether people came by car, public transport or on foot. Although the inspector recommended that both permissions be refused, in July 1988 the Environment Secretary granted permission for the Asda superstore, upholding the inspector's recommendation regarding the Bushbury store (Planning 1988a).

4 The Prospect of Massive Out-of-centre Developments

4-31

While the above factors have been important factors in determining Wolverhampton's retail vitality, they pale in comparison to the threat of non-central regional shopping centres. The failure of any rational planning system to operate is obvious, as single planning consents made at the local level and for local reasons threaten repercussions that go way beyond a given borough's boundaries. As we have seen in Chapter 3 on South Hampshire, rather than presenting a common front to the proposals, those boroughs with little to lose grant permission to these vast centres, while those with vulnerable town centres can only watch from the sidelines or join in an attempt to secure some of the monopolistic development for themselves. At present there are several major out-of-centre proposals in the West Midlands in various stages of planning consent. The locations of these proposals are shown in Figure 4-5, and they are described below:

4-32

A: Sandwell Mall, on the site of the former Patent Shaft Steelworks in Hollyhead Road, Wednesbury. The scheme originally proposed by Color Properties was along the lines of West Edmonton Mall in Canada with both retail and leisure facilities totalling 185 000 m^2 and 210 000 m^2 respectively. While outline planning permission was granted by Sandwell MBC in June 1986, development has been delayed because of problems in assembling a consortium of developers (Cameron Hall, developers of the Metrocentre, pulled out). Sandwell MBC are determined to see the 125 acre site developed as a national tourist attraction, and have entered into a partnership with the Black Country Development Corporation to find a suitable developer. Delays have also been caused by the existence of substantial coal reserves on the site which will now be mined by British Coal before development starts. Drivers Jonas, in a study of retailing in the West Midlands (1987) estimated that the development of Sandwell Mall (in its original form) would have seriously jeopardised Wolverhampton town centre's viability. The current brief is for a centre with approximately 93 000 m^2, and

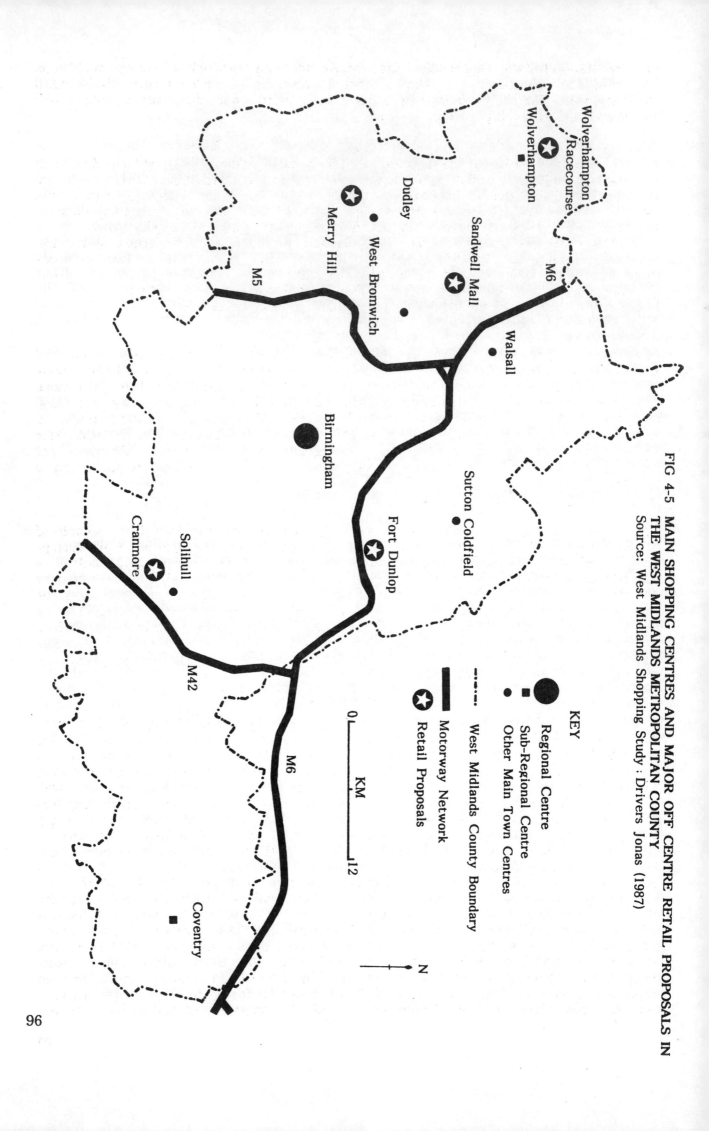

FIG 4-5 MAIN SHOPPING CENTRES AND MAJOR OFF CENTRE RETAIL PROPOSALS IN THE WEST MIDLANDS METROPOLITAN COUNTY
Source: West Midlands Shopping Study : Drivers Jonas (1987)

KEY

⬤ Regional Centre
■ Sub-Regional Centre
• Other Main Town Centres

—·—·— West Midlands County Boundary
▬▬ Motorway Network
✪ Retail Proposals

0 ————— KM ————— 12

N

Wolverhampton Racecourse
Wolverhampton
Dudley
Merry Hill
West Bromwich
Sandwell Mall
M5
M6
Walsall
Birmingham
Sutton Coldfield
Fort Dunlop
Cranmore
Solihull
M42
M6
Coventry

in late 1988 it was announced that Speyhawk and the Alton Group had been appointed as developers. Their scheme comprised both leisure and retail facilities, the latter including an indoor mall with four department stores and 100 shop units (Planning 1988b).

4-33
B: Fort Dunlop. An outline application for a new shopping centre together with a retail warehouse park, a factory and recreational facilities was made to Birmingham City Council in October 1986 by the Australian based George Harris Group. The retail floorspace is planned to total 117 000 m^2. The application includes a substantial 'carrot' for Birmingham City Council in the form of up to £15M worth of road building. The Council however are concerned about the potential impact on other existing shopping centres. The scale of the development has been reduced, and it is proposed that the centre would include about 78 000 m^2 of retail floorspace. The proposal has been called in by the Secretary of State and an inquiry is likely late in 1988 or in 1989.

4-34
C: Cranmore, Solihull. Two outline planning applications have been submitted for adjoining sites between the Monks Path Industrial Park and the A34 Stratford Road. The first was submitted in July 1986 by Standard Life Assurance Company for a 37 000 m^2 regional shopping centre with car parking for 3250 vehicles. the application was refused by Solihull Borough Council early in 1987. The second proposal was made by Canberra Developments Ltd in September 1986. The plan was for a non-food development of 13 000 m^2 with parking for 720. Both applications were considered at the April 1988 Public Inquiry, and a decision is awaited.

4-35
D: Wolverhampton Racecourse. A planning application has recently been submitted by Richardsons Developments for a retail development on the site of Wolverhampton Racecourse. The scheme, which would total 23 000 m^2, would include a superstore, a number of retail warehouses and several shop units. Development on this site would require the relocation of the racecourse, and the application is linked to one submitted to South Staffordshire District Council for a new racecourse together with other retail and leisure facilities. Given Wolverhampton MBC's concern for the viability of the town centre, it seems unlikely that permission for the racecourse redevelopment will be granted, and that it may therefore go to appeal.

4-36
E: Merry Hill, Phase 5, Dudley Enterprise Zone. In 1986, Dudley MBC granted outline planning permission for 112 000 m^2 of retail in addition to the 54 000 m^2 which Richardsons Developments had already built under the terms of the Enterprise Zone scheme. A total of almost 6000 parking spaces will be provided. Although the shopping centre was not due to be completed until September 1989, by June 1988, 85% of the centre had been let. A study of Merry Hill's implications for Wolverhampton, by Edward Erdman and Company (1986) indicated that the effects of this development could be quite profound. Essentially, Wolverhampton (about 10 km to the north) would be faced with a completely new competitor whose comparison floorspace equalled its own. Moreover, while 55% of Wolverhampton's comparison floorspace comprises national multiples, in the Merry Hill scheme the figure will be closer to 90%. This combined with the modern design of the new centre together with large amounts of free car parking will constitute a major challenge to the continued success of Wolverhampton. The consultants estimated that by 1990 the impact on comparison shopping in the borough as a whole would be 9.5%, though the effect in the town centre, where most comparison shopping is located, could be higher. Some stores, which act as important anchors could lose up to 20% of their trade. Overall, it was estimated that the effect of the development would be subtle, and spread over a few

years, rather than being immediate and obvious. As rental growth slowed still further, and vacancy rates increased, investment would be insufficient to keep the centre in good repair, thus initiating a cycle of decline. The impact of the Merry Hill scheme will be second only to that of the Sandwell Mall proposal, should it be realised.

4-37

In addition to these regional shopping centre scale proposals, there has been a proliferation of retail warehouse park schemes. Thus, after several applications by the CEGB and the Carroll Group for major regional shopping centres, plans for the site of the former Walsall Power Station together with neighbouring railway land have been scaled down. Following the withdrawl of the original developers, Rush and Tomkins proposed 28 000 m^2 of retail development. This scheme was called-in and dealt with at the Public Inquiry in April 1988. The decision is awaited. Consent has been granted for a retail park in Marshland Road Solihull.

RESPONSES

4-38

Following abolition of the West Midlands County Council in April 1986, decision making passed to the district councils. However, the 1985 Local Government Act ensured that policies set out under the Approved Structure Plan (as amended in January 1986) still apply until districts have prepared their Unitary Development Plans. District authorities have generally followed policies that echo the tenor of the structure plan and which tend to reinforce the rôle of town centres. Faced with such a large number of out-of-centre proposals, the West Midlands Joint Committee commissioned Drivers Jonas to conduct a shopping survey of the West Midlands. However, despite the attempt at cooperatively researching and planning what is a strategic issue, some district councils, most notably Sandwell MBC, have issued planning consent for large out-of-centre developments that threaten any concerted approach.

4-39

In December 1986, perhaps realising that a 'free for all' was becoming likely, the Secretary of State for the Environment issued Article 10 directions on nine proposed developments in the West Midlands. These directions prevented local authorities from granting approval on Fort Dunlop, Reedswood, and Cranmore. Since outline consent had already been granted for Sandwell Mall and Merry Hill, these developments fell outside the restriction. The article 10 directions were in addition to the requirement under Circular 12/86 that local authorities should refer retail proposals over 250 000 ft^2 (23 325 m^2) to the Secretary of State if they wish to grant permission.

4-40

Drivers Jonas submitted their West Midlands Shopping Study in March 1987. The study concluded that there was only scope for one new regional shopping centre with a maximum size of 650 000 ft^2 (60 645 m^2). Any more than this would damage existing town centres which themselves needed to increase turnover to fulfil spare capacity brought about by more efficient retail methods. The consultants estimated that an out-of-centre development would not increase the total employment in the region, but would only lead to a redistribution of jobs. It is significant that planning consents already granted for Sandwell Mall and Merry Hill total about 280 000 m^2, five times the amount recommended by the consultants.

4-41

In May 1987, the West Midlands Districts Joint Committee endorsed the findings of the Drivers Jonas Study. It was suggested that member authorities should not grant planning consent for out-of-centre shopping developments, that schemes where consent had been granted should be reduced in scale, or alternative land uses found, and that outstanding proposals should be dealt with to restore certainty for local authorities and traders.

CONCLUSION

4-42
Wolverhampton is a town centre whose vitality and continued success are threatened. Problems have been created by Wolverhampton's historical development and its location within the shopping hierarchy. Other centres have consolidated their retail provision, thus narrowing the gap between Wolverhampton and its smaller competitors. Meanwhile, Telford has eroded the town's traditional catchment to the northwest, and Birmingham has experienced renewed interest from developers, retailers and shoppers.

4-43
All these influences (perhaps with the exception of the rapid development of Telford) might be expected given the normal operation of the retail market. The changes occurred over a period of time, so their effects tend to be incremental rather than dramatic. However, the introduction of new forms of retailing, initially in the shape of superstores and retail warehouses but latterly, and more significantly, as out-of-centre regional shopping centres threaten to shatter the traditional market hierarchy. In its place would be a small number of highly profitable, car-based centres and a larger number of declining and decaying town centres.

4-44
Suddenly the future of centres such as Wolverhampton is in the hands of single development companies who stand to make enormous profits by the development of new centres. Local authorities are in disarray, lacking a single voice and enforcable strategic policies. Central government has helped create an atmosphere where local authorities are fairly certain that some out-of-centre development will occur, and each is under pressure to attract such development or suffer competition from a new centre located in a neighbouring district. The planning system has been forced to abandon rationality and adopt monopoly as its underlying philosphy. The gainers from this change are primarily the developers, but also the national multiples and some car-borne consumers. The losers are smaller town centre retailers, together with car-less consumers. In the West Midlands, the Merry Hill regional shopping centre is already under construction, while outline consent has been granted for a massive development in Sandwell. Retailers and shoppers in Wolverhampton are likely to suffer as the centre declines and the range of shops contracts.

4-45
Wolverhampton MBC's shopping policies have been designed to maintain retailing within the town centre, an easily identifiable area encircled by the town's inner ring road. Such policies have been a response to the borough's belief that this location is good for retailers, shoppers and the town as a whole, and, as such, they have received the strong support of the local Chamber of Commerce which represents local retailers and landlords. In line with these principles, the borough has carried out a series of environmental improvements in the town centre, including further pedestrianisation, and 'traffic calming' in order to make the centre more attractive to pedestrians. If all the proposals are implemented, Wolverhampton will have one of the most extensive pedestrian schemes in Britain, and will rival many European towns where the link between a good physical environment and a good economic environment has long been recognised. Proposals to improve public transport, particularly by effective use of light rail systems have the potential to reinforce these benefits.

4-46

Despite Wolverhampton's commitment to the town centre, its policies have been forced to bend to the will of an uncontrolled market. As surrounding districts permitted the development of non-central superstores and retail warehouses, the borough saw much of its trade drawn out of Wolverhampton. In order to retain this trade it was felt necessary to allow similar developments within the borough. Additionally, it was becoming obvious that the prevailing political climate meant that planning refusals on such developments were more likely to be overturned at appeal. Factors which were seen as justifying refusal were becoming fewer in number. Rather than lose increasing amounts of trade, or end up with unwanted developments in the wrong locations, Wolverhampton MBC, like so many local authorities, was forced to compromise its principles and allow a limited amount of such development in carefully chosen locations.

4-47

The conclusions of this case study are pessimistic, both for town centres such as Wolverhampton whose vulnerable positions are threatened by a new wave of development, and for those who believe that local planning should be an effective way of regulating the excesses and inequalities of the market. Town centres are left to cycles of decline, reducing choice and accessibility for a large number of consumers, while the historical investment in centres such as Wolverhampton is abandoned in favour of sources of quicker economic return.

REFERENCES

Department of the Environment (n.d.) **Strategic Planning Guidance for the West Midlands** Birmingham

Drivers Jonas (1987) **West Midlands Shopping Study**

Edward Erdman & Company (1979) **The County of West Midlands Structure Plan Shopping Study**
- (1986) **Merry Hill (Phase V) : An Assessment of the Implications for Wolverhampton**

Goad (1986) **Out-of-centre shopping directory**

Jones, P (1987) **Evidence to Molineux/Electric Construction Company Public Inquiry** Bernard Thorpe & Partners

Joyce, R (1987) **Personal Communication** Drivers Jonas

Lillywhite, John (1987,1988) **Personal Communication** Wolverhampton Metropolitan Borough Council

Office of Population Censuses and Surveys (1984) **Census 1981 : Key statistics for Local Authorities** London HMSO

Planning (1988a) **Wolves store battle is over** No 779 29 July p40
- (1988b) **Developers named for Sandwell Site** No 797 2 December p8

TEST (1988) **Quality Streets – How traditional urban centres benefit from traffic calming** London TEST

West Midlands County Council (1976) **West Midlands County Council Household Survey**
- (1978) **County Structure Plan Report of Survey**
- (1980) **West Midlands County Structure Plan**

Wolverhampton Metropolitan Borough Council (1987) **Wolverhampton Town Centre Local Plan : Written Statement**

5 YORK

SUMMARY

5-01
This chapter paints a very different picture of retailing from those of the previous two chapters. With a prosperous city centre which has become aligned to the needs of visitors, out-of-centre retailing has gradually become accepted as a way of serving the local population. However, as surrounding local authorities have been prepared to permit a limited amount of off-centre development, so the pressure for further development has increased.

5-02
York has benefitted from the boom in tourism which has occurred during the last two decades. Tourists visiting the Minster, the Mediæval streets and the many museums have bolstered the town centre's economy. The industrial economy however has suffered continued decline. York's retailing has exploited the tourist market. The town centre has large numbers of gift shops, tea shops and other outlets primarily meeting the needs of visitors. Although local authorities in the Greater York area have worked together to develop a strategy to cope with out-of-centre pressures, recently the cooperation has ceased as two districts gave consent for major off-centre schemes. York City Council has embarked on a major programme of pedestrianisation designed to enhance still further the city's environment.

5-03
York city centre's orientation toward tourism ensures that it will not suffer the kind of decline that out-of-centre retailing threatens in places such as Wolverhampton. However, the kinds of problem that result from York's emerging retail structure are relevant to other centres whose history and/or environment is seen as the answer to off-centre competition. The first problem is that of access. York's population has below average incomes and car ownership rates, and with a poorly developed public transport system a dispersed pattern of retailing means that access to it is not always easy. Dispersal of retailing to non-central locations therefore does not represent the most efficient and rational strategy. In addition, by capitalising on its historic environment the city centre is at risk of becoming little more than a heritage theme park. While this will secure the continued existence of the centre in physical terms, it means that its function will have been transformed as radically as that of a declining centre elsewhere.

INTRODUCTION AND BACKGROUND

5-04
The historic city of York is located in the predominantly rural county of North Yorkshire. The city could be described as freestanding with the nearest settlement of any significant size being Leeds 40km to the south west. Unlike many other places with similar historic environments, York's economy has been founded on heavy industry; in particular British Rail has been the source of many jobs in both engineering and administration. Average incomes are lower than the national average, and in 1981 York was overrepresented among semi and unskilled workers. Car ownership is considerably lower than the national average (in 1981 52% of households did not own cars compared to a national figure of 39.5% [OPCS 1984]), while cycling has remained a popular means of transport. The city does not have a particularly well developed public transport system. Because of the compact nature of the city, and the focus of roads on the city centre, many people walk or cycle to the centre.

5-05

Local politics in York have maintained an atmosphere of consensus. At the present time York City Council is controlled by the Labour Group who have a thirteen seat majority, but the Conservatives had a majority between 1975 and 1984. In practice there is a fairly peaceful coexistence between the two main parties, with party political issues only coming to the fore in the more volatile full committees of the council. The urban area of York (see Figure 5-1) extends further than the City boundaries, largely the result of post-war suburbanisation. The result is that policies affecting the whole area have to be drawn up in the context of Greater York, which includes the districts of Harrogate, Selby and Ryedale as well as the City and County Councils. Despite the differing interests of these local authorities, until recently there appeared to be cooperation and understanding between them, allowing the development of policies which cover the whole area.

CHANGE IN THE RETAIL MARKET AND THE DEVELOPMENT OF RETAIL POLICIES

5-06

In the early 1970s York's retail sector was experiencing stagnation (Pearson 1987). The town centre was suffering low trading levels and there was a relatively high vacancy rate. Gillygate for instance was largely derelict and the City Council planned to demolish much of it to build a new road system and to reveal the city walls. Many of the shop units in Micklegate were empty.

5-07

It is not suprising therefore that the concept of out-of-centre retailing was strongly opposed by York City Council who feared that if large stores were allowed outside the city centre other forms of retailing would follow leaving inefficient (to retailers) retailing space in the town centre. This approach had been supported by Viscount Esher (Esher 1968) who suggested that the health of York depended on business and housing being kept in the city centre. In 1971 Asda made an application to build a superstore (6 000 m^2 gross 3500 m^2 net) at Huntington in the north east of the city. York City Council refused permission for the development, a seemingly rational decision given the high proportion of people who walked or cycled, and relatively compact nature of the city. However, permission was subsequently granted on appeal, the inspector concluding that the Asda superstore would not damage the city centre and would actually improve the area, since the site in question was currently a knackers yard. The Secretary of State granted permission in February 1973; the store opened in September of the following year (Lee Donaldson Associates 1986)

5-08

Asda's impact on the local market was closely monitored both by the local Junior Chamber of Commerce and by the Centre for Urban and Regional Research, University of Manchester. The Junior Chamber of Commerce (1977) examined changes in shoppers' behaviour which occurred after the new store opened. The new Asda had a significant effect on shopping patterns; 65% of shoppers came from districts around the store in the north east of York, the remaining 35% coming fairly evenly from the rest of York. Many of the shoppers had previously used supermarkets in the city centre, while some trade was taken from local supermarkets and specialist stores. Whereas before Asda opened 50% of shoppers used cars, 30% walked, 10% used public transport and 10% used bicycles, the Junior Chamber found that 90% of shoppers came to the new store by car, only 1-2% using a bus service that called at the store. Given the fact that most consumers would previously have shopped in the city centre, and travelled there by foot, bike or bus, the new superstore therefore generated a large number of new car journeys, together with their associated externalities.

102

5-09

The Junior Chamber argued that many supermarkets in York were suffering as a result of the competition from Asda (see Table 5-1). The only store which managed to maintain customer levels while increasing spending per head was the Co-op in New Earswick, probably because of its customers' loyalty and lower car ownership. It was stated that, between 1974 and 1977, two city centre supermarkets and two food halls in department stores closed. The Junior Chamber argued that the opening of the new Asda was only one element in the town centre's decreasing attractivenenss to convenience shoppers. Equally important, in their view, was the failure of the city centre to accommodate car borne shoppers. They argued that policies designed to restrict vehicular access to the historic core of York had 'prevented the casual shopper from coming into York, with the effect that fewer local people are shopping in York.' Thus they felt that the Asda store, while affecting other stores, was allowing dissatisfied city centre shoppers to shop elsewhere using their cars.

Table 5-1 : Estimated weekly trading per square foot of retail selling area

	PRESTO City Centre (2400 m^2)	HILLARDS SE Suburb (1500 m^2)	ASDA NE Village (3500 m^2)	Food Price Index
Sept 1974	£2.40	£3.00	–	107.5
Sept 1975	£2.00	£3.10	£3.10	130.7 (+21.6%)
Sept 1976	£1.90	£4.40	£5.40	157.0 (+20.1%)

Source: York Junior Chamber of Commerce (1977)

5-10

The conclusions regarding the Asda development that were drawn by Bridges (1976) of the University of Manchester differed somewhat from those of the Junior Chamber. Looking at the patterns of spending in York before and after Asda opened its store, Bridges argued that the city centre had lost trade from outside the city, but had gained it from inside. By diverting away some of the car-borne shoppers coming from outside York, the new superstore actually made the city centre more attractive to the large population living within York. Thus while the city centre took 19.5% of the potential food trade of people living within 15 miles in 1974 (the year Asda opened), in 1975 this had only fallen to 18.0%. Huntington had gained 7.1% of the market thanks to the new Asda, a figure four times that of the city centre's loss. Losses of non-food 'Asda-type' goods by the city centre showed a similar pattern, and Bridges concluded that the city centre had in fact fared reasonably well. Given fairly stable population and expenditure levels, the gains sustained by Asda had to be losses suffered elsewhere. Bigger losses were sustained by those suburban centres located close to the new Asda store. Overall however Bridges argued that at least 20%, if not more of Asda's trade must have been at the expense of shops outside York.

5-11

The Junior Chamber concluded that convenience shopping to the north east of the city was now well provided for, but that there was a continued and pressing need for more such facilities on the western side of the River Ouse. However, they were adamant that the City Council should oppose an application by Tesco to build a superstore at Foss Bank close to the city centre. It was felt that this location would have a significant impact on the remaining supermarkets in the town centre and would increase road congestion for motorists approaching the city centre from the north east. The City Council did refuse planning permission for this store, and when the application was taken to appeal the inspector supported the local authority arguing that the combination of the proposed Tesco store with the existing Asda could lead to supermarket closures and serious economic consequences for the city centre. The appeal was dismissed (Lee Donaldson Associates 1986).

5-12

While York City Council were opposing the development of any form of out-of-centre retailing, North Yorkshire County Council was drawing up its structure plan policies. In 1978 NYCC published a Draft Written Statement in which it set out its proposals. The shopping policies were aimed at maintaining the present hierarchy of shopping provision throughout the county and the role of each existing shopping centre. The policies themselves were quite clear; 'new shopping developments should be accommodated within town centres or their acceptable extensions' (Policy S1); hypermarkets, superstores supermarkets and retail warehouses would only be accommodated within town centres (Policies S4, S5). By the time the North Yorkshire Structure Plan was approved in November 1980, the shopping policies had become somewhat diluted.

5-13

The structure plan allowed for new shopping developments in town centres or existing residential areas which currently had shopping deficiencies, provided that they did not prejudice the continued existence of established shops, and that they did not cause unacceptable traffic and environmental impact (Policy S1). It also stated that shopping developments over 1500 m^2 would only be permitted outside shopping centres where a need had been created by a growing population, where existing shopping facilities were inadequate and the new scheme could not be incorporated into it, and where it could be readily served by public transport (Policy S3). In addition it would have to satisfy the requirements outlined in Policy S1. Thus North Yorkshire County Council's policies had shifted from prohibiting retail development outside established centres, to allowing it where certain provisos were met.

5-14

During the 1970s York began to experience a tourist boom. Traditional attractions like York Minster and the Castle were gradually joined by new developments such as the National Railway Museum, and latterly Jorvik Museum. Tourists have also been attracted to the historic core of York, in particular to streets such as Stonegate and The Shambles. While the tourist season is fairly pronounced (half the visitors to the Castle Museum come between June and August), York's cultural/historic character has meant that the season is not as polarised as in other centres. Despite this seasonality, tourism has provided an important boost to the town centre economy. Many retail outlets specifically aimed at the visitor have opened and streets which were once derelict have become full of gift shops, jewellers and tea shops. From a low point in the early 1970s, town centre retailing has become a boom sector. In some streets, rents are approaching £100 per ft^2 for the prime pitch (Chartered Surveyor Weekly 1987).

5-15

The regeneration of the city centre and its move from convenience towards speciality shopping can be seen by examining the retail composition between 1970 and 1986. Data on the number of shops differentiated by type are presented in Table 5-2 below.

104

Table 5-2 : York city centre retail composition 1970-1986

Retail Type (%)	Number of shop units				
	1970	1975	1980	1983	1986
Convenience Goods	73(16.6)	57(12.5)	48(10.5)	56(11.7)	45 (9.4)
Books	6 (1.4)	13 (2.8)	11 (2.4)	15 (3.1)	15 (3.1)
Footwear	27 (6.1)	34 (7.4)	31 (6.8)	31 (6.5)	25 (5.2)
Clothing	90(20.4)	108(23.6)	99(21.7)	110(23.0)	99(20.7)
Furniture	15 (3.4)	20 (4.4)	18 (3.9)	20 (4.2)	17 (3.6)
Floor Coverings	6 (1.4)	7 (1.5)	4 (0.9)	4 (0.8)	1 (0.2)
Household Txtles.	7 (1.6)	6 (1.3)	6 (0.2)	12 (2.5)	17 (3.6)
Electrical & Other Durable Goods	14 (3.2)	18 (3.9)	17 (3.7)	22 (4.6)	24 (5.0)
China, Glass etc	1 (0.2)	6 (1.3)	5 (1.1)	5 (1.0)	5 (1.0)
Hardware/Tools	11 (2.5)	8 (1.8)	7 (1.5)	11 (2.3)	11 (2.3)
DIY	12 (2.7)	8 (1.8)	6 (1.3)	7 (1.5)	9 (1.9)
Chemists' Goods	9 (2.0)	9 (2.0)	6 (1.3)	8 (1.7)	9 (1.9)
Recreation & Misc Goods	103(27.9)	123(26.9)	134(29.3)	143(29.9)	137(28.7)
Dept & Variety Stores	8 (1.8)	8 (1.8)	8 (1.8)	8 (1.7)	10 (2.1)
Vacant Stores	23 (5.2)	7 (1.5)	13 (2.8)	12 (2.5)	31 (6.5)
Unknown	36 (8.2)	25 (5.5)	42 (9.2)	14 (2.9)	24 (5.0)
TOTAL	441 (100)	457 (100)	455 (100)	478 (100)	479(100)

Sources: York City Council (Unpublished); Goad Shopping Centre Plans (1970 1975, 1980, 1985, 1986); Kelly's Directories (1970, 1975)

5-16
Tables 5-2 and 5-3 relate to streets within the central area of the city (listed in the Appendix); for streets on the periphery of the city centre data were only available for 1975 and 1983, making any longer term comparisons impossible. This is unfortunate because streets like Gillygate and Micklegate probably experienced the most significant transition from dereliction to retail bouyancy. It should therefore be noted that changes described in Table 5-2 and 5-3 are likely to err on the conservative side.

5-17
The clearest trends to emerge from the tables are the decline of convenience goods outlets and the growth in the number of shops meeting demands of the tourist (gift shops and jewellers which are classified as Recreation and Miscellaneous Goods, Books and China and Glass). While Hardware and Tools outlets have remained fairly constant in number, the number of DIY outlets has dropped both in absolute and percentage terms, perhaps reflecting the develop-ment of DIY retail warehouses outside the city centre and the movement of builders' merchants into the DIY market. This change is mirrored among city centre carpet shops, which fell in number from six to only one. Trends among shops selling DIY goods and carpets therefore run counter to the argument that the 'First Wave' of retail warehouses had no effect on town centres. The most significant decline however has been experienced amongst convenience stores, falling from over 16% of the total number of shops to just under 9.5%. In real terms the number of stores has dropped from 73 to 45. This must reflect the movement of shoppers to out-of centre stores, be they superstores or simply

supermarkets located in district centres. These patterns of change are confirmed by data for peripheral streets such as Gillygate, Micklegate and Walmgate for 1975 and 1983. During this period the number of convenience stores dropped from 33 to 25 and the number of shops selling 'Recreation and Miscellaneous Goods' increased from 37 to 46.

Table 5-3 : York city centre floorspace 1970-1986

Retail Type	Total floorspace (m^2)				
	1970	1975	1980	1983	1986[1]
Convenience Goods	12 648	14 404	12 509	13 566	11 934
Books	943	2 013	1 960	2 109	1 881
Footwear	5 445	6 692	6 205	5 922	7 080
Clothing	16 591	17 995	16 002	19 357	15 922
Furniture	9 197	10 446	10 170	8 994	6 688
Floor Coverings	1 430	1 381	920	1 044	460
Household Txtles.	1 703	1 045	1 816	1 230	3 091
Electrical & Other Durable Goods	5 289	5 485	5 651	6 127	6 249
China, Glass etc	388	897	609	1 009	801
Hardware/Tools	3 295	2 601	2 743	2 549	2 337
DIY	2 960	2 666	2 334	2 334	2 620
Chemists' Goods	3 093	3 599	2 807	3 016	2 473
Recreation & Misc Goods	13 920	15 776	16 359	17 587	14 733
Dept & Variety Stores	25 666	25 666	25 666	23 816	23 100
Vacant Stores	3 469	2 477	3 735	4 499	9 121
Unknown	4 775	3 036	4 843	3 529	5 650
TOTAL	110 812	116 179	114 329	116 688	114 140

Note : 1 Does not include Coppergate development
Source: York City Council (Unpublished Data)
        Goad Shopping Centre Plans (1970, 1975, 1980, 1985, 1986)
        Kelly's Directories (1970, 1975)

5-18
Information was only comprehensively available for the main city centre, so peripheral streets such as Gillygate, Micklegate and Walmgate, where the transition from dereliction and vacancy may have been most pronounced, have therefore been excluded from the main analysis. The figures presented in Tables 5-2 and 5-3 are important for two reasons. First, they show the extent to which the centre of York has benefitted from economic revival. Many vacant and derelict premises have been brought back into use, while the total stock of retail floorspace has increased. In addition, many of the shops which serve the tourist market have specialised in more expensive goods, rather than the down market souvenirs characteristic of many tourist areas.

5-19
The second point that should be made is that by specialising at the top end of the tourist market, many of the town centre shops no longer serve the local population. Shops selling convenience goods have declined in number, while gift shops and jewellers have multiplied. Thus there is a growing gap between the local demand and the supply of speciality shopping. This gap has undoubt-

edly increased pressure for out-of-centre shops which can serve local needs. At the same time, the buoyancy of city centre retailing has meant it is less threatened by any out-of-centre shopping that may occur than many other towns. This is fortuitous because pressure for out-of-centre retailing has increased since York's outer ring-road was completed.

5-20

By the late 1970s York City Council had come to the conclusion that out-of-centre superstores were not such a threat to exisiting trade as they had anticipated. This was partly due to the buoyancy of the city centre. Reversing the decision they had earlier made on Tesco's application at Foss Bank, they granted planning permission for Sainsburys to build a superstore and DIY store on the same site. Pressure for non-central convenience retailing continued to grow however. York's City Planning Officer persuaded the County Council that a strategic study should be carried out in order that applications could be evaluated in the context of existing retailing. Since York's urban area extends further than the York City Council boundaries, a working party was set up with officers from the City, North Yorkshire County Council, Harrogate Borough Council, Ryedale District Council, and Selby District Council (1983).

5-21

The working party first considered future convenience expenditure in Greater York. The growth of demand for convenience goods by 1991 was calculated as £18M pa, taking annual turnover from £86M in 1983 to £104M. The working party went on to see how this growth could best be accommodated within the city, considering two policy options that were open: retail development in district centres, and out-of-centre retailing. It was argued that the former option was more attractive because it conformed to policies set out in the County Structure Plan, and that out-of-centre development should only be considered if the convenience retailing deficiencies could not be accommodated in local centres.

5-22

Possible locations for new convenience shopping were then considered. There was already a feeling that the western side of the city was underprovided with this type of shopping, there was already a large Asda at Huntingdon, while the Sainsburys superstore at Foss Bank was under construction. There were proposals for superstores at Bishopthorpe Road (1900 m^2 net), Acomb (Sainsburys 2500 m^2 net), Foxwood (York City Council 1300 m^2 net), Clifton (Henry Boot 7300 m^2 net) and Boroughbridge Road (2400 m^2 net). Three potential locations were identified by the working party: in the existing Acomb shopping centre (up to a maximum of 1300 m^2 net), in the developing residential area at Foxwood (up to a maximum of 1300 m^2 net), and at Clifton where major residential and industrial development was proposed on a disused air field (up to a maximum of 2000 m^2 net). Three stores in the above locations would absorb £12.2M of the estimated £18M leaving £5.8M for small scale developments and extensions. The working party concluded that large out-of-centre developments would generate a turnover well in excess of the maximum expenditure available, seriously prejudicing the continued existence of established shops and undermining the economic basis of the city centre conservation policy. Existing superstores are shown in Figure 5-4.

5-23

Local authorities in Greater York were therefore gearing themselves up to cope with a surge in convenience applications. However, an increase in pressure for comparison shopping followed hard on its heels and at this stage there was little information regarding durable expenditure trends which could be used to develop policies to sensibly cope with the pressure for development. The 1983 policy document concluded that any decisions on large applications should be postponed to a time when the effects of current commitments were known. It also recommended that the member authorities should conduct a study of durable retailing.

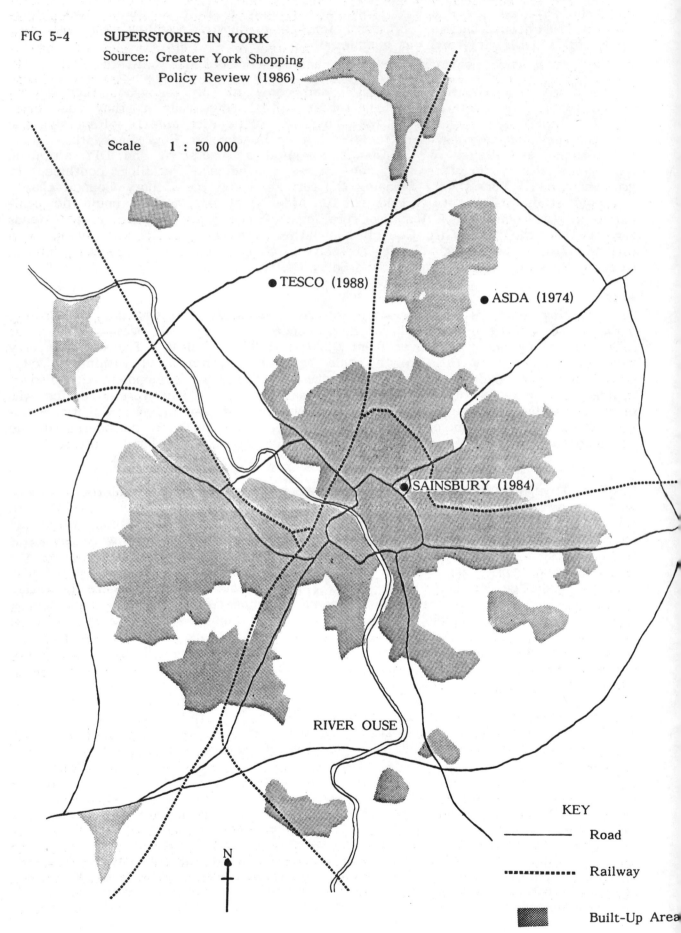

FIG 5-4   **SUPERSTORES IN YORK**
Source: Greater York Shopping
Policy Review (1986)

Scale   1 : 50 000

● TESCO (1988)

● ASDA (1974)

● SAINSBURY (1984)

RIVER OUSE

N

KEY

——————   Road

••••••••••••   Railway

▓▓▓   Built-Up Area

5-24

In 1984 the economist Harvey Cole was commissioned by the Greater York Shopping Study Working Party to assess the future floorspace requirements for comparison retailing. Cole examined the pattern of comparison retailing in 1971, the date of the last Census of Distribution, and updated it to take account of changes in the goods sold, population, inflation and expenditure per head in York. He concluded that there was a requirement for 120 000 m^2 in 1984 and almost 140 000 m^2 by 1991. Given a total of 105 500 m^2 of comparison floorspace in 1984, this left a deficit of 15 000 m^2 with a further 17 500 m^2 by 1991. Cole's calculations gave the working party a base from which to develop policies on comparison shopping.

5-25

The Greater York Shopping Study Working Party produced a policy document for comparison shopping in April 1985. The study underlined the need to safeguard the shopping function of the city centre while at the same time recognising that the buoyancy of the retail sector and the limited capacity of the city centre meant that some consideration would have to be given to some form of out of centre development.

5-26

The working party argued that any policy for comparison shopping would have to take account of the following factors:

- existing Structure Plan Policies;
- the changing demands of shoppers;
- the environmental importance of the existing City Centre;
- traffic congestion and parking facilities in central York;
- the importance of appropriate competition;
- the availability of sites for shopping development;
- population trends;
- expenditure trends;
- future development already committed in terms of planning consents

5-27

There were two substantial comparison shopping developments under construction at the time. The City Council were partnering Wimpey in the development of the award winning Coppergate scheme on the western edge of the city centre. The scheme centres round an open square and totals 9 500 m^2 including two department stores and twenty two other shop units. Included in the scheme is the highly popular Jorvik Viking Museum. The second scheme under construction was the Sainsbury development at Foss Bank which was to include a 2 700 m^2 DIY and garden centre. Also with planning permission was a 1 600 m^2 retail warehouse on Foss Islands Road, which had a condition restricting its use to the stock and sale of furniture.

5-28

In order to estimate future growth of retail floorspace, the working party examined expenditure trends within the city's catchment. If expenditure growth was insufficient to support new forms of out-of-centre retailing in addition to existing and future comparison shops in the centre, it was felt that the former would have the advantage of lower overheads (land costs, construction costs and rates) and easy access for car users. In such a situation it was argued that non-central retail development could only be viable at the expense of existing facilities. In addition to gauging demand, the working party also sought to identify areas of York which were relatively underprovided with comparison shopping. It was assumed that adequate provision existed when expenditure and turnover estimates were roughly equal.

FIG 5-5

COMPARISON OF MAJOR SHOPPING PROPOSALS
SUBMITTED BETWEEN 1/1985 AND 6/1986
Source: Greater York Shopping
        Policy Review (1986)

Scale   1 : 50 000

•2   △6   △11
                           •3
                        7△

                    5• △9
                4• △8   •1

N

↑

River Ouse

△10

KEY

△ Permission Refused   ▦ Built-Up Area   —— Road

● Permission Granted   ------- Railway

110

Developments
1=Hull Road,Osbaldwick
2=Clifton Airfield
3=Pigeon Cote Industrial Park, Huntingdon
4=Foss Islands Road, York
5=Foss Islands Road/Layerthorpe, York
6=N.York Trading Estate, CLifton
7=Society Lane/New Lane, Huntingdon
8=Foss Islands Road, York
9=Ebor Industrial Estate, York
10=Eastfield Farm, Askham Bryan
11=Pigeon Cote Industrial Park, Huntingdon

5-29

Examining expenditure projections, the working party concluded that Greater York might be expected to sustain up to 30 000 m^2 of additional comparison sales area by 1991. This figure is in line with Cole's figure given above. Comparison retailing was then split up into two types: Group A comprised those goods which could easily be sold from existing centres, while Group B goods were those which the working party argued were more easily sold from outside existing shopping centres because of their bulky nature and their dependence on car based sales (DIY, furniture). Group A retailing development would only be given planning permission if it was located within a town centre, and the total amount that would be permitted up to 1991 was set at 10 000 m^2. Group B retailing would be allowed to expand by 20 000 m^2 by 1991. These totals were in addition to current committments.

5-30

Meanwhile, demand for new retail space continued to grow. Eleven applications, all for out-of-centre developments, were determined in the light of the above policies (see Figure 5-5). Outline approval was given for five schemes totalling just over 20 000 m^2, the agreed amount that Group B goods would be allowed to grow up to 1991. Two retail warehouse units were given consent in Osbaldwick for occupation by MFI and Harris Queensway. A larger proposal at Clifton Airfield (a site identified in the convenience shopping study) totalled 7000 m^2 (this development included a 3 700 m^2 Tesco superstore which was granted planning permission on appeal). At Pigeon Cote Industrial Park outline consent was given for three retail units totalling 3 700 m^2. Two separate schemes gained outline permission at Foss Islands near the new Sainsbury site. The permissions allowed two units of 3 100 and 1 000 m^2, to be occupied by B&Q and Allied Carpets respectively. Six other proposals, totalling 44 000 m^2 were refused consent. All the applications received were for developments outside the city centre despite the retail policy's attempt to limit out-of-centre development.

5-31

Despite the fact that permissions representing the floorspace growth up to 1991 had been granted, the pressure for further approvals continued. By October 1986 a further four comparison applications were awaiting determination. In addition there were several informal proposals for shopping development under consideration relating to sites in the Clifton and Hull Road areas and within the city centre. The scale of the pressures for out-of-centre retail development, and their relation to city centre retailing are clear from Figure 5-6.

5-32

This wave of applications marked a change from the retail warehouse format that had characterised earlier proposals. In particular the Monk's Cross development represented a type of development which would compete with the city centre to a much greater extent than the retail 'sheds' selling DIY and flat pack furniture. The Monk's Cross scheme was hailed as a 'tourist free' alternative to the city centre, and as such highlighted both the perceived problems of the city centre, and the potential damage that existing shopping could sustain if such developments were to go ahead.

5-33

By late 1986 the retail working party considered that an increase in the overall floorspace limit for comparison shopping was justified. They argued that the 1985 floorspace survey suggested that floorspace earlier identified may have been understated. Secondly, all the floorspace which was built and committed under the policy related to Group B sales. As a result it would be likely to operate at below average turnover level for all comparison shops. In addition, the working party stated that about 10 000 m^2 of new floorspace could be built in and around the city centre. If this land was developed the scale

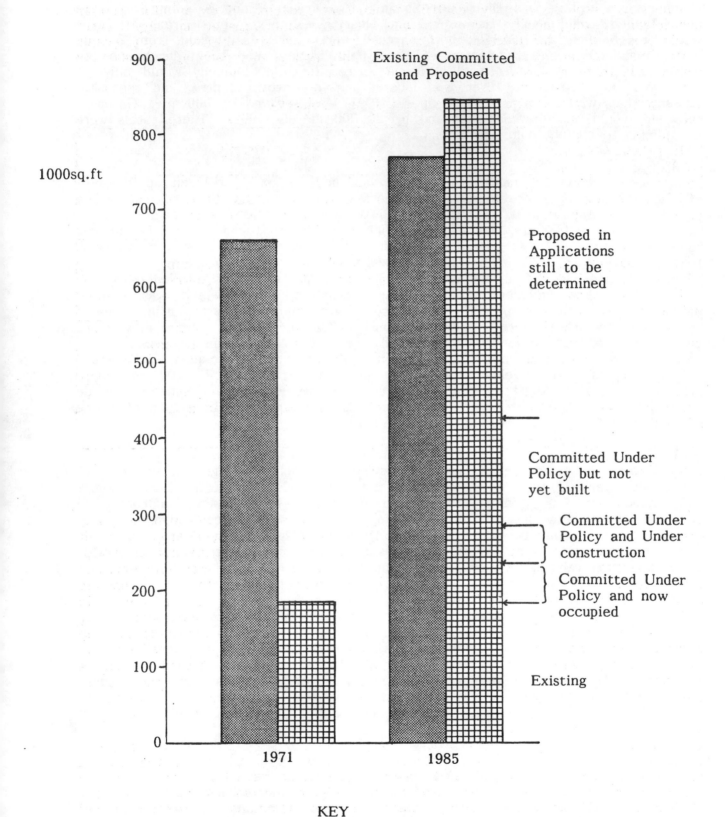

FIG 5-6   COMPARISON OF SHOPPING FLOORSPACE IN
GREATER YORK BETWEEN 1971 AND 1985
Source: North Yorks County Council et al (1986a)

Existing Committed
and Proposed

Proposed in
Applications
still to be
determined

Committed Under
Policy but not
yet built

Committed Under
Policy and Under
construction

Committed Under
Policy and now
occupied

Existing

KEY

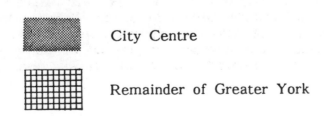

City Centre

Remainder of Greater York

112

would exceed the overall floorspace limit. It was decided that the limit on floorspace growth between 1985 and 1991 should be increased to 40 000 m^2. Of this total, 23 000 had already been built or was committed, leaving a further 17 000 m^2 to be provided. The working party stated that 10 000 m^2 of this should be reserved for city centre development, leaving 7000 m^2 for further non-central development. Sales in new developments outside the city centre would continue to be limited to Group B goods. If no town centre proposals were received during the next two years, the policy of reserving 10 000 m^2 would have to be reviewed.

Table 5-7 Applications awaiting determination in October 1986

PROPOSALS	SIZE	NOTES
Clifton Airfield	9 300 m^2 gross non-food retailing	Adjacent to Tesco development
Pigeon Cote Industrial Park "Monk's Cross"	21 000 m^2 retail with 5 400 m^2 leisure uses	would replace earlier approval for 6 600 m^2
Huntington	11 000 m^2 retail	Adjacent to Asda superstore
Askham Bryan	9 300 m^2 gross non-food & 7 000 m^2 gross food	In Green Belt

Source: North Yorkshire County Council et al 1986

5-34
Given the difficulty in estimating floorspace requirements, the working party agreed that the floorspace limits would be treated only as guidelines, and not strictly adhered to. Regular monitoring would have to be carried out to evaluate the success and appropriateness of the policy. Finally, it was recommended that applications to make outline planning permissions into full consents should take place within twelve months of the former having been granted. In addition, building work should commence within a year of full permission being granted. This aim of this measure, which would be achieved using conditions on planning permission, was to prevent the whole of the floorspace allocation up to 1991 being absorbed by one permission which was not being realised. Such a situation would increase pressure for further development and thus over-provision.

5-35
By November 1986 three additional applications for large scale shopping development had been received. Estates and General Investments plc proposed an additional 16 000 m^2 retail and leisure development at Clifton on a site to the west of the approved Tesco development. Polar Motors proposed 8 400 m^2 (6 000 m^2 net) at Pigeon Cote Industrial Estate adjoining the other proposal for this site. In the city centre a proposal was put forward for the redevelopment of Yorkshire Evening Press's works in Coney Street. The proposal involved the relocation of the printing works, but would provide 9 000 m^2 (6 300 m^2 net) of retail space. The scheme was greeted by the working party as evidence that there was still interest in retail development in the city

113

centre. The working party reiterated its commitment to floorspace limits, and argued that while York might be better equipped to fight off out-of-centre competition because of its tourist functions, the development of retailing that would directly compete with the city centre would put its future investment and viablility in jeopardy. It was therefore concluded that the benefits of confining Group A retailing to the central shopping area outweighed any benefits of decentralisation.

5-36
Before the constituent local authorities had even agreed to implement the recommendations of the retail working party, the Secretary of State for the Environment issued an Article 10 Direction which prevented the district councils from deciding applications until he had decided whether they should be referred to him.

5-37
In January 1987 the revised policies for both convenience and comparison shopping were set out in a new policy document (NYCC et al 1987). That for convenience retailing allowed for one additional superstore with a preferred location in the south-west quadrant of York. The working party identified the proposed Foxwood local centre as a suitable location for such a store. Elsewhere development would be limited to supermarket or small convenience shopping in or adjacent to existing or proposed local shopping centres. Monitoring would ensure that the policy was in line with changing conditions. The policy document recognised that there should be an expansion of comparison shopping in Greater York to keep in line with projected expenditure levels. Preference would be given to proposals within or adjacent to the city centre or local centres. It was agreed that planning permission would only be granted where developers entered a Section 52 agreement which limited the life of the consent to twelve months. The policy stated that, in addition to development committed but not yet constructed, 21 000 m^2 of conventional comparison retail floorspace, or its equivalent, could be permitted within Greater York without undue concern for its impact on existing or proposed centres.

5-38
On 7 January 1987 North Yorkshire County Planning Committee approved the policies for convenience and comparison retailing. The meeting also noted that, in accordance with the now approved policies, Ryedale District Council had resolved to grant planning permission for the 8 400 m^2 proposal at Pigeon Cote Farm. Consent would be conditional upon the developer entering into the Section 52 agreement. However, this proposal was included within the Secretary of State's Article 10 Direction preventing the local planning authority from determining it. It was decided that all the Greater York local authorities should support Ryedale's request that the Article 10 direction should be lifted for this case. Since planning decisions would be based on the policy established by all the Greater York local authorities, it was decided that in the event of a local authority having to pay costs as the result of an appeal, the member authorities would share the costs between them. The Secretary of State did decide to remove the Article 10 Direction from all the proposals, allowing permission to be granted for the Pigeon Cote Farm proposal (with a condition limiting the life of the permission). In the light of this decision, permission was refused on the other outstanding applications.

Recent Developments

5-39
Recent interest in the city centre suggests that retailers and developers believe there is still scope there for further retail growth. Wimpey are currently building a 6 000 m^2 store for Marks & Spencer on the site of the former ABC cinema. The City Council had refused permission for the scheme on

the grounds that the cinema was a valued local amenity, but were overruled by the Secretary of State at appeal. General Accident has gained outline planning permission for the refurbishment of a number of properties in Little Stonegate, Grape Lane, Back Swinegate and Swinegate. These streets are close to the already successful Stonegate, and would be converted to form about 3 500 m^2 of speciality retailing. There are also plans to include a Roman museum in the scheme. Close to the Coppergate Centre, and the Marks & Spencer extension, Laing Properties has acquired the property which includes the Tesco supermarket, and has submitted an application for a 4 500 m^2 department store and six smaller shop units (Estates Times 1988). A mixed scheme under construction close to Lendal Bridge includes approximately 3 000 m^2 of speciality retailing.

5-40

Until recently, a significant aspect of planning in Greater York was the cooperation that operated between different districts. It has been shown that the districts, together with the County Council came together in an atmosphere of apparent consensus to determine where out-of-centre retailing should be permitted. Recent events have ended this consensus, and have shown the weakness of voluntary groupings of local authorities. By granting permission for one large out-of-centre shopping scheme in Ryedale, it was thought that expenditure growth up to 1991 would be accommodated. After this date development might be allowed in another district. Despite apparent commitment to the shopping policy, Selby District Council have granted planning consent for a second large shopping scheme on the site of the former Fulford and Naburn Hospital.

5-41

With two local authorities willing to allow major out-of-centre schemes, and the possibility that both may reach fruition, the agreed shopping policy no longer holds. It may be that earlier cooperation reflected the fact that most proposals were located within Ryedale, and that as soon as schemes come forward in other areas the consensus breaks down. The competition between authorities in the York area is now akin to that operating in South Hampshire where Eastleigh BC is keen to allow development on the fringe of Southampton (Chapter 3) and in the West Midlands where regional shopping centres have been granted permission in Sandwell and in Dudley.

The Future

5-42

Until very recently Greater York had an agreed shopping policy for both convenience and comparison retailing. Before the policy even had a chance to be tested at a planning appeal, it was undermined by Selby's decision to allow development at the former Fulford and Naburn hospital. The policy's rôle in the future is uncertain, although its flexibility may mean it is still applicable. It recognises that the floorspace limits are only indicative, and are subject to change given different forms of retailing and changing conditions. Additionally, the policies are constantly being monitored to check that they are in line with expenditure levels and changing retailing conditions.

5-43

York's rôle as a tourist centre has both encouraged out-of-centre retailing to develop as a means of serving local needs, and has meant that the city centre has been able to find a means of surviving in the new retail climate. The City Council cautiously welcomes the relief that out-of-centre retailing has brought the city centre, although officers are aware that two separate retail markets are beginning to develop: one for tourists and one for local people. The more that the centre develops shopping for the visitor, the greater will be the pressure to allow out-of-centre retailing. However, because of the relatively small size of York and its isolation, the County and City Councils believe that

FIG 5-8   PEDESTRIAN AREAS IN CENTRAL YORK
Source: WALK April 1988

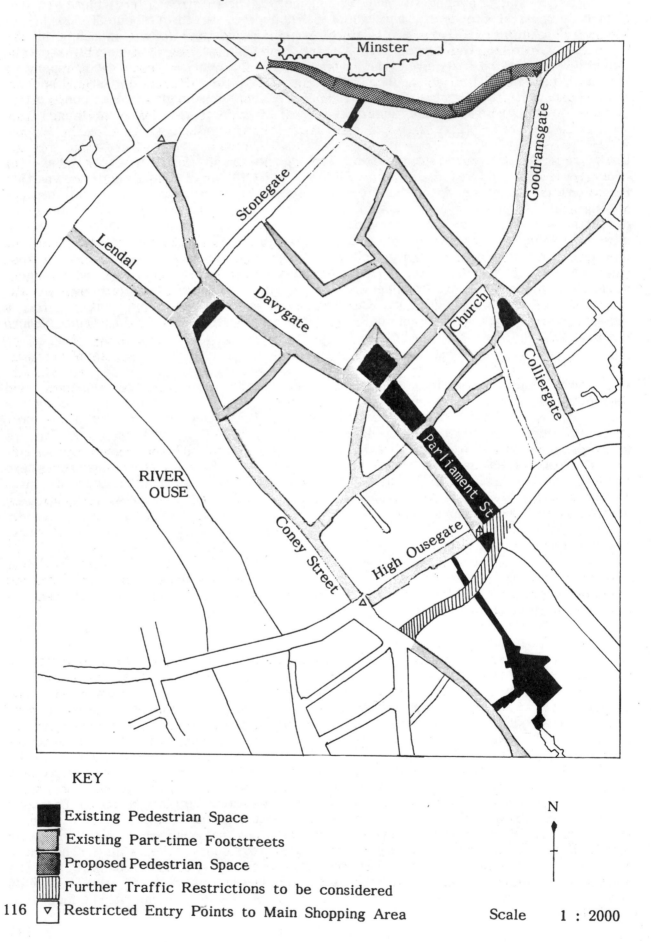

KEY

▮ Existing Pedestrian Space

▨ Existing Part-time Footstreets

▨ Proposed Pedestrian Space

▨ Further Traffic Restrictions to be considered

▽ Restricted Entry Points to Main Shopping Area

N

Scale   1 : 2000

there is insufficient population to attract the massive 'regional-shopping-centre' type of proposals that are currently common near motorway junctions and ring-roads around other large urban areas.

5-44

Meanwhile, York City Council is further enhancing the attraction of the city centre by pursuing ambitious pedestrianisation plans (see Figure 5-8). The exclusion of vehicles from the city's streets during the day is primarily a response to their congestion, and also the aesthetic effects of removing cars and trucks from otherwise picturesque mediaeval shopping streets. Plans to develop a network of paved 'footstreets' are complemented by a park and ride scheme designed to discourage visitors from bringing their cars into the centre in an attempt to gain access to the centre. Already one park and ride scheme has been operating on Tadcaster Road to the south of the centre. A large car park is linked to the city centre by a frequent and inexpensive bus service during school holidays.

5-45

While the pedestrianisation plans are not the cornerstone of the centre's defence against out-of-centre retailing, it has already been demonstrated that the removal of traffic from streets in York substantially enhances retail turn-over. In the mid-1970s Stonegate, one of the primary shopping streets, was pedestrianised, and rents leapt from £20 per ft^2 to £80 per ft^2. Any measure which can boost the town centre economy in such a way must be strengthening it against out-of centre competition. Despite the strong evidence in favour of pedestrianisation, and the existing congestion in the narrow mediaeval streets, there is apprehension among retailers in the centre who fear that pedstrianisation will cause delivery problems and make things difficult for shoppers who buy bulky goods.

5-46

A solution sometimes suggested for town centres which are threatened by out-of-centre retail developments is the development of speciality shopping along the lines of Covent Garden in London. The aim is for a centre to exploit its hist-oric character by specialising in small scale, high income retailing that new out-of-centre developments are unable to compete with. Clearly, town centres' ability to capitalise on their environment and historic character will vary, but for some centres such a course promises to maintain its viability. In York this process has already gone quite far. Pressure for out-of-centre retailing has been partly a response to changing retailing conditions and the relaxed planning approach of Marsham Street, and partly a result of the city centre's concentration on the tourist market.

5-47

While it is recognised that speciality retailing developed in York as a response to the tourism boom rather than as part of a 'save the centre' policy, the city's experience does show the problems that could be created by the development of a speciality based town centre able to survive alongside non-central retailing. The physical structure of the shopping centre may survive intact, but its function may change as dramatically as if out-of-centre retailing had caused its demise. People unable to reach a new superstore by means of a car will find little solace in a selection of quaint shops which now grace the town centre. A town centre might find itself transformed into some kind of retail museum which served only those people with enough money to spend on speciality goods. Even the town centre retailers who had not been threat-ened by out-of-centre developments would be squeezed out as speciality retailers paying higher rents moved in. And of course the situation is self-perpetuating: as more of a town centre goes over to speciality shopping, so the pressures to develop an alternative shopping centre in a non-central location arise.

CONCLUSION

5-48
Retail policies in York have changed quite considerably since the 1970s when there was total resistance to any form of out-of-centre retailing. Today local authorities in Greater York have adopted a more pragmatic approach, allowing a limited amount of non-central development, while maintaining a flexible approach to floorspace limits and future development of the policies. This change has been the result of the interplay of several factors. In the early 1970s retailing in the city centre was suffering decline. Out-of-centre retailing was opposed by the City Council who argued that it would further weaken the centre's economy. However, tourism began to develop into a major industry, and many of the city centre's shops became oriented towards the visitor market, and the centre began to experience an economic revival. At the same time, the non-central retailing which had gained planning consent at appeal was seen to have less of an impact than had been predicted.

5-49
Today York is beginning to develop two retail markets, one geared to local people and one geared to visitors. While the city benefits in terms of the health of the existing centre, issues of equity remain. Car ownership is low, many people are dependent on public transport, bicycles or walking, so the development of non-central shopping as an alternative to the tourist city centre will increase problems of access for many people. To maintain equal levels of access there would have to be major shopping schemes in each sector of the city. It is unlikely that the market could sustain such a level of provision which would effectively replicate town centre retailing at a number of points around the periphery. In any case, higher levels of car use, longer journeys to the shops and the abandonment of York's radial network of communications would significantly increase road congestion, pollution, road accidents and energy consumption.

5-50
The newly approved Greater York shopping policy is already in disarray as the result of Selby's approval of development on the site of the Fulford and Naburn Hospital. The policy aim is to keep a mixture of standard comparison and speciality retailing in the city centre. If substantial out-of-centre schemes do develop, large town centre retailers may be tempted to move to non-central locations where they will attract York's car owning population. Provision in the centre would then become increasingly for the tourist, reinforcing pressures for other retailers to move out. The City's pedestrianisation plans, which are undoubtedly justified in terms of safety and environmentally, may speed this retail gentrification. On the other hand, the removal of traffic from the dense network of shopping streets is very likely to increase the city's popularity with local shoppers as much as with visitors. Any non-central shopping will then be faced with the challenge of providing an equally attractive environment as well as easy access for car users.

5-51
This case study has highlighted the failings of a planning system which increasingly depends on cooperation between neighbouring local authorities to resolve strategic issues. In York's case, it had been thought that the newly established planning policy would first be put to the test by a developer appealing against refusal of permission. What has happened in reality is that after a long period of cooperation leading to its recent approval by districts in Greater York, the policy has disintegrated as individual local authorities react to the the pressure for out-of-centre retailing individually, and in terms of their own interests. The need for statutory regional planning bodies could not be clearer.

118

Appendix

Streets analysed in Tables 5-2 and 5-3

Back Swinegate	Feasegate	Kings Court	Patrick Pool
Blake Street	Finkle Street	Little Shambles	Piccadilly
Bridge Street	Fossgate	Lord Mayor's Walk	St Sampson's Sq
Clifford Street	George Hudson St	Low Ousegate	Shambles
Coney Street	Goodramgate	Low Petergate	Spurrier gate
College Street	Grape Lane	Market Street	Stonegate
Colliergate	High Ousegate	Minster Gates	The Stonebow
Coppergate	High Petergate	Nessgate	Whip-Ma-Wop-Ma-Gate
Davy Gate	Jubbergate	Parliament Street	

References

Bridges, M (1976) **The York Asda : A Study of Changing Shopping Patterns Around a Superstore** Centre for Urban and Regional research, Manchester University

Chartered Surveyor Weekly (1987) **Plenty in Store for Prosperous York** 9 July

City of York (1986) **A City for the Pedestrian** York

Cole, Harvey R (1984) **Greater York Shopping Study : Future Floorspace Requirements of Comparison Goods Shops** (Study Commissioned by the Greater York Shopping Study Working Party)

Esher, Viscount (1968) **York : A Study in Conservation - report to the Minister of Housing and Local Government anf York City Council** London HMSO

Estates Times (1986) **North Yorkshire and Humberside** Supplement 27 June
- (1988) **North Yorkshire and Humberside** Supplement 24 June

Goad (1970 - 1986) **Shopping Centre Plans**

Kelly's Directories Ltd (1970, 1975) **York Directories**

Lee Donsaldson Associates (1986) **Superstore Appeals Review 1986** London

May, A D and P M Weaver (1980) The impact of traffic management on retailing activity - a case study in York In PTRC **traffic & Environmental Management Seminar** (Proceedings of Summer Annual Meeting 7 - 10 July)

North Yorkshire County Council (1978) **Structure Plan : Draft Written Statement**

North Yorkshire County Council, York City Council, Harrogate Borough Council, Rydale District Council and Selby District Council (the Greater York Shopping Study Working Party) (1983) **Greater York Shopping Policy**
- (1985a) **Greater York Shop Survey**
- (1985b) **Greater York Shopping Study : A Policy for Comparison Shopping**
- (1986a) **Greater York Shopping Policy Review**
- (1986b) **Shopping Policy Review Background Paper**
- (1987) **Policies for Convenience and Comparison Shopping**

Office of Population Censuses and Surveys (1984) **Census 1981 : Key statistics for local authorities** London HMSO

Pearson, E (1987) **Personal Communication** City of York

Rigby, John (1987,1988) **Personal Communication** City of York
- (1988) Pedestrian Power in York in **Walk** Vol 6 No 4 April pp6-10

Unit for Retail Planning Information (URPI) (1980) **Shopping Centre Profile : York** Reading URPI

Webber, Derek (1987) **Personal Communication** North Yorkshire County Council

York Junior Chamber of Commerce (1977) **A Study of Shopping with Particular Reference to the Impact on Food Shopping of an Out-of-town Superstore** York

WEST GERMANY

POPULATION :	AREA :
1975 61.8 million 1980 61.4 million 1985 61.0 million	248 600 km^2

POPULATION DENSITY :

1975 249 persons per km^2
1980 247 persons per km^2
1985 245 persons per km^2

PER CAPITA GROSS DOMESTIC PRODUCT

1975   5 176 ECU
1980   9 555 ECU
1985 13 488 ECU
(in current prices)
(1985 1 ECU = DM 2.22)

EMPLOYMENT :

1975 25.9 million
1980 25.3 million
1985 25.0 million

UNEMPLOYMENT :

1975   4.2
1980   3.4
1985   8.4
(% of civilian workforce)

CAR OWNERSHIP

1975 290
1980 377
1984 420
(per thousand population)

PASSENGER TRAFFIC BY MODE

	Cars	Buses	Rail
1975	405	68	38
1980	508	74	38
1985	482	62	44

(billion passenger kilometres)

FINAL CONSUMPTION BY HOUSEHOLDS, PER HEAD IN ECU 1985 (% of total)

Convenience Goods	1443 (17.3)	Health	1176 (14.1)
Clothing/Footwear	663 (7.9)	Transport/	
Rent/Fuel/Power	1650 (19.8)	Communication	1180 (14.1)
Household Goods/		Education/Recr	731 (8.8)
Furniture	695 (8.3)	Misc Goods &	
		Services	797 (9.6)

Source: EUROSTAT (1988)

Source: EUROSTAT (1986)

Chapter 6 : West Germany

Chapter Structure

```
Summary          Introduction      Definitions
 6-01      ───────   6-10     ───────   6-12
                                          │
        ┌──────────┬──────────┬──────────┼──────────┬──────────┬──────────┐
  Department   Law          Data      Retail      Gainers    Views      References
  Stores       on Location   6-37     Trends      and Losers  of the Future
  6-14         6-18                    6-44        6-61        6-77
                  │           │                      │           │
               Other      ┌───┴───┐              Large
               Factors    The     European       Store Lobby
               6-33       HGZ     Research        6-73
                          6-37    6-42
```

Note : numbers refer to paragraphs

6 GERMANY

SUMMARY

6-01

There are clear differences between Britain and Germany in retail policies. Germany has maintained a firmer control on the location of large new superstores, hypermarkets, shopping centres and retail warehouses since modification of the construction laws in 1977 and 1986; Britain is following *laissez-faire* policies. German retail data are more comprehensive than British ones, disposable income and car ownership are much higher, but shop opening times are shorter than in Britain. German out-of-centre retail development preceded Britain by eight years (though the British case was an isolated example - the full flood of development took some years to happen) and, by the time the late 1970s were reached, new developments were much less in evidence. Department stores are more important in Germany than Britain, they establish wherever there is a suitable location, and both they and hypermarkets offer many of the goods that previously could only be obtained in traditional centres. Department stores have lost substantial trade in city centres and have introduced new remedial policies which have had some success.

6-02

Traditional German town and city centres appear more stable than their British counterparts, but without comparative data this cannot be confirmed: while some British town centres have 'to let' signs these are rarely visible in German ones - space is at a premium. Some say German large city centres have recently experienced a boom, because of new investments by firms; the law constraining out-of-town development has had some effect. This Law was strengthened in 1977 and 1986: retail developments over 1 200 m^2 gross or 800 m^2 net can normally only develop in core areas or in specially designated areas - such as those zoned for industry or mixed use. Even those who used to prefer outer locations are moving to main or district centres, generally with a smaller floorspace. Most city centre stores have discovered the value of urbanity and all favour pedestrianisation, though controversy still surrounds traffic calming. There appears to be less pressure for parking spaces, particularly in cities with good public transport and substantial housing in and around the centre from which people can walk to the shops.

6-03

There is a plethora of German retail statistics that are not always comparable, because the bases on which they were collected and disseminated differ. However analyses of the data, from the literature and carried out for this report, are presented. Nationally, for the period 1978/9 to 1984/5, the number of firms and of outlets reduced while the number of outlets per firm increased slightly. Employment fell 2.9% overall - it reduced by 5.5% among firms with 1-4 outlets, and increased by 7% in firms with 10 or more outlets. Turnover increased, in real terms, by about 3%.

6-04

The three top-performing areas for turnover and number employed, in 1984/5, were Hamburg, West Berlin and Bremen; the three worst performing *Lände* were *Baden-Württemberg, Rheinland-Pfalz* and *Niedersachsen*. Comparing 1984/5 with 1978/9 cities with populations between 100 000 and 1 000 000 performed worse than smaller towns, very large towns, and counties in terms of number of shops, number employed, turnover and floorspace additions. By 1982, West Germany had 72 out-of-centre shopping centres larger than 30 000 m^2. As in other countries, Germany has seen a concentration of retailing into larger stores. This has been more pronounced 1978/9 to 1984/5 in convenience retailing than in comparison retailing. In convenience retailing, firms with more than 500 employees increased from 7% to 12% of all firms, and those with 50 or more outlets increased from 8 to 12% over the period. The corresponding changes in comparison retailing were from 2% to 3% in each category.

6-05

When comparing the situation 1978/9 to 1984/5 according to type of retail outlet, and using turnover per employee as the measure, we find that hypermarkets and superstores did best, increasing from 271 000DM to 351 000DM. Supermarkets came next, followed by department stores and smaller chain and independent stores. Turnover per outlet reduced for department stores and had a slight increase for smaller chain and independent stores. Supermarkets scarcely did any better, but hypermarkets and superstores increased by 31%.

6-06

Those who gain and lose from major retail developments are considered. Both are evident at all levels of society, though the gainers may cluster more among suburban, affluent car users, and the new store owners. Losers range from small central non-multiple shops, through department stores (though the principal losses have been in convenience rather than comparison shopping), to those lacking a high level of mobility. Outside traditional centres the community incurs environmental disbenefits from newly generated traffic - and the corollary of newly built roads and very large parking areas. Local authorities do less well in trade taxes than was anticipated. A number of questions are asked about outer-site developers' contentions in support of their proposals.

6-07

It is found that 'job creation' more often means job redistribution, that these stores 'are what the public want' may be more related to peer-group pressure and advertising, and while they are efficient operationally they are not in terms of the effective use of floorspace. Turnover, for all goods, is only just over 2% higher than consumer price increases 1978-84: it was therefore largely static during that period. However, it increased for convenience goods and decreased slightly for comparison goods. This suggests both concentration of retail trade and a redistribution from which some shopkeepers (notably small independents selling food, alcohol or tobacco) suffer.

6-08

Views of the future suggest on the one hand that traditional centres should be protected and on the other that retail outlets should go where the people have moved to. Feelings differ on whether central place theory is still relevant, but there is a majority in favour of the multiplicity of activities that city centres generally have. Views also differ on how the traditional centre should be reached - some want to control the car, others to improve access routes and provide more car parking. The vote for improved public transport is quite solid, however, and others want access by bicycle and on foot to be emphasized. The improvement of environmental quality, and the retention or reintroduction of public buildings and their associated life were seen to be vital.

6-09

In terms of retailing, it was felt that department stores could regain their eminence, with fewer discount stores constructed. A growth area would be shopping in sub-centres and in smaller towns. There would be a continuing tendency toward concentration, and in the city centre a particular problem would be the attempts of large chain stores to establish wherever they could - but the narrow streets of historic centres made this impractical. There were varied views on the importance of arcades and of glazing over existing streets. The most important features of city centre shopping were seen to be the quality of goods available; personal advice and service; information; ability to exchange goods; and provision of crèches, places to change nappies and rest.

INTRODUCTION

6-10

This chapter concerns what Mayr (1980) has called planners' desire for organised addition to town development and 'the shaping of multifunctional urban centres in place of monofunctional product distribution centres.' Perhaps the most significant difference in retailing trends between Germany and Britain is one of time: Germany established its largest out of centre shopping facility, the Ruhr Centre in Bochum, in 1964. By 1977, lessons had been learnt and the law had been changed to make such developments more difficult to achieve. Britain, in comparison, had to wait another eight years for its first hypermarket at Caerphilly in 1972: seemingly fewer lessons have been learnt and the law has been relaxed.

6-11

Other differences between British and German retailing are similarly less of principle than extent. They may be summarised in four interrelated phrases: type of store (including definitional differences), the law which aids or constrains development, investment in traditional centres, and operational 'territory' of developers. There is also one difference in principle: in Germany, statistics are irregularly available on retail firms and their outlets, turnover, floorspace and employment statistics, while in Britain the two-yearly retail enquiries provide national information about turnover for retail firms aggregated by type of goods sold and/or organisational type. And there are subsidiary differences, eg in trading hours, disposable income, car ownership, and the lack of a very large city. Because of the important differences between the two countries' response to the retail revolution, and the cultural differences which engender this response, this Chapter will first discuss them in some depth before undertaking a general review of retailing trends in West Germany.

DEFINITIONS

6-12

In everyday use it is not customary to distinguish between *Verbrauchermarkt, Hypermarkt, SB-Warenhaus, SB Centre* but in the literature distinctions are made. Shopping Centres (also called *Einkaufszentren/EKZ*) are an agglomeration of retail shops and services located in a purpose-built complex (Mayr 1980). The *Deutsche Industrie- und Handelstag* (DIHT) defined shopping centres as having at least 15 000 m^2 net or 25 000 m^2 gross of floorspace. Falk (1983) considered a regional shopping centre only required 15 000 m^2 gross floorspace. Shopping Centres are either **integrated** with other shops, offices, hotels or even residential land uses, or not. This term **integrated**, which is akin to **'planned'** is of considerable importance in Germany, and also applies to the location of hypermarkets, superstores, etc. A retail warehouse newly added to other retail warehouses on a particular site is not integrated, for the concept of 'retail warehouse' did not appear on zoning plans - they are most likely to have been permitted to establish on industrial or mixed use zones. Out-of-centre developments usually have much higher parking provision than traditional centres. In 1983 West Germany had 72 so-called regional shopping centres (Hatzfeld 1986). This is an increase of only 5 on Hatzfeld's 1980 figure of 67, mapped by Mayr and reproduced as Figure 6-1; these centres are generally over 15 000 m^2. In 1980, apart from a cluster of 13 centres in the Ruhrgebiet, nearly half of the total were in the Frankfurt-am-Main sub-region or south Germany. (Further analysis may be found in Table 6-6).

6-13

According to Mayr (1980) shopping centres developed in Britain and Germany from 1964 onwards, in France from 1969 onwards: he may have included traditional centres. As we have seen above, Britain's first hypermarket, at Caerphilly,

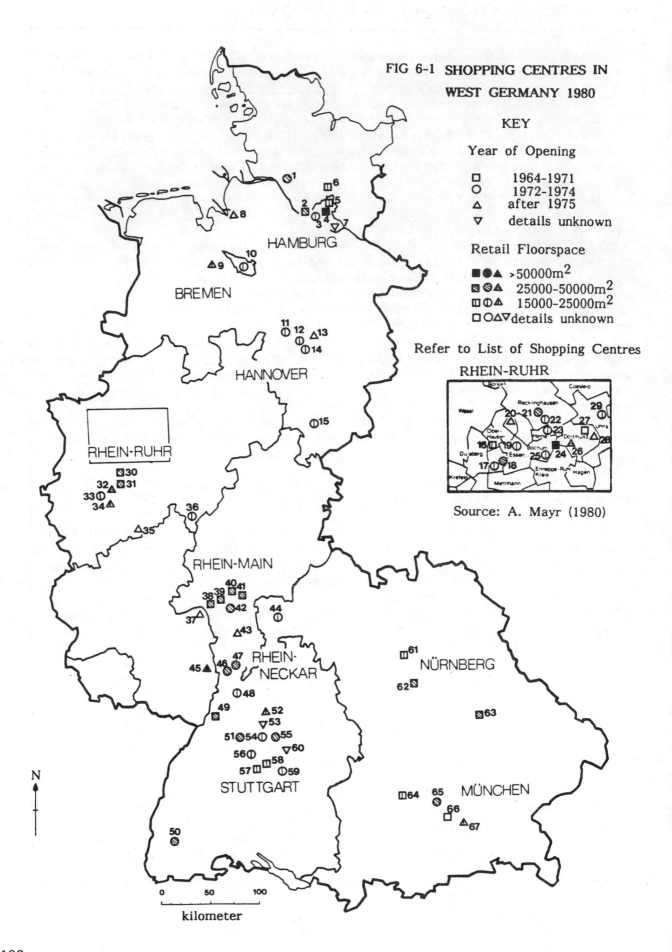

FIG 6-1 SHOPPING CENTRES IN
WEST GERMANY 1980

KEY

Year of Opening

□   1964-1971
○   1972-1974
△   after 1975
▽   details unknown

Retail Floorspace

■●▲ >50000m^2
◩◪▲ 25000-50000m^2
▣◔▲ 15000-25000m^2
□○△▽ details unknown

Refer to List of Shopping Centres
RHEIN-RUHR

Source: A. Mayr (1980)

LIST OF SHOPPING CENTRES IN WEST GERMANY 1980
Refer to Figure 6-1 Shopping Centres in West Germany

Key Number	Name and Location	Year of Opening /Expansion
1	Holstein-Center, Itzehoe	1972
2	Elbe-EKZ, Hamburg-Osdorf	1966/1973
3	Neue City von Altona, Hamburg	1973
4	EKZ Hamburger Straße, Hamburg-Barmbek -Uhlenhorst	1970
5	Alstertal-EKZ, Hamburg-Poppenbüttel	1970/1975
6	Herold-Center, Norderstedt bei Hamburg	1971
7	EKZ Billstedt, Hamburg	*
8	Columbus-Center, Bremerhaven	1978
9	Famila-EKZ, Oldenburg	1976
10	Roland-Center, Bremen-Huchting	1972
11	EKZ Garbsen, Garbsen bei Hannover	1973
12	Ihme-Zentrum, Hannover-Linden	1974
13	Kröpcke-Center, Hannover	1975
14	Leine-EKZ, Laatzen bei Hannover	1973
15	City-Center Grafenhof, Northeim	1973
16	Bero-Center, Oberhausen	1971/1978
17	City-Center, Mülheim	1974
18	Rhein-Ruhr-Zentrum, Mülheim-Heißen	1973/1977/1978
19	EKZ Altenessen, Essen-Altenessen	1973
20	City-Center, Gladbeck	1980
21	Marler Stern, Marl	1974/1975
22	Löhrhof-Zentrum, Recklinghausen	1975
23	City-Center, Herne	1974
24	Ruhrpark-EKZ, Bochum-Harpen	1964/1969/1974 /1977
25	Uni-Center, Bochum-Querenberg	1973
26	Wertkauf-Center, Dortmund-Oespel	1975
27	Westfalen-EKZ, Dortmund	1971
28	Plaza-Markt, Dortmund-Aplerbeck	1975
29	City-Bergkamen	1974
30	Turm-Zentrum, Solingen	1969
31	City-Center(City-A, City-C), Leverkusen	1969/1972
32	EKZ Chorweiler, Köln-Chorweiler	1976
33	EKZ Aachener Straße, Köln-Weiden	1972
34	EKZ Hürth-Mitte, Hürth bei Köln	1977
35	EKZ St. Augustin, St. Augustin	1976
36	Siegerland-Zentrum, Sieger-Weidenau	1973
37	Dom-Rathaus-Zentrum, Mainz	*
38	Wertkauf-Center, Wiesbaden	1970
39	Main-Taunus-Zentrum, Sulzbach bei Frankfurt	1964/1969
40	Nordwest-Zentrum, Frankfurt-Nordweststadt	1968

* = Data unavailable

Key Number	Name and Location	Year of Opening /Expansion
41	Hessen-Center, Frankfurt-Bergen-Enkheim	1971
42	Isenburg-Zentrum, Neu-Isenburg	1972
43	Luisen-Center, Darmstadt	*
44	City-Galerie, Aschaffenburg	1974
45	Rathaus-Center, Ludwigshafen	1979
46	Wertkauf-Center, Mannheim-Vogelstang	1972
47	Rhein-Neckar-EKZ, Viernheim	1972
48	Famila-EKZ, Heidelberg-Rohrbach	1973
49	Wertkauf-Center, Karlsruhe-Durlach	1970
50	Schwarzwald-City, Freiburg	1973
51	Famila-EKZ, Pforzheim	1974
52	EKZ Wollhausplatz, Heilbronn	1975
53	Kronen-Zentrum, Bietigheim	*
54	Marstall-EKZ, Ludwigsburg	1974
55	EKZ Breuningerland, Ludwigsburg	1973
56	Leo-Center, Leonberg	1973
57	EKZ Böblingen, Böblingen	1966/1968/1973 /1974/1975
58	Filder-EKZ, Leinfelden-Unteraichen	1971
59	Neckar-Center, Esslingen-Weil	1974
60	Rems-Murr-Center, Fellbach	*
61	EKZ Neuer Markt, Erlangen	1970
62	Franken-EKZ, Nürnberg-Langwasser	1969
63	Donau-EKZ, Regensburg-Weichs	1967/1974
64	Schwaben-Center, Augsburg	1971
65	Olympia-EKZ, München-Moosach	1972
66	Stachus-EKZ, München	1971
67	Perlach Einkauf Passagen, München-Neuperlach	1980/1981

* = Data unavailable

did not open until 1972, and London's Brent Cross - the first true freestanding shopping centre - arrived in the late 1970s. Britain's New Towns did of course have their own newly built shopping centres well before these dates. As noted above, the first German Shopping Centre opened west of Frankfurt (Main-Taunus Zentrum) in 1964. Six months later the Ruhrpark Shopping Centre, between Bochum and Dortmund, opened. Both were located near motorways. The Ruhrpark today, after several extensions, is the largest in Germany, with a net floor space of 52 500 m^2, and a gross of 75 000 m^2.

1. RETAIL WAREHOUSE DEVELOPMENTS (*Fachmärkte*) vary in size. According to Hatzfeld (1986) retail warehouses are concentrations of warehouses carrying 'medium or long term' goods. They are located outside the city centre with good accessibility by car, and started in the early 1970s as DIY and garden centres. Furniture, textile and carpet warehouses followed. Knee (1986) discussed Professor Bruno Tietz' (of the University of the Saar) findings. Tietz detected an extremely rapid growth of the Fachmärkte with virtually no category of merchandise outside their selling range: this dispels the idea that they are a response solely to the needs of bulky goods retailing. The diversification is apparent through a look at the share of the total accounted for by building materials and DIY: 5.5bn DM of a total of 15.5bn DM in 1982 to 6.5bn of a total of 30.5bn DM in 1985. Particularly significant increases took place in drugs, paints and household cleaning materials, wine, furniture, clothing and sports goods, and photo, optical, audio, computers and software.

2. HYPERMARKETS (*SB Warenhäuse*) are large superstores (see below) with an aggressive price policy. The selling area is differently defined to start at either 3 000 or 4 000 m^2, though some have opened rather larger with a gross floorspace of 12 000 to 15 000 m^2 (recall that URPI in England define hypermarkets as having a selling area starting at 5 000 m^2 [URPI 1986]). Since 1980 their size has increased further - in 1980 the largest was at Schwabach/Mittelfranken with 27 000 m^2 (assumed to be selling) floorspace (Mayr 1980). Apart from food they also offer other goods as long as they are suitable for self-service. In 1966 Germany had 66 hypermarkets; 11 years later it had 1 408, an increase of over 2 000%. By 1980 its retail market share was 15%. The large hypermarkets sell goods similar to those available in city centre department stores; sometimes they 'contain' otherwise independent specialised retailers. These stores are typically located at the edges of towns and cities, though some - eg Bielefeld - are close to the city centre. Taking superstores and hypermarkets together, Mayr (ibid) reported that 66% are located at the edge of towns and cities, 25% in a suburban location, and 9% in city centres.

3. SUPERSTORES (*Verbrauchermärkte*) are large discount stores with a selling area of at least 1 000 m^2 (URPI's minimum size is 2 500 m^2). They sell mainly food, though they also have non-food articles. Superstores used to be located at the edge of towns and cities, with large parking facilities: now there is a tendency for them to move inward (reflected to an extent in Britain), to district centres in particular. They have also moved away from solely cheaper goods toward higher quality (compare with Tesco in Britain whose policy used to be 'pile it high, sell it cheap': they now compare in quality with Sainsbury). It is worth noting that the average size of superstore/hypermarket in Germany has fallen from a peak of 3 900 m^2 in 1976 to the 1986 figure of 3 180 m^2, and the number of stores opened in 1985 was the smallest number since the early 1970s (Knee n.d.) The same source says that units under 1 500 m^2 have become more common, doubtless as a result of the 1977 amendments to the BauNVO Law (see para 6-23, subsection 4 below); presumably since the 1986 amendment 1 200 m^2 is now the critical size. In 1985-86 10 superstores and hypermarkets over 5 000 m^2 opened in West Germany and 8 closed (Wichmann 1987). The new ones were

most likely within existing shopping centres.

4. MAIL ORDER FIRMS (*Versandhäuser*) developed in Germany from 1925 onwards, mostly in the textile sector. After 1950 a wider variety of goods became available. These firms increased their market share from 3.4% in 1956 to 4.9% in 1978. The mail order firm Quelle also has 27 department stores; it is the largest mail order firm in Europe (Mayr 1980). Finally in this listing (which has excluded Department Stores - see below - and Supermarkets), and varying considerably in size, are the Discount Stores, with a limited range of goods, mainly food. In 1978 there were 2 640 shops. Aldi, the main discount store chain, had 1 200 (Mayr 1980).

THE STATE OF DEPARTMENT STORES

6-14

Department stores are particularly important in Germany where they were first established about 1850, and traditionally located in the main shopping streets of city centres. Today there are four main groups: Karstadt, with headquarters in Essen, Kaufhof in Köln, Hertie in Frankfurt and Horten in Düsseldorf. In 1978 these four groups had a total of 536 stores and earned a high proportion of the department stores' 13.5% of the total retail market (Mayr 1980). During their period of expansion, stores of about 3 000 m^2 opened in many inner city subcentres serving a catchment of 30-40 000 people. Most department stores also had a low price chain - Karstadt had Kepa stores until they were given up in 1977, and Kaufhof had Kaufhalle. The biggest store chain is Karstadt. The list below includes others with chains; while Quelle and Otto are primarily mail order, they also have department stores.

	Turnover in DM bn, 1984
Karstadt	12.0
Kaufhof	8.5
Hertie	5.9
Horten	2.9
Quelle	8.5
Otto	4.0

6-15

After more than one hundred years of comparative euphoria, some unease developed. At first department stores did not realise the danger of the range of out-of-town or fringe superstores and hypermarkets (*SB Warenhäuser* and *Verbrauchermärkte*) which developed toward the end of the 1960s. These developments did not challenge the slogan of the department stores, up to the 1970s, that the customer could buy anything needed in one store - eg *Kaufhof bietet tausendfach alles unter einem Dach* (Kaufhof offers everything a thousand times under one roof): they were simply cheaper. The fight against the new developments thus did not start until the 1970s, with attempts at trading up (and down, at times) of department store goods. It was believed that department stores as large and comprehensive as Harrods (the German equivalent of which is the KaDeWe, called the Department Store of the West, in Berlin) could save the stores from the decline in both number of visitors and turnover.

6-16

Between the end of the 1970s and the beginning of the 1980s selective marketing promoted department store sections which made high profits, and abandoned those with low profits. New design standards in department stores were established to improve the appearance of buildings inside and out. Colours changed from dark to light tones. Marketing, customer service and image were improved - important improvements took place in treatment of customers, and in staff clothing.

6-17

Since 1986, recession and decline in turnover in department stores has been reversed. Kläsener (1987) pointed out that Karstadt achieved an annual turnover increase of 6.7% during 1986: it had been in decline from 1981. It is believed that about 3.5% of the increase resulted from new design standards and the rest from the improved economic situation. During the more difficult years Hertie experienced large structural problems which led to the closure of some department stores, for example in Dortmund and Würzburg.

THE LAW AFFECTING RETAILING LOCATION

6-18

The Law affecting retailing is complex; much of it is determined through construction laws. It is not intended that a comprehensive overview will be presented here, rather that there will be sufficient to explain differences between Britain and Germany. Although many German local authorities still complain about the weakness of existing legislation to deal with new forms of retailing, in comparison with Britain the legislation can appear dramatic.

6-19

There is one law, the *Bundesbaugesetz (BBauG)*, or Federal Construction Law, which is supreme on decisions where new forms of retailing, such as shopping centres, hypermarkets and superstores, may locate. It is supplemented by the *Baunutzungsverordnung (BauNVO)*, or Construction Use Regulation. While being complex, the legal situation also permits some flexibility in negotiations between local authorities and shop owners or developers. Complexity is increased because the *Land* Planning Laws, and to a lesser extent the Federal Planning Law, are included in the interpretation of the BBauG. Several *Länder* (States) have amended their Planning Laws to recognise recent retail developments.

6-20

Under the existing planning law (section 1.1 BBauG) local authorities are required to put forward two kinds of master plan, one of which shows the main land use functions: housing, industry, forestry, agriculture, etc (*Flächennutzungsplan*). The second, much more detailed one which is also legally binding, is called a 'construction plan' (*Bebauungsplan*) (Hass-Klau 1982). Generally one such construction plan covers only a small area of a local authority, and it is a time-consuming process to set up and have such a plan approved. The BauNVO is an additional aid which helps clarify special aspects of the construction plan.

6-21

According to the BBauG, a local authority's land has to be designated according to land use. This procedure is dealt with by the BauNVO, providing much greater detail than the land use designation used in the first type of master plan. The BauNVO describes in detail the possible legal use for each part of the land, and also includes the permitted heights of buildings and the ratio of open to built-up land (BAG 1986). The BauNVO experienced several amendments after it was implemented in 1962: in 1968, 1977 and 1986, largely to cope with problems occurring with large-scale retailing developments. However these later changes in the BauNVO are only of importance to construction plans which were approved **after** the date when amendments in the BauNVO had been agreed. Therefore a construction plan agreed **before** 1977 does not have to comply with the BauNVO of 1977 or 1986, which include much stricter regulations on the location of large-scale retailing development.

6-22

At present the Federal Republic has **five** different legal requirements showing how to handle large scale retail developments (Hatzfeld 1986; BAG 1986). The type of legal requirement which is applied depends on a range of factors, of which the most obvious are:

- does a construction plan exist?
- if so, in what year was it implemented?
- the desire of the local authority to prevent large-scale retail developments because they can decide to modify an old, or set up a new, construction plan or simply **intend** to do this, so legally avoiding establishment of a planned retailing unit
- on the attitude of the Land Government toward such retailing schemes; in this case the exceptions described in paras 6-26/27 below are important.

The different Länder have interpreted the contents of the BauNVO, particularly section 11.3, according to their political attitude toward these new forms of retailing. The Länder also give advice to local authorities on how to interpret these different regulations. These interpretations are published and circulated by the Land Minister responsible for Planning (*Runderlaß*).

6-23
The five different legal requirements are:

1 The legal status before 1962 where no special regulations existed on how to deal with large scale retail developments

2 The first implementation of the BauNVO occurred in 1962. It still allows large retail establishments of any size to locate in the core, in areas of mixed use, or in areas designated for industry and manufacturing. However, large scale retail establishments may **not** be permitted in such areas - Section 15.1 BauNVO - if they do not fit into the designated area, or if a disturbance may be expected that is unacceptable for its surroundings. For example, the new establishment might create so much new traffic which negatively impacts an adjacent residential area. According to BAG (1986, p73) this opportunity to prevent the siting of such establishments has not often been used.

3 For the first time, regulations about the construction of large scale shopping centres and superstores were included in the 1968 amendments (section 11.3). According to these amendments, shopping centres and superstores serving more than the market area of a local authority, are only allowed to locate in so-called central core areas, or areas which have to be specially designated. Problems occurred very soon with the legal interpretation of what was understood by a market area.

4 A further tightening of the law occurred with the 1977 revision of the BauNVO. Apart from shopping centres and superstores, other forms of retailing such as hypermarkets, department stores, discount shops and retail warehouses were now included. These forms of retailing can only locate in either the core areas or in specially designated areas. (See paras 6-24 to 6-27 for further information about the 1977 amendment).

5 Since December 1986 there has been a further change in BauNVO. Several Länder had attempted to reduce the critical size of retailing units from 1 500 to 800 m^2 (Saarland) or 1 000 m^2 (Nordrhein Westfalen). In the event, the reduction agreed for the 1986 amendment was to 1 200 m^2.

6-24
The 1977 amendments (section 11.3) assumed that any of the forms of retailing above **would** have an effect on both the urban structure and on the objectives of regional and Land planning if they were larger than 1 500 m^2 gross floorspace (1 000 m^2 net). According to section 11.3, effects on the urban structure or regional/Land objectives could be:

- noise and air pollution in nearby residential areas

- infrastructural problems, eg if the street network could not cope with newly created traffic flows
- negative effects for the population on the provision of convenience goods (*Nahversorgung*)
- negative effects on the urban structure, eg expected problems in other retailing centres (DIHT 1986)
- protection of nature is endangered, eg use of open green land and sealing of open land by concrete, etc (*Flächenversiegelung*).

Clearly what effects are possible depends on the location, type of shop and the suggested size. If one of these effects was damaging, then the local authority could refuse construction of a shopping development larger than 1 500 m^2.

6-25

Retail establishments with **less** than 1 500 m^2 gross floorspace also cannot be allowed outside specially designated or central areas if adverse effects on the urban structure can be expected. However, in this case the **local authority** has to **prove** that negative urban or regional effects will occur. In retail developments of more than 1 500 m^2 the **applicant** has to **prove** that section 11.3 is not operating, which is rather more difficult. If several retail units of **under** 1 500 m^2 want to locate together then the sum of gross floorspace is decisive. If there is already one retail unit, occupying a gross of 1 500 m^2, additional retailers may not be allowed because section 11.3 could become operative.

6-26

There are also regulations if a wholesale dealer wants to change into retailing, or if a factory building is changed into retailing. In both cases special permission is needed for the change, and section 11.3 may be applied. As always there are certain exceptions:

- the gross floorspace can be larger than 1 500 m^2 if the net floorspace is well below 1 000 m^2
- the shop has a limited product range, eg a garden centre
- the articles sold are connected with artisan or manufacturing trades.

The first two of these particularly encouraged the growth of retail warehouses which specialised in a few goods only.

6-27

There are further exceptions with reference to an area's urban structure, eg:

- the area has insufficient goods offered in new forms of retailing
- there is no retail centre planned in any other nearby urban location
- the new shopping facility is planned in a central location which can easily be reached by the whole population of the area.

In these cases it is assumed that retail establishments do not have significant effects on the urban or regional structure and hence can be located in other urban areas (DIHT 1986). Thus, the regulations allow some controls on excessive growth while encouraging new developments where they are seen to remedy deficiencies: nevertheless, such developments could adversely affect transport, land use and environmental aspects.

6-28

About 80% of local authority land lacks construction plans. These are largely the areas which had been built up before the construction plan legislation came into force (1960). In such areas, section 34.3 BBauG regulates the possibility of settlements of retail units. According to a recent legal decision, which is binding for any future negotiation on retailing (the *Bundesverwaltungsgericht*), the BauNVO can be applied despite the absence of a construction plan if an area in question can clearly be classified - eg into a housing or industrial area. In such cases section 11.3 of the BauNVO will be applied. If the area cannot be classified then section 11.3 cannot be used. However this would still not allow construction of large scale retail developments because section 34.1 BBauG could be applied. This states that it has to be proved that a retail unit 'fits' into the surroundings - admittedly a vague formulation.

6-29
According to the *Hauptgemeinschaft des Deutschen Einzelhandels* (main German retailing organisation) the legal changes of the BauNVO have had some effect: the trend of large scale shopping developments to settle at non-integrated urban locations has weakened (DIHT 1986). However the main criticism has been that these regulations have only resulted in smaller-scale shopping developments, without solving the problem as such. At the Prisma Seminar (1979) A Klöser said the locational decision of a few individuals conceals the danger of corruption of the public administration 'which enables a deliberate negation of the concept "public interest" and a rejection of a project even against the shopping preferences of the consumer.'

6-30
Since 1986 the requirements of that year's amendment to the BauNVO have had to be observed; they substantially follow the detail of the 1977 amendment (see above) though reducing the area permitted on non-integrated sites to a gross of 1 200 m^2. A report from the *Bundesminister für Raumordnung und Städtebau* (1986) shows the political difficulties of balancing the support of one's small shopkeeper constituency (who considerably influenced changes in the BauNVO) and developer interests against a realisation that matters were getting out of hand. The report decries the rise of subcentres and small towns in the urban fringe and is apprehensive about qualitative change in retail business. It then expresses 'sorrow' at the appearance of stores on what Germans term the 'green meadow' (Green Belt, urban fringe); at trading-up trends toward high class retail business in some locations; at what is called 'textilisation' or the introduction of cheap textile stores in city centres; at the buying-up of small businesses; at chain stores and junk food; and at the expansion of superstores on non-integrated or fringe locations. These used to be DIY. Now they cover shoes, textiles, garden centres, etc.

6-31
To return to the difficulties of the urban planner and the law, the above report was written in the context of the 1986 changes to the BauNVO: clearly there was a desire to make stronger measures, but politically this was not expedient. The *Lände* have all given guidelines to their towns and cities on how to handle retail applications of less than and greater than 1 200 m^2. *Bayern* and *Nordrhein Westfalen* have been much more direct than the other *Lände* in trying to influence their local authorities against large out-of-centre retail developments, and some local authorities, for example Dortmund, have introduced their own regulations to control retail development. What, it might be asked, is the point of this when the BauNVO states the legal position? Essentially, it states that developments greater than 1 200 m^2 will not be permitted on non-integrated land but it does not wholly exclude them - if the developer can assemble a powerful case it might be listened to. But, affirmation of the local authority's position, through local laws on retail development and other policy statements, can deter many would-be applicants.

6-32
There is no doubt that these rather complex legal requirements for large scale retail establishments have changed the size, and possibly also the nature, of these new forms. Mega shopping centres as proposed all over Britain are not legally possible in the Federal Republic. This implies that with these regu-

lations one could attenuate changes in retail location. New forms of retailing have moved into established city and subcentres and can adversely affect the shops which have been there for a long time (Jahn 1986).

OTHER FACTORS AFFECTING RETAIL INVESTMENT AND LOCATION

6-33
The British per capita GDP was only 75% of that in Germany in 1984; in 1975 (at current prices) it was only 62% of the West German figure. This can be expressed through two examples: car ownership is 40/100 inhabitants in Germany and 32/100 in Britain. And, using 1980 prices, per capita consumption on a range of retail goods (food, beverages, tobacco, clothing, footwear, furniture, furnishings, household equipment and operation) was as follows (Eurostat 1986):

1980 prices, consumption/capita in ECUs

	1975	1983
West Germany	1825	2070
Britain	1368	1519

6-34
Trading hours tend to be 09.00-18.30 Monday to Friday and 09.00-14.00 on all Saturdays except the first in each month which is similar to a weekday. No shops, except a few catering for travellers' needs at railway stations and airports, are open outside these times. Here too there are considerable differences with Britain, which turns a blind eye to illegal, but widespread, Sunday trading, and where weekday trading is less rigorously regulated. But Wolf (1988) says the German law is likely to be relaxed, allowing one evening a week's opening; he also notes the Bill is facing considerable opposition from trade associations and trade unions.

6-35
There has been a different attitude toward traditional town centres, because of respect for the past (which meant that most of those destroyed in the second world war were rebuilt as they had been). Another factor was the revered principles of Christaller's central place theory, the major planning determinant in retailing: to give just one example, Dischkoff (1979) said 'Where the (hierarchical) system breaks down, however, is when new retailing developments are built without due regard to the general principles of centrality.' The effect of these causes has been a level of investment in traditional German centres higher than in most British cities. This is evident in public transport (detailed in Chapter 10), in roads and car parking, in pedestrianisation and traffic calming, and in the public and private sector buildings themselves. If you express this kind of faith, you do not easily disavow it.

6-36
Perhaps this is why, in Germany, the out-of-centre developers tend to be different financiers and entrepreneurs from those operating in the traditional centres, as was noted in Chapter 2. This is not wholly true, as certain department stores have been active out-of-centre as both developer and part-occupant: Breuninger in and around Stuttgart is a case in point.

DATA

The Handels- und Gaststättenzählungen (HGZ)

6-37
These surveys are a seemingly unique source of data on retailing. They have been carried out in 1960, 1967/68, 1978/79 and 1984/85, throughout the Federal Republic. Data have been collected by the *Länder* (States), analysed by the

Statistisches Bundesamt in Wiesbaden, and returned to the *Länder* and cities. Confidentiality of information is guaranteed by the level of disaggregation which is made available - never at less than the level of one complete street. Data are provided on the number and area of establishments, the number employed and the annual turnover of the establishments. There are problems in this apparently halcyon statistical world, however. First, it is not always possible to compare parts of the series because the rules were changed from one survey to another. Second, certain of the larger local authorities disagreed with the results of the 1984/85 survey, preferring data they had collected themselves while realising they could not be read within the larger context of county or region. Third, the level of disaggregation that can be achieved often depends on what a local authority's *Statistisches Amt* is prepared to give you.

6-38
Fourth, some HGZ data are not easily accessed. There are four variants. The first uses as its areal measure **gross** floorspace (*Geschäftsfläche*). The second uses **net/sales** floorspace (*Verkaufsfläche*). For the 1984/5 HGZ, gross floorspace, which adds confidentiality, is quoted by some cities, while others quote net floorspace. In 1978/9 gross and net were generally available. The third variant presents all retail trade, and includes shops and stores, and the service sector attached to retailing, depots, storehouses, employee car parks, etc. The fourth is specific to shops and stores (*Ladengeschäfte*). Variants one and two are variously permed with three and four. These are designated:

All retail trade	HGZT
Shops and stores only	HGZL
No specific information	HGZ

and it is indicated (where known) whether the data are gross or net floorspace.

6-39
Sometimes, but not always, a straight comparison can be made between the 1979 and 1985 HGZ (turnover data were collected for the previous years 1978 and 1984). Some broad results of the two surveys are presented here; most of the analysis will be found below in the 'Gainers and Losers' section, and in Chapters 7, 8 and 9. **Most significantly, retailing overall has been nearly static over the 1978-84 period, though it has differed considerably in its distribution between types of store.** The consumer price index increased by 26.4% 1978-84 while the overall change in retail turnover, in current terms, was 29.5%. Within this, turnover on convenience goods increased by 38.4% and by 25.8% (just below the consumer price index) on comparison goods. From 1979 to 1985 there were 1.9% less firms, 1.4% less establishments and 2.9% less employees connected with retailing throughout the Federal Republic (all data are HGZL and are from HDE 1987 and Krockow 1988).

6-40
Table 6-2 defines the size of firm (the controlling interest) by the number of outlets (actual selling locations) it has. The size of **outlet** could vary considerably from a small boutique to a one-off hypermarket. From the Table we can see that the great majority of firms only had one outlet, at both survey periods. They had three quarters of all the outlets, half the employees, and nearly half the turnover of all German retail firms. On the other hand their turnover per outlet was relatively poor. As the number of outlets per firm increases, so does the turnover per outlet, until one reaches 50 or more outlets per firm, when the turnover per individual outlet in 1984 was nearly seven times that for a single outlet firm.

Table 6-2 : Number of firms and their outlets, employment and turnover, and
(percent) 1978/79 to 1984/85: HGZL (see para 6-38 for definition)

Outlets per firm	1000 firms in category		1000 Outlets		1000 Employees		Turnover Total bn.DM		Turnover 1000DM/outlet	
	1979	1985	1979	1985	1979	1985	1978	1984	1978	1984
1	320.0 (92.5)	316.5 (93.3)	320.0 (77.5)	316.5 (77.8)	1325.5 (54.5)	1309.1 (55.5)	117.3 (48.4)	226.5 (47.8)	554	715
2-4	23.6 (6.8)	20.8 (6.1)	54.7 (13.2)	47.6 (11.7)	370.6 (15.2)	293.8 (12.4)	58.3 (15.9)	59.0 (12.5)	1066	1242
5-9	1.6 (0.5)	1.3 (0.4)	9.9 (2.4)	7.9 (2.0)	109.7 (4.5)	89.5 (3.8)	19.9 (5.4)	21.4 (4.5)	2007	2694
10-49	0.6 (0.2)	0.6 (0.2)	11.6 (2.8)	11.7 (2.9)	180.4 (7.4)	187.7 (7.9)	36.2 (9.9)	52.9 (11.2)	3112	4508
50+	0.1 (<0.1)	0.2 0.1	16.5 (4.0)	23.0 (5.7)	444.6 (18.3)	480.6 (20.4)	74.6 (20.4)	113.9 (24.1)	4522	4946
Totals	346.0 (100)	339.3 (100)	412.7 (100)	406.8 (100)	2430.8 (100)	2360.7 (100)	366.3 (100)	473.8 (100)	888	1165

Source: HDE 1987

Table 6-3 : Percent change 1984/5 on 1978/9 for convenience goods (food, drink
and tobacco) by HGZ variables and population of *kreisfreie Städte*
(independent towns): HGZL

Population range	Shop businesses	Employment	Turnover	Net Floorspace
under 100 000	- 1.6	+18.0	+66.4	+44.1
100 000-500 000	-18.8	-10.3	+18.9	+ 5.0
500 000-1 000 000	-17.9	- 4.7	+14.4	+ 5.9
over 1 000 000	- 6.5	+ 5.6	+31.6	+22.8
Counties	-16.7	- 2.8	+34.0	+19.2
All areas	-15.8	- 2.7	+30.1	+16.8

Source : Krockow 1988

Table 6-3 looks at changes between the two survey periods in terms of the size
of town, by population, in which retail outlets are located. It shows that the
smallest and largest towns performed best in all categories, while those with a
population between 100 000 and 1 million performed worse than the Districts and
the Federal average. However, there are very few cities over 1 million population: West Berlin, Hamburg, München and Köln (according to some definitions).

6-41
Table 6-4 looks only at the 1984/5 HGZ, comparing the 11 *Länder* in terms of
outlets, employment and turnover per 10 000 population. The rich area of
Baden-Württemberg performs poorly and the relatively poor areas of Bremen and
Saarland perform well: this is because of population density.

Table 6-4 :   1984/5 HGZL retail results by *Land*, per 10 000 population, ranked
by turnover

| | Population mill. | < per 10 000 population > | | |
		Workplaces no.	Employment no.	Turnover mill.DM
FRG	61	66	372	77.1
Hamburg	1.6	79	531	121.1
West Berlin	1.8	78	437	93.1
Bremen	0.7	73	461	89.0
Saarland	1.1	82	415	79.0
Bayern	11.0	71	368	78.4
Schleswig-Holstein	2.6	63	388	77.9
Hessen	5.5	66	370	77.1
Nordrhein-Westfalen	16.7	65	371	75.6
Baden-Württemberg	9.2	57	338	73.3
Rheinland-Pfalz	3.6	67	351	71.6
Niedersachsen	7.2	65	364	70.9

Source: Krockow 1988

THE EUROPEAN SHOPPING CENTRE RESEARCH

6-42
Further data have been analysed by Falk (1983), some being shown in Table 6-5.
The rise in the number and annual addition of gross floorspace peaked in the
period 1970 to 1974, and in 1977 and 1980.   The average size of a shopping
centre has consistently fallen through the time period.

Table 6-5 : Number and size of German Shopping Centres: HGZT

| Year | Total no. | Gross area m^2 | | |
		Area added this year	Cumulative area	Ave. area per centre
1965	3	170 500	170 500	56 833
1966	5	52 000	222 500	44 500
1967	6	48 000	270 500	45 083
1968	8	51 579	322 079	40 260
1969	11	95 687	417 766	37 979
1970	15	208 233	625 999	41 733
1971	21	181 074	807 073	38 432
1972	26	211 684	1 018 757	37 732
1973	37	315 743	1 334 500	35 118
1974	44	267 206	1 601 706	35 593
1975	47	53 000	1 654 706	34 473
1976	49	43 000	1 697 706	33 954
1977	56	176 400	1 874 106	32 879
1978	58	55 400	1 929 506	33 267
1979	61	94 000	2 023 506	33 866
1980	69	152 000	2 175 506	31 044
1981	72	66 275	2 241 781	30 665
1982	72	22 067	2 263 848	31 442

6-43

Falk also gave the progression of gross floorspace in German shopping centres according to their location:

Table 6-6 :   Location of German Shopping Centres, opened in 1970, 1975 and 1982
              HGZT

Year	Gross area m^2			
	Inner city	Suburbs	Between town & greenfield*	New housing area
1970	37 447	34 500	75 000	30 000
1975	33 067	34 262	52 972	36 825
1982	29 907	31 979	40 283	31 050

*   'Greenfield' should not be taken too literally.   These are areas outside an urban boundary which have been zoned for industrial or mixed uses.

Table 6-6 shows a reduction in inner city locations, a modest fall in suburban sites, a consistent fall in the urban fringe location, and some fluctuation in shopping centres built adjacent to new housing developments.   At all three years the most popular location for centre developers was the urban fringe one, with no pronounced bias among the other three.   Falk makes the point that the substantial development in the city centre and inner city is very much in contrast with United States' policies.

RETAIL TRENDS IN WEST GERMANY

6-44

During the 1960s shopping at the periphery was generally thought to be positive.   The concept came from the US, was thought to be progressive, and was generally established by foreign and German firms in combination;   over the years the foreigners were largely bought out and now exert little influence. The idea that out-of-town/fringe shopping could negatively affect the city centre or sub-centre retailing took some time to develop.   Because the city centre had a prime position it was very slow to react - the outer shops were simply not seen as serious competition.

6-45

In 1988 opinion appears to be split on whether, and how much, German city centres will lose to out-of-centre developments (out-of-centre meaning both suburban and at the edge of town);   out-of-centre includes district centres, and in all these locations one can find new shopping centres, hypermarkets, superstores and discount stores. Another topic is whether the city centres are experiencing a new boom period.   By and large, retailers are more inclined to see a dangerous situation for city centres (and among these retailers the representatives of department stores cry loudest), while planners and academics see the danger to be overemphasized.   It certainly appears that Germany is not following the US in retail trends even if its cities have succumbed to MacDonalds, as most European cities have.   Undoubtedly major changes have taken, and are taking, place in retailing in Germany, as in other European countries, but the expression of change is different.   There is no doubt that strict legal regulations, and other planning guidelines, which control out-of-centre developments play a crucial rôle in ameliorating change.

6-46

Before examining the conflicting views some contextual data are desirable.

Kläsener (1985) reviewed BAG's market research between 1965 and 1984; in 1984 588 stores, members of BAG in 249 cities, participated. During the 20 year period:

1 the number of private cars rose from 9.3 to 25.2 million
2 the residential population increased very modestly from 58.6 to 61.3 million (and is now declining)
3 the number of dwellings increased from 18.3 to 26.5 million
4 concentration of the population in large cities reduced from 37.4% to 33.2%
5 net retail floorspace per inhabitant doubled from 0.5 to 0.99 sqm
6 large cities' share of retail turnover decreased from 50.9% to 44.3%
7 department stores' share of retail turnover decreased from 8.3% to 6.6%
8 share of superstores and hypermarkets increased radically from 0.4% to 14%

All the above events were of course significant for existing centres. Interestingly, 4 and 6 may be causally related. 1 seems to have damaged city centres' retailing (though not their environment) far less than its great increase would suggest; the modest increased use of cars for access to the city centre 1980-1984 (+1.9% on Saturdays and +1.3% on weekdays - Triesch & Kläsener [1985]) does not relate to the 8.4% increase in the number of cars over that period.

6-47
Kläsener points to other, rather more meaningful, measures of the deterioration of traditional shopping centres. Their floorspace, as a proportion of the total, fell from 94% to 81.6% and their market share from 91.3% to 79.4%. Both the number of customers (1980 to 1984, down 8.3% on a Thursday and 10.4% on a Friday) and turnover per customer declined. While the latter had increased to 1980 in current (but not real) terms, it declined over the whole period: in real terms 1984 'is substantially below the value of 1965.'

6-48
Mössner (1986), as Chairman of the Federal Association of Hypermarkets, has said that the exodus of shops from the city centre in principle does not exist; there is virtually no empty retailing floorspace in any German city centre; the slogan of the 'dead' city centre is no more than a slogan and has little to do with reality - he does not know a dead city centre; he also does not know any city centre that confirms the predicted increase in sex shops. Against these popular claims he believes reality to comprise: part of the purchasing power has moved outwardly because people have moved in that direction; rents in city centres have not increased as strongly as in the past: department stores have lost customers and experienced a fall in turnover; city centre retailers (except big food retailers who never located there) have become stronger. Therefore, the crisis of the city centre is the crisis of the department store. Mössner's view on department stores is supported by Adrian (1986) in a similar phrase; he believes that turnover has largely shifted from department stores to sustain increases in superstores and hypermarkets: we return to this claim below. In Hannover (TEST 1988) 'Planners believe that specialised shops in the city centre will not be significantly at risk from ... out-of-centre retailing. More at risk are city centre department stores together with traditional shopping streets and centres throughout the inner city and suburbia.'

6-49
According to Adrian, stabilisation can best be seen in urban streets which still possess high quality - Severinstraße in Köln, and the Lister Meile in Hannover and Bergerstraße in Frankfurt, for example. In the suburbs he thinks retailing is dying, though he believes peripheral superstores and hypermarkets are expanding. He also says the centres of large cities will decline in importance though retailing is tending to increase in middle-sized towns and cities; this is particularly so in historic town centres. Contrary to

Adrian's views, Dr Hermanns from Köln Chamber of Commerce believes that large city centres are booming again. For many years they stagnated, while smaller town centres became more prosperous, but to-day strong investment has recurred in city centres - in retailing, cultural developments, hotels, housing and banks. He cited a 20% increase in the number of new retailing firms in Köln (Hermanns 1987)

6-50

We have noted in para 6-12 that superstores are tending to move inwards and Somogyi (1986) adds to this 'On the Continent, where the hypermarkets and commercial centres had developed fastest till the mid-seventies, the attention is switching to the town centres and the inner city.' Difu (1982) carry the discussion further: 'The development of retail locations shows a continuing trend toward the town centre as the area of easiest access (public transport) and of spatial concentration of retail outlets, which is specially preferred by businesses serving medium- and long-term needs, because here the concentration of different types of business in one place enhances market attractiveness. However, as the size of a town increases, the significance of the centre drops in favour of decentralised shopping centres and new forms of business for short and medium term needs, exploiting the problems of town centre retailing such as increased traffic volume, altered structures and poor growth of purchasing power. This development of a shopping centre hierarchy is detrimental to areas of low population density as well as to provision in urban residential areas.'

6-51

One further locational comment: Knee (n.d.) affirms that the smaller stores are not locating peripherally or out-of-town, but rather in a town's secondary shopping district, in smaller and medium sized towns, and in the main shopping districts of small communities. He refers to a study by the *Land Nordrhein Westfalen* Institute for Research into Rural and Urban Development which shows these locations to be preferred by superstore firms, intent on stabilising their base. Knee also mentions 'numerous examples of new downtown development schemes, including shopping centres and pedestrian precincts, which include superstores and hypermarkets.' Clearly a major reason for the increased interest in traditional centres is that they are exempt from the 1986 BauNVO regulations - in theory a new shopping centre of 25 000 m^2 could be built there. The fact that this does not happen is explained by opposition from existing traders. There is some evidence of developers' increased interest in traditional British centres, too - Birmingham has been mentioned in Chapter 4.

6-52

Knee also refers to the phenomenon of self-service department stores (the title sometimes given to hypermarkets) in traditional town centres. The Massa Company of Alzey believes such stores can now be profitably run downtown; it opened its first in Offenbach in 1984. It has 9 400 m^2 selling floorspace and is located only 100 metres from the main shopping street to which it is connected by a pedestrian walkway. This was followed by the 1985 takeover of the Hertie department store in the town centre of Troisdorf, which Massa then enlarged from 11 000 to 15 000 m^2. Hertie itself, after closing a number of its stores, is now running its own city-centre hypermarket division: the first of 9 000 m^2 has been opened in Oldenburg. The Horten department store opened just one of these stores, in 1983, in Recklinghausen.

6-53

While these innovations take place, in Stuttgart the Breuninger department store is building more conventional department store floorspace. Other stores will still invest in city centres. New department stores or substantial extensions are planned. Often the new stores replace old ones - Karstadt pulled down an old and built a new one in Münster which opened in 1986. In Lübeck similar plans are approved; extensions are planned in Karlsruhe and Berlin-Tempelhof.

141

These new stores are sensitively integrated into the existing streetscape. Karstadt in Nürnberg used several connected original historic house façades to make the department store exterior. The CASH-Haus in Düsseldorf, dating from the 1920s, was restored by Horten to regain its original form. 100 million DM were spent in 1983/84 in Köln by the department stores Hertie, Karstadt and Kaufhof to restore their original stores (Heyer 1985).

6-54

Attitudes toward parking provision are changing. While some stores feel a great deal of parking continues to be vital to them (Hertie's Oldenburg store has 480 spaces), the Stuttgart Breuninger store is not adding further spaces. Hötteker (1987) said Kaufhof consider they have enough spaces except for Saturday, and they do not plan to build more spaces. Sieverts (1987) said the main danger for city centres is to accept retailing organisations' demand for more parking facilities. TEST's (1988) study of parking provision in 10 German city centres underlined what may be nascent trends: it showed no relationship between the number of spaces provided per square metre of retail floorspace and either the turnover achieved for that square metre, or the rent paid for it. In other words, the constant cry of retailers, most politicians and many urban planners, for ever increasing amounts of car parking space may not be borne out by available evidence. Indeed, the reverse may be true - beyond a certain threshold additional car parking provision can reduce retail turnover. While more work needs to be done on this, an explanation may be that as land is set aside for storing cars it is sterilised for other and more profitable uses.

6-55

Perhaps the most extreme case in the TEST parking study mentioned in the previous paragraph was München: it had both the lowest CBD car parking provision (the highest amount of shopping floorspace in m^2 per parking space) and by far the highest turnover per m^2 of shopping floorspace. This is particularly interesting because the CBD of München is considered to be almost too successful. Its urban design quality is high, it has exemplary access by public transport: U-Bahn, S-Bahn, tram and bus, and many people live in and close to the CBD. (U-Bahn is an underground rail system; sometimes a heavy rail like the London Underground, and sometimes a light rail as in Dortmund or Stuttgart; S-Bahn is an urban heavy rail system run by *Deutsche Bundesbahn*, the Federal railway). TEST would argue it possesses a near perfect combination of those elements needed for a successful traditional city centre.

6-56

The policy of Karstadt and Kaufhof is strongly in favour of improving the urban environment, in part through pedestrianisation and traffic calming. Both store groups see it to be an important factor for promoting turnover. The new trend of building arcades is also greatly favoured. Karstadt has developed new designs for streets containing their department stores; these are discussed with local planning departments. General retail policy of Hertie, Karstadt, Kaufhof and Horten department stores is interesting. Since 1986 the decline in department store turnover (Hertie had large structural problems which led to the closure of city centre department stores in Dortmund and Würzburg) has been partly reversed. Competition for department stores still comes mainly from specialised retailing shops in the city centre, whereas superstores and hypermarkets are seen (by the department stores) to be stagnant economically. The strength of department stores still lies in their city centre location, and in the vast range of goods they carry - Karstadt has about 200 000 items, not including colour and size variants, whereas an average superstore only has about 80 000.

6-57

Turning to food stores, Dr Hermanns, Chairman of the Köln Chamber of Commerce, is concerned about the departure of stores like Aldi from the city centre and inner city to suburban locations. Aldi is the largest food store chain (of the aggressive type) in Germany, with a turnover of 20 billion DM in 1985. It developed during the 1960s with a completely new concept. The shops were to have few items - about 500 - of very high quality. The service is poor and the articles are provided in cardboard boxes, with no special design to attract customers; at the same time, prices were low, and no other retailer could compete on price. Many other retailers have tried to copy Aldi, though none have succeeded. The company is privately run by two brothers, so no one has insight into their policies. They tried to expand into other countries, succeeding in the Netherlands but failing in the US and Austria. From an original size of 500 m^2 net with 500 articles, they have enlarged to 800 m^2 net, adding fresh fruit and vegetables. This means that Aldi, smaller than a superstore or hypermarket, escapes the 1986 BauNVO restrictions.

6-58

We conclude this section with the rather different views of two key persons in the retail movement, obtained in interviews: Dr Weitz, of the Federal Organisation of Retailers, and Dr Wichmann, Chairman of the Association of Superstores. Dr Weitz believed that cities with over 100 000 people had no real problems with out-of-centre retailing. It was the medium-sized cities, specially those without historic centres, which were in danger. The main reason for this disparity was that the larger cities have a better functioning planning system with officially-agreed land use plans. Furthermore, the medium cities located close to the larger cities wanted a share of the investment (see the discussion on South Hampshire in Chapter 3, and Sandwell MBC's grand gestures in the face of nearby Birmingham in Chapter 4). The medium-sized cities were also less selective about whom they attracted.

6-59

Weitz felt the future of city centres was now less bleak than it had appeared. Large cities have done a lot to make their centres attractive and the new fad for arcades had helped. These trends were more visible in cities that had experienced a decline in the number of visitors and in turnover, or where there were substantial out-of-town developments, or both. Cities like Stuttgart and München which had not had such problems had not made investments of this kind (this is debatable: Stuttgart has an arcade, and both have invested heavily in public transport). Wichmann, unsurprisingly, believed that decisions in favour of superstores should be left to the customer, and that central place theory was a concept of the past and should be abandoned. He noted that the political position of the superstores and hypermarkets was weak, because they had not developed a political lobby. In fact, the strength of chambers of commerce in Germany greatly contributed to the restrictive policies within the German law.

6-60

Wichmann then maintained that shopping in superstores and hypermarkets was the shopping form of modern people, that the planning laws distorted free competition and were in favour of the conservation of existing structures. Department stores had tried too late to establish out-of-centre stores: superstores and hypermarkets had discovered the niche between traditional retail firms and department stores. Wichmann added that the new self-service stores felt their rights had been cut: they are not allowed to settle on remaining interesting locations. Perhaps more significantly, they compete in a limited way. They had started by selling convenience goods and had become expert in this. In the non-food sector traditional retailers were much better than the new stores, partly because suppliers are often reluctant to provide high quality goods. Many radio and record/tape player firms have been reluctant and Philips have only recently agreed to supply after a long legal battle. There were also difficulties with other electrical goods, and with clothing and cosmetics - often because wholesalers still determine prices of goods in the shops: the new stores cannot accept this.

6-61
It would require another report the size of this one properly to enumerate the gainers and losers from major retailing changes, but some are listed here, with comments from the literature. Gainers and losers are likely to be represented in the following groups and concepts:

a International, national, regional and local economies; public administrations; fiscal effects; quality of urban life (*Urbanität*)
b Employment
c Commercial interests at various structural levels, from the multi-national to the corner shop; effects on competition, distribution, number of shops
d Consumers, particularly the poor and those without some form of personal mobility; choice, range of goods, price
e Physical environments, through land use changes; transport infrastructure (road, rail, parking, servicing, control systems); severance caused by transport routes, accidents, energy use, pollution; time used to reach the shops

6-62
It is difficult to discuss these subject areas discretely, as they overlap into others. They will therefore be dealt with more holistically within this section, which will be followed by a critique of the big store lobby's self-justification. In order to provide more background information, two further Tables are presented first, to expand on Tables 6-2 to 6-4. Table 6-7 (next page) shows the significance of store location within a particular part of town and country.

Table 6-7 : HGZL characteristics by location, 1979/1985 (turnover 1978/1984)

Location	Employees per outlet	Turnover (1000DM) per outlet / employee		Turnover per sales m^2	Sales area m^2/outlet
In towns+cities					
1979	6.8	1 026	150.9	5 707	179.8
1985	6.6	1 298	196.2	6 345	204.5
Inner areas of above					
1979	7.6	1 090	143.8	5 958	182.9
1985	7.0	1 355	192.4	6 488	208.9
Small towns+villages					
1979	4.7	671	143.6	4 912	136.6
1985	5.0	949	188.5	5 348	177.5
Outside built-up areas					
1979	7.4	1 523	207.0	4 159	366.1
1985	10.0	2 847	284.6	4 578	621.8

Source: Krockow 1988

Table 6-7 displays a clear progression (low to high) from the small town and village through towns and cities at large, to their inner cities, to the 'greenfield' sites - in terms of employment turnover and sales area per outlet - though the differences between towns+cities at large and their inner areas are not great. The much greater size of the 'greenfield' stores is reflected in the lowest efficiency of land use, expressed as turnover per sales area. The area of the outlet is reflected in the employee and turnover measures per outlet. **In fact, is success in the 'greenfield' stores largely a function of the quantity of sales floorspace?** The answer must be 'yes' because it allows extensive retailing, and internal economies of scale. For these stores (often for convenience goods) the mean sales area increased by 70% 1979 to 1985, but the turnover per m^2 of sales area only increased by 10% over that period. While floorspace (in 1985) is just under three times the inner city's, turnover (in 1984) is only just over twice the inner city's. Viewed in this way the 'greenfield' stores perform worse than (but damage) the inner city ones. Arguably both make great demands on the environment, and on the transport infrastructure.

6-63

Table 6-8 is centred on sales area and whether a store is self-service, or conventional-service (where a store is labour-intensive).

Table 6-8 : Characteristics of self-service and conventional-service stores
according to their sales area: HGZL

Sales area m^2		Turnover			Employees per outlet
	MillionDM	% total	employee 1000DM	per m^2 sales area DM	
All stores	388 065	100.0	195.7	5 940	6.1
Self-service	150 598	38.8	277.0	7 064	9.6
Conventional-serv.	237 467	67.4	165.0	5 395	5.3
under 100					
S-service	8 286	2.1	148.2	7 064	2.7
C-service	76 078	19.6	127.8	8 461	2.9
100-399					
S-service	39 052	10.1	255.9	7 893	6.4
C-service	53 479	13.8	165.8	6 167	6.2
400-999					
S-service	39 006	10.0	290.1	7 899	15.7
C-service	26 028	6.7	199.3	4 843	14.3
1000-2999					
S-service	27 159	7.0	285.0	5 884	33.1
C-service	30 059	7.7	215.5	3 757	27.9
3000 and more					
S-service	37 094	9.6	352.1	6 572	114.0
C-service	51 823	13.4	206.2	3 993	122.4

Source: Krockow 1988

The Table shows that 39% of all German retail turnover depicted here (the full total for 1984 was 473 762 million DM - HDE [1987]) was attributable to self-service stores. With only 17% of the outlets, the self-service group had 27% of the employees and 33% of the sales floor area. Turnover per employee was 1.7 times higher in self-service than other stores and 1.3 times higher per square meter of sales floorspace. Self-service employed 1.8 times more people per outlet than other kinds of store: this is because self-service stores have on average 2.3 times the sales floorspace as conventional stores - 377 m^2 against 163 m^2, itself caused by the very large absolute number (202 396 – ten times the number of self-service stores at that floor area range) of conventional stores with sales floorspace under 100 m^2.

6-64

Standing back from numerical analysis for a moment, and taking a positive view first, those who discuss gainers include Mössner (1986), quoted above to the effect that out-of-town developments are not adversely affecting city centres, and Wichmann's eloquent partisanship for superstores and hypermarkets, also above: it is not surprising that the support group is strongly influenced by the large store owners! Sollner (1984) claims that the retail revolution has increased variety of choice in city centres, and the number of comparison stores has increased in five Bavarian medium-sized towns that were studied. For the car-owning consumer group all forms of out-of-town store tend to be welcomed (though they continue, often, to use the city centre): Alles et al (1983) examined three superstores in Hessen. They found a shift in retail demand in favour of these stores - the store was preferred by 35% of those interviewed to traditional stores with service (23% supported them); the superstore ranked close to self-service shops (38% supporting) as the most important shop for the satisfaction of short-term needs.

6-65

Because of the large number of users of superstores, hypermarkets, retail warehouses and new shopping centres, the number in favour probably outweighs those against (as in car ownership, support of out-of-centre large stores doubtless owes a lot to peer group pressure and advertising) - in other words those who lose - who seem to be more vocal. Sometimes the losers, or antagonists, say positive things about city centres as a way of countering outer retail developments: 'Possible measures against the development of decentralised forms of retail business can be implemented by local authorities and local city retailers...improve access to their premises (parking places, cycle parking, delivery, luggage storage)...(and) the city can be made more attractive by pedestrian zones and passages, and integrated shopping centres' (Depenbrock-Naumann 1981). Diametrically opposed is Hoffmann's (1984) investigation of the extent to which the BauNVO 1977 amendment had negative effects on competition, and was therefore adversely affecting the out-of-town developer. Hoffmann is not at a loss however: he suggests 'in order to get round the strong limitations on expansion imposed by BauNVO (try) looking for older building areas not covered by the restrictions, setting up markets under $1\ 500\ m^2$, choosing locations with integrated facilities, and acquiring existing businesses instead of newbuild.'

6-66

Hoffmann (ibid) also noted '...these new retail businesses and their possibly undesirable effects have necessitated new planning regulations (against) potentially damaging environmental effects - noise nuisance, traffic problems, the danger of depleting existing centres, visual intrusion etc.' Hoffmann listed many adverse effects: 'shift of demand from retail locations to the larger types of business, because of price advantages; disadvantages for less mobile social groups; the possible threat to the rôle of other central places as providers; taking custom away from city centre shops; loss of attractiveness of the city (centre); a decreasing number of specialist shops, and job losses. This type of effect can be expected where the existing balanced relationship of available purchasing power with the supply of retail areas falls into disequilibrium because of newly established hypermarkets: this must be stopped by means of planning controls.'

6-67

A study in Saarbrücken (Landeshauptstadt Saarbrücken 1980) listed the effects of concentration in retailing, which the city considered as negative: decreasing density of provision in residential areas, withdrawal of shoppers threatening central businesses, costs of increasing the road network and increased distances, traffic nuisance for residents and impairment of the townscape. A study in Hessen (Alles et al 1983) noted 'the extension of superstores has accelerated the structural change in retailing in Hessen ... in districts with superstores the number of businesses and jobs reduced more sharply than in others, while the growth in turnover per business and per inhabitant was slower.' In only one region studied, Grosszimmern, could negative effects for local trade be ruled out. The authors continue 'In general, superstores are seen by retailers as competition in pricing and marketing policy, not so much by shops serving medium-term needs as by grocery shops and by medium-sized shops serving short-term needs...tried to counter the danger through modernisation, special offers and marketing which has however had little significant effect in increasing turnover (apart from specialist shops).' The choice of location of superstores in Hessen has, the authors say, largely followed central place theory, preferring large and medium-sized centres, with negative consequences for surrounding centres. 'The edge of town position favourable to traffic was a prime motive, but attempts to integrate the superstores into the surroundings have largely been neglected.'

6-68

While local authorities may do well out of trade tax (but see below), they may lose in other fiscal directions with the development of out-of-town stores. Mayr (1980) pointed out that *Lohnsummensteuern* (employment taxes) are lower in business categories with fewer staff than in labour-intensive retailing. Alles et al (1983) also discussed *Gewerbesteuer*, or trade tax. **They** concluded: 'the increase hoped for by local councils is limited; with a revenue of DM3-4 000 per million of turnover, large and productive specialist grocery shops have contributed an equal proportion, and specialist shops for medium and long-term needs a significantly higher proportion, than the superstores and hypermarkets.' Mayr (ibid) noted that 2000 small local authorities no longer had a grocery shop - but British village shops have also declined rapidly. Smaller businesses often do badly; Regierung von Unterfranken (1983) showed that superstores and self-service markets in their area had a strong market position, varying with location. In core areas with one third the population they accounted for 60% of turnover, in more suburban areas with two thirds the population, they accounted for 40% of retail turnover. They also noted that '3% of the 6 000 shops in Unterfranken account for approximately 58% of the floorspace.'

6-69

Heckl (1981), when investigating retail locations in Bavaria, showed how the cash and carry movement had declined in parallel with the rise of superstores, yet he felt the development of large retail businesses was not always negative, believing that consultation with shoppers had effected a reorientation of several larger businesses. Nevertheless, where existing stores could not change the type of goods they sold so as to compete better, the large stores often forced closure of the smaller shops. Sollner (1984) was more trenchant: 'Significant effects of superstores on city centre locations cannot be proved; however, slightly weakened shop development in outer areas can be expected. Convenience goods shops are threatened as much in inner as in outer urban locations (there have been numerous shop closures, especially grocery branches), this process being accelerated by openings of new superstores in outer urban locations.' Sollner added that choice was less in outer areas (fewer food shops, rare new openings) with the exception of areas within walking distance of the new businesses. However, TEST (1988) showed that in Freiburg Benetton shops, for example, were opening in small towns, diminishing the magnetism of Freiburg's central shopping area as a place of specialist retail attractions.

6-70

The number of convenience goods retailers declined by 15.9%, a loss of 18 387 firms. Size of firm also changed considerably. While the number of medium-sized firms (200-499 employees) decreased very slightly (-2%), the number of outlets operated by this group increased by 20%. The number of firms with 500 or more employees increased by 17%, and their total number of outlets by 47%.

At the other end of the scale, the number of small firms (less than 200 employees) declined by 16%. There was a similar decline in the number of outlets operated by these firms. There has therefore been a process of concentration within the convenience goods sector, with large retailers expanding at the expense of smaller ones. This is reflected in Table 6-9 showing the growing share of market turnover commanded by large firms. We noted above that convenience goods turnover had increased somewhat faster than the retail price index, but that turnover on comparison goods had not kept pace with the index. It appears therefore that the large convenience goods firms have gained at the expense of the smaller ones, and that convenience goods retailing generally has gained at the expense of comparison retailing - all within a static market.

Table 6-9 : Large firms selling convenience goods

| | Firms with more than | | | |
| | 500 employees | | 50 workplaces | |
	1979	1985	1979	1985
Number of firms	100	117	85	100
% of total:				
workplaces	7.0	11.6	7.5	12.4
employees	27.3	39.2	23.0	34.1
turnover	37.1	50.0	31.6	44.8

Source : HDE (1987)
*Note that in this sector of convenience goods, superstores and hypermarkets are included if more than 70% of their turnover is attributable to the sector

6-71
Turning to comparison retailing (ie that other than food, drink and tobacco), the number of firms of all sizes increased 1979-85 by 5.1%. In contrast to the convenience goods sector, the smallest firms (with 1-9 employees) experienced a growth in numbers of 6.6%. Firms with more than 9 employees decreased in number by 6.2%, while the number of outlets of such firms declined by 4.4%. Although firms with more than 200 employees decreased in number by 9.3%, they operated 15.3% more outlets in 1985 than in 1979. This again represents a process of concentration within the sector. Table 6-10 shows comparable data to Table 6-9 (the source is also HDE 1987).

Table 6-10 : Large firms selling comparison goods

| | Firms with more than | | | |
| | 500 employees | | 50 workplaces | |
	1979	1985	1979	1985
Number of firms	143	136	54	57
% of total:				
workplaces	2.0	2.6	2.2	2.7
employees	24.0	22.2	16.7	15.2
turnover	26.2	26.6	16.1	15.4

*This sector of comparison goods includes department stores, mail order houses and some of the hypermarkets.

148

6-72

DIfU (1982) end this discussion with a concern for urban quality: 'The city centre has always been accorded special significance as 'heart and brain' of the town, because here the lifestyle associated with urban life – *Urbanität* – is centred (liveliness of communal life, variety of social contacts, communication). However, in recent times a loss of *Urbanität* has been noticeable as a result of depopulation in areas close to the city centre, traffic nuisance, parking problems, the difficulty of accommodating delivery vehicles, air and noise pollution. Here, in order to establish a new *Urbanität* planning and organisational measures must be produced.' The conclusion is that urbanity cannot be produced by planning alone.

The Large (non-Department) Store Lobby

6-73

This brief survey of the gainers and losers might usefully be ended by examining the self-justifying contentions of the large store lobby. The case for such stores is often stated in England, and to some extent in Germany, to the effect that they create employment, they are efficient, they provide what people want. To take the last first, paragraph 6-64 showed that an interview survey gave support for such stores; similar results could easily be obtained for Britain. They relate strongly to personal justification for ownership of a car. This does not mean that these stores are to the advantage of society at large. On the first two contentions, lack of data makes their exploration difficult if not impossible for British stores. Table 6-11 provides German evidence about the first two contentions.

Table 6-11 : HGZT data 1978/9 to 1984/5 by type of retail outlet, fixed premises only

Type of shop	1000 employees Employees/outlet		MillDM Turnover Turnover/outlet		Turnover/employee 1000DM	
	1979	1985	1978	1984	1978	1984
All fixed premises	2202	2175	341770	447053	153	206
	5.8	**5.8**	**0.91**	**1.19**		
Not included below	1708	1555	241759	275523	142	177
	5.2	**4.9**	**0.72**	**0.87**		
Supermarkets+other self-service food	134	196	34207	59620	255	304
	24.0	**21.1**	**6.12**	**6.43**		
Hypermarkets+ superstores	41	72	11081	25400	271	351
	106.3	**107.9**	**28.86**	**37.91**		
Department stores	188	159	23172	27522	123	173
	360.5	**227.0**	**44.48**	**39.32**		
Other (eg filling stations)	130	192	31551	58988	242	307
	3.3	**4.0**	**0.80**	**1.22**		

Adapted from Krockow 1988

FIG 6-12 RETAIL SECTOR EMPLOYMENT AGAINST CONSUMER EXPENDITURE

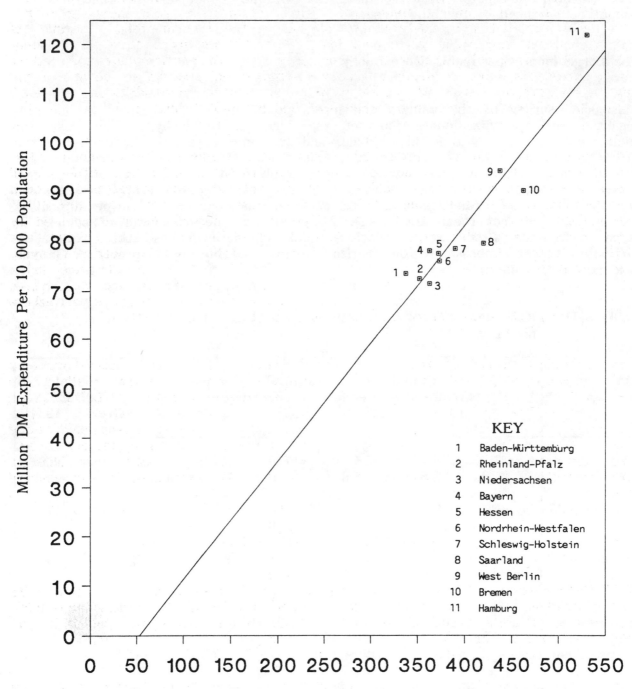

150

6-74

On the question of employment gain, Table 6-2 shows a 2.9% loss overall in retail employment 1979-1985 at the same time as the total sales floorspace and turnover were increasing. Table 6-3 shows an 18% rise in employment in convenience goods retailing in independent towns of less than 100 000 population and of 5.6% in cities larger than 1 million population. At other city levels and in counties there were losses as great as -10.3%. Table 6-11, covering all branches of retailing, shows that supermarkets etc gained 61 938 employees 1979-1985, and hypermarkets and superstores gained 31 485 employees. But the 'not included below' category lost 153 000 employees and Department Stores lost 28 941. The losses exceed the gains. What we are seeing is therefore redistribution of a relatively fixed number of jobs - the supermarkets, hypermarkets and superstores gain while all others lose. One further point about employment - there is a geographical shift that employees have to accommodate too: their city centre jobs have suddenly migrated to the outer suburbs or beyond incurring new transport costs to locations which are often more difficult to reach by public transport, and possibly a change of residential location.

6-75

What else does Table 6-11 tell us? Department stores performed better than other stores in terms of absolute figures, but turnover/outlet fell 1978-84 and turnover/employee was poor - half that of hypermarkets and superstores at both points in time. The Department Stores improved turnover/employee by 40% 1978-84, but they started from a low base. Hypermarkets and Superstores improved by 30% from a high base. The small outlets (often one per firm) in the 'not included below' category regressed except for turnover/outlet per employee. Turnover/outlet increased by 14% in current terms, but the retail price index increased by nearly twice that amount. Only hypermarkets and superstores exceeded the index change with a current terms increase of +31%; supermarkets only achieved +5% and Department Stores lost by 11%.

6-76

The misleading nature of the 'job creation' claim by the large, non-department. stores clearly needs addressing. But have these store owners not realised the principle that Figure 6-12 demonstrates? That there appears to be a direct link between the number employed per 10 000 population and turnover? As one increases, so does the other - at least as far as these data for each *Land* show. And what of efficiency? It certainly appears that the hypermarkets and superstores are more efficient than other types of store. But their benefits and disbenefits to the community at large need to be considered in any balance sheet.

SOME VIEWS OF THE FUTURE

6-77

Wolf (1988) forsaw changes in the structure of German retailing. Using 1978 data and changes that took place by 1982, he predicted the situation in 1990. He used 7 different types of retailing: their market shares in 1978, 1982 and 1990 are shown in Table 6-13.

The Table shows that while the classifications are more disaggregated than those used elsewhere in this chapter, department stores, voluntary chains, retailer cooperatives and mail order are shown scarcely to change over the period 1978 to 1990, the share of multiples is predicted to rise by 2.6% and that of superstores and hypermarkets by 1.3%. The main losers are the unaffiliated independents, by 6.1%.

Table 6-13 : Actual and predicted structural changes in German retailing

Retail type	% share of market in		
	1978	1982	1990
Superstores and hypermarkets	6.2	6.8	7.5
Department stores	7.6	7.0	7.3
Mail order	5.2	5.3	5.5
Multiples	18.4	19.1	21.0
Retailer cooperatives	29.0	29.6	30.5
Voluntary chains	13.5	13.5	14.2
Unaffiliated independents	20.1	18.7	14.0

6-78

Wolf also predicted some new developments. One is specialists, created by conversion of some superstores and hypermarkets, and by umbrella stores accommodating a number of specialists. Another is 'fast fashion' modelled on the fast food concept, and another the 'concessionaire concept' where retailers let surplus floorspace, thus acting as property managers. Interestingly several of Wolf's 'new' concepts already operate in Britain. He also believed that shopping centres would increase by two or three a year from the 83 in 1986, with more than 15 000 m^2 floorspace (unspecific on whether gross or net floorspace). Wolf noted the slow growth of these centres, attributable to lack of suitable sites, building regulations which 'hinder the erection of large-scale retail developments outside town centres; building costs and land values have risen faster than the rents retailers are prepared to pay; and 'overprovision of retail floorspace at the regional level has reduced the need.'

6-79

Kläsener (1985) was concerned to protect retail investment in traditional centres. His recommendations are set out below.

1 The concept of central place must remain the basis for planning and development: he gives the example of Langenfeld, a medium-sized town whose self-service market experienced a decrease in real turnover 1978-84, of about 20%. 'The expected improvement of mixed businesses did not take place... there was a parallel weakening of the main centre and (surrounding) purchasing areas'
2 All possible legal planning avenues must be explored
3 City and regional planning has to refer to promotion of urban settlement: housing construction has to make city centres more attractive to live in. 'There is no need for prolonged shop opening hours in the vital city centre of Aachen with 40 000 inhabitants, of which 8 000 are students, within a total population of around 245 000.'
4 Public transport must be made more attractive. This applies to the larger cities - there seems little point in improving public transport in medium and small cities, where it is used less and less for shopping.
5 Access to city centres as well as to parking places has to be improved. Kläsener supports this contention with a 1985 estimate that private vehicle traffic will increase by 20% 1980 to 1990. '54% of customers...drive into the city centre on Saturday and 40% on weekdays.' (This represents a smoothing of the BAG survey's findings: for example in 1984 on Thursday 22.4% of shoppers used a car to travel from Hannover to its centre, and 41.3% from the hinterland to the centre. On Saturday the figures were 32.0% and 58.0% respectively. **All of these represented considerable reductions on the 1976 proportions** [Triesch & Kläsener 1985])

6-80

Weitz (1987) believed there would be a further increase in the concentration of retailing not only in food firms, but also in other areas. There is a division between middle-sized retailers (*mittelständische Firmen*) - the so-called traditional firms - and the large, often international, firms. The number of middle-sized retailers depends both on the size of a city and its history. Köln has a large number of traditional firms whereas Dortmund does not. These smaller firms do not have the financial 'muscle' to invest in marketing skills, and these firms find misjudgements difficult to survive. The biggest danger for them comes from retail warehouses, and some of the middle-sized firms have nearly totally disappeared - ironmongers and joinery firms for example.

6-81

Another prescription was written by Depenbrock-Naumann (1981). She suggested 'in order to confront the competitive pressure of lower prices in the decentralised businesses' (it is extraordinary the number of terms used) 'ie to win back customers and not lose them, the inner city retail trade must compensate in other areas: in selecting a range of products particular emphasis should be placed on higher quality products which need advice - matching the changed requirements of customers for speciality products.' A specialised range might be added to an existing specialism, she noted: for example, a chemists could add cosmetics or health foods. In her view, smaller retailers had the advantage of this flexibility over large-scale shopping centres. More certainly the medium and small retailers could present their products attractively and provide information for customers using window displays and interior decoration, and a greater effect could be obtained through a collective effort with other retailers: these were less easy to achieve with the large self-service stores.

6-82

Depenbrock-Naumann continued to suggest that a variety of services could influence the consumer's choice of shopping location: ability to exchange clothes, technical information, facilities for changing nappies, crèche, rest rooms, etc. And consumer credit cards for particular stores (for example Hertie's Golden Customer Card introduced in Stuttgart in 1973) enabled an increased turnover as well as a stronger relationship between the customer and shop in question. Depenbrock-Naumann maintained that here was a substantial difference between these retailers and discount shops. Alles et al (1983) were more prosaic: size of stores should remain in balance with local population, and for town planning and traffic reasons not exceed 7 000 m^2 gross floorspace; there should be liaison with neighbouring districts in drawing up plans for superstore development.

6-83

A view of 1990 as seen from 1983 by a sub-region (*Regierungsbezirk Unterfranken* - the northwest part of Bavaria) is illuminating: 'Consumer behaviour will change because of smaller households, more people with jobs as potential customers with higher value needs, increasing expenditure on accommodation, decreasing expenditure on food and clothes.' The authors argue this changes the structure of retailing in the following ways:

* a slight increase in floorspace, a continuing trend toward smaller units integrated into the urban structure, a 10-15% decrease in the number of establishments, and development of neighbourhood shops as a new trend
* the wave of expansion of superstores and hypermarkets weakens in favour of traditional department stores
* medium and small town locations are strengthened while the dominant position of city centres for high quality goods (both needing advice, and exclusive) is further extended
* residential and neighbourhood shopping centres become more significant.

153

They conclude: 'In view of these trends, the goal of a balance between large and small shops is hardly possible' (Regierung von Unterfranken 1983).

6-84

For a city's view of a future where out-of-town developments needed to be resisted - and which retains relevance to-day for the future of city centres - we can turn to Hannover (TEST 1988). Positive support for traditional shopping streets and centres centred on providing them with space for expansion, together with:

* improvement of environmental quality and standards of urban design in shopping streets and nearby residential streets. Mainly through pedestrianisation and traffic calming
* improvement of access to shopping streets by bicycle, public transport and on foot
* provision of sufficient parking spaces although numbers do not attempt to mirror provision in out-of-centre shopping centres
* improvement of housing and the environmental quality in the neighbouring areas so as to retain a local catchment for traditional shopping facilities.

6-85

Heckl's (1981) future suggests a further expansion of superstores which will then go into decline as did the cash and carry stores: they would give way to newly evolving types of business. He also felt that an increase in petrol prices would perhaps bring central shopping areas to the fore again: what he did not allow for was the changed land uses and low density outer developments that have followed or caused out-of-town retail developments. These are inimical to public transport for access to city centres, and those centres would find it impossible to accommodate all the cars whose owners felt impelled to take them there. Perhaps more to the point is the DIfU (1982) approach: 'While the process of concentration of retail areas in the centres of large towns can be taken as conclusive, there still appear to be possibilities of growth in well functioning medium-sized centres; even in stagnating retail areas, expansion for economic reasons will necessitate an increase in retail floorspace.'

6-86

Sieverts (1987) was critical about certain current trends and their possible blanket adoption. As we have noted above he felt the main danger confronting city centres was to give way to retail organisations' demands for more parking facilities. He also criticised the vogue for glazing over shopping streets in order to replicate shopping centres outside traditional urban centres. He felt this would destroy the contrast between public street space and private space. It would also increase conflict within the city centre by introducing high rents in the covered places: only firms with high turnover could locate there. A further problem was that if everything had to be modernised, the historic centres would be at a disadvantage - large stores cannot be fitted into narrow streets, nor can deliveries be made from large trucks. In fact the encroachment of large chain stores into city centres was the main problem he foresaw for the future; he suggested this could be controlled through strict planning regulations.

6-87

Kossak (1988) had an entirely different view of arcades and their value to the city centre. He discussed the centre of Hamburg, showing how three concentric rings, each with shopping centres, surrounded the CBD to the outermost parts of the city. These had had such a profound impact on the CBD that by about 1975 the latter was declared dead. In fact, as Kossak shows, there were several other factors contributing to the decline. But then, two things happened: 'an audacious young mayor...pushed through his idea of an elegantly redesigned city hall square' and the manager of an insurance company noted indicative lines on maps which showed potential arcades, cut through several building blocks in the western part of the city centre. Seven different firms of architects were given freedom to develop imaginative schemes, their schemes were built, and the centre has recovered much of its original significance.

6-88
DIfU (1982) suggest 'The internal competitive struggle in town-centre retailing will intensify because of poor increases in purchasing power and saturated markets. This will favour large stores and specialised businesses and, because of increasing land prices, other land uses (gastronomic and leisure). This situation will only be contained by "trading up" or improving accessibility for car-users. However, for some years there has been strong criticism not only of the one-sided support of the town centre, but also of the exclusive emphasis on the city's (assumed to be city centre's) economic function. In this sense one aim for town-centre planning will be development of other public, cultural and political institutions - as economic uses, and the spatial differentiation according to function - diminish. This would be necessary to preserve what remains of public life in town centres, as well as to retain and enhance *Urbanität* and the diversity of urban functions that town centres represent. It would also be necessary to work against the process of alienation and depersonalisation.'

6-89
Türke-Schäfer (1988) presented three scenarios to an Anglo-German Foundation Conference. He quickly dismisses his first, 'naive image of the future', The Liquidated City Centre. It decentralises the city, with its inhabitants connected by cable and computer terminal. The city centre has decaying tower blocks and office buildings, yet, while the office space is up for sale 'urban life is going on in the pedestrian zone all around, with leisure pursuits for pleasure. City cafés, games, grass lawns for sunbathing have replaced the city traffic.' It sounds eminently acceptable, except that these are presumably the flawed concepts of idealists.

6-90
His second and third scenarios 'are not trend setters - they strengthen trends.' Scenario 2 is entitled The 'Brave New (Neocapitalist) City'. This city is young, urbane, professional, as is the social pattern of its inhabitants...high performance technologies...physical traffic concentrated on inter-regional and international high-speed links in air and rail transport.' Superficial though this may sound, it certainly echoes 1989 interests in rail transport, rather than road, by developers who see it as the new profitable investment. Türke-Schäfer's third scenario reads 'The Post-modern City for Living and Working'. The functions of living have been reintegrated, and are close to each other spatially. ' Comparatively small production sites (do not cause) undue strain on the environment.' The people 'who work here and live nearby are able to spend their (growing) leisure time mainly in the vicinity of their homes or make use of the extensive social and cultural facilities available. The city centre (is) the main junction in a wide network of neighbourhoods ...The "urban dominants" are shopping, cultural events or just to serve as meeting-places. The inhabitants of this city find it quite natural for these areas to be reserved for pedestrians, cyclists and local public transport.'

6-91
While Türke-Schäfer's third scenario is some distance from the disintegrating cities, bits centrifugally flying off into rural space and the pockets of developers, that we are accustomed to now, it is still a very attractive vision. His paper was found well after the reflections in the first part of Chapter 11 were written. The reader may wish to compare the two.

REFERENCES

Adrian, Hanns (1986) Was wird aus der Stadt, wenn der Handel sich aufs Land zurückzieht? **Urbanicom IX: Studientagung der Deutschen Sektion** Dortmund 4-6 June

Alles, R H Sautter et al (1983) **Erfahrungen mit Großbetriebsformen des Handelsökonomische, städtebauliche und regionalplanerische Auswirkungen** Darmstadt Institut Wohnen und Umwelt GmbH

BAG (1986) **Standortfragen des Handels** Köln

Depenbrock-Naumann, Eva Maria (1981) **Einzelhandel und Stadtentwicklung - eine Marketing-Konzeption für den City-Einzelhandel zur Förderung der Urbanität** München Hofbauer Verlag

Der Bundesminister für Raumordnung und Städtebau (1986) **Städtebaubericht Umwelt und Gewerbe in der Städtebaupolitik** Bonn

Deutscher Städtetag (1986) **Die Innenstadt: Entwicklungen uns Perspektiven** Köln

Deutsches Institut für Urbanistik (DIfU)(1982) **Die City als Einzelhandelsstandort; Räumliche Entwicklungsplanung, Teil 2** Berlin

DIHT (1986) **Baurecht für den Handel, Wegweiser für die Ansiedlung großflächiger Betriebe** Bonn

Dischkoff, N (1979) Retail Planning in West Germany in RL Davies (ed) **Retail Planning in the European Community** Saxon House

Eurostat (1986) **Review 1975-1984** Luxembourg

Falk, B (1983) **Europäische Shopping-Center-Untersuchung - Deutschland-Überblick** Urach, Baden-Württemberg Institut für Gewerbezentren

Hass-Klau, C (1982) **Planning Research in Germany** London SSRC

Hatzfeld, U (1986) **Der Einzelhandel in der Stadtentwicklung** Dortmund DASI Stadtforschung/Stadtplanung

Hauptgemeinschaft des Deutschen Einzelhandels (HDE) (1987) **Unternehmensergebnisse der Handels- und Gaststättenzählungen 1979 und 1985** Köln

Heckl, FX (1981) **Standorte des Einzelhandels in Bayern - Raumstrukturen im Wandel** Regensburg Lassleben/Kallmünz

Hermanns, Heinz (1987) **Meeting in Köln**

Heyer, HW (1985) Investitionen des Handels zur Erneuerung der Städte in **Urbanicom VII Lebendige Stadt - der Beitrag des Handels** Frankfurt

Hoffmann, K (1984) **Auswirkungen der 1977 neugefaßten Baunutzungsverordnung auf die Ansiedlung von Handelsbetrieben und die räumliche Struktur des Handels** Dissertation Universität Mainz

Hötteker, Herr (1987) **Meeting in Köln** Kaufhof Marketing Division

Jahn, F-A (1986) **Das Baugesetzbuch ist mittelstandfreundlich** BAG Nachrichten 2/1986 pp4-5

Kläsener, Robert (1985) **Growing Danger in the Inner City - Result of the Investigation into the Movement of Customers 1984** BAG Bundesarbeitsgemeinschaft der Mittel- und Großbetriebe des Einzelhandels eV Köln
- (1987) **Meeting in Essen** Marketing Division, Karstadt

Knee, Derek (n.d.) **West Germany - New Policies for Superstores and Hypermarkets: Smaller Stores and More Downtown Locations** Oxford Institute of Retail Management
- (1986) **West Germany - The Rise of the 'Fachmarkt'** as above

Kossak, Egbert (1988) The City is Dead - Long Live the City in Carmen Hass-Klau (ed) **New Life for City Centres** London Anglo-German Foundation for the Study of Industrial Society

Krockow, Albrecht (1988) Ergebnis der Handels- und Gaststättenzählung 1985 **Wirtschaft und Statistik 1/1988**

Landeshauptstadt Saarbrücken (1980) Grundsätze zur Entwicklung des Einzelhandels und zur Ansiedlung großflächiger Einzelhandelseinrichtungen in **Saarbrücken Materialien zum Standtentwicklungsprogramm** Heft 11 Saarbrücken Amt für Standtentwicklung und Statistik

Mayr, A (1980) Entwicklung, Struktur und planungsrechtliche Problematik von Shopping-Centern in der Bundesrepublik Deutschland in Heineberg, H (ed)

Einkaufszentren in Deutschland Paderborn Shöning

Mössner, Günther (1986) Der Exodus des Handels aus den Städten **Urbanicom IX**

Prisma (1979) Seminar: **Staatliche Rahmensetzung für Handel und Verbraucher - Ordnungsinstrument oder Zwangsjacke?** Hamburg Institut für Handels-, Stadt- und Regionalforschung

Regierung von Unterfranken (1983) **Tendenzen im Einzelhandel - Erfahrungen der Landesplanung in Unterfranken 1976-1982** Würzburg

Sieverts, Thomas (1987) Kulturpolitik und Städtebau - Planungsperspektiven für die Innenstadt paper to **Entwicklungsperspektiven der Innenstadt - Folgerungen für die Planung** Berlin 12-15 May

Sollner, JT (1984) **New superstores and their consequences - an empirical investigation of the structural change in retailing in five medium-sized towns in Bavaria** Nürnberg Friedrich-Alexander-University (only English title available)

Somogyi, Jan de (1986) Retail Planning for the Next Ten Years in **Retail and Distribution Management** September/October pp9-13

TEST (1988) **Quality Streets** London

Triesch, Günther and Robert Kläsener (1985) **Gefahr für die Innenstädte wächt** Köln BAG

Türke-Schäfer, Klaus (1988) Technological Change and the Future of City Centres in Carmen Hass-Klau (ed) **New Life for City Centres** London Anglo-German Foundation for the Study of Industrial Society

Unit for Retail Planning Information (1986) **List of UK Hypermarkets and Superstores** Reading

Weitz, Dr (1987) **Interview** Hauptgemeinschaft des Einzelhandels, Köln

Wichmann, Dr (1987) **Interview** Bundesverband der Selbstbedienungs-Warenhäuser Bonn

Wolf, Jakob (1988) Retailing in the FR Germany - Trends and Prospects for the 1990s in Alan West (ed) **Handbook of Retailing** Aldershot Gower

7 DORTMUND

SUMMARY

7-01

Dortmund is at the eastern, and Köln (see Chapter 8) at the southern, extremity of the densely populated industrial belt most of which is filled with the Ruhr. Dortmund only has half the population of Köln, and in most other respects it is dissimilar - higher unemployment, less prosperity, coal and steel in comparison with lighter industry and tertiary employment, etc. But the interest of this book is much more to do with retail policies (and their effects) of the two cities' local government, and their interpretation of Federal law.

7-02

In terms of central place theory Dortmund and Köln are two of four 'upper centres' in the area, the other two being Düsseldorf and Essen. But the theory has been displaced by the accretion of out-of-centre shopping; between Bochum and Dortmund lies one of the largest such centres in Germany, the Ruhrpark, and several others have appeared in the Ruhr area. Bochum (much more affected by the Ruhrpark than Dortmund) has fought back by establishing new city centre shopping. Dortmund's retail policies have differed from those of Köln perhaps mainly because the former's Chamber of Commerce is much less powerful. Since 1977 large-scale retail development has not been permitted on non-integrated sites within the city, one effect of which was the establishment of new retailing just outside the city boundary. In 1985 the City set aside 5 hectare sites for retail warehouses that could not be integrated with traditional centres and have, relatively recently, started to improve both the City Centre and several sub-centres.

7-03

The City Centre is not a statistical unit; it is contained within the Western Inner City area. Between 1978 and 1984 retail turnover in this area, in real terms, declined by 23.5%; this may be compared with Bonn and Stuttgart which both declined by 12%, and Hannover which declined by 10%.

THE REGION OF NORTH RHINE WESTFALIA

7-04

The *Land Nordrhein Westfalen* has the highest population of all the Lände (16.7 million). In terms of retail spending, it ranked eighth among the 11 Lände in 1984 (Krockow 1988) with DM76 million per 10 000 inhabitants, against DM121m in Hamburg, the highest. This presumably is a reflection of its relatively depressed state, with high unemployment in places. However, these comments may be more appropriate to the Ruhr than to Düsseldorf and areas to the south of there. Yet, in terms of spending in hotels, restaurants and 'pubs' the population of this Land spent the least (DM6.5m per 10 000 inhabitants, against the highest, DM10.7m in Hamburg). NR-W was fourth in wholesale trade turnover.

7-05

Figure 7-1 is a map appropriate to this chapter and chapter 8. It shows the system of central places for the Region. There are four 'upper centres' with a catchment of more than 2 million people: Dortmund, Düsseldorf, Essen and Köln, the distance from Dortmund to Essen to Düsseldorf to Köln being almost the same on the map, as if it had been planned before the cities were permitted to establish themselves. Bielefeld, Duisburg and Münster come into the next level (1-2 million people), and Aachen, Bonn and Wuppertal in the third (0.75 to 1 million people).

FIG 7-1 **THREE TIER SYSTEM OF CENTRAL PLACES (CPs) IN NORTH RHINE WESTPHALIA (1979)**
Source: Nordrhein Westfalen Landesentwicklungsplan 1/11

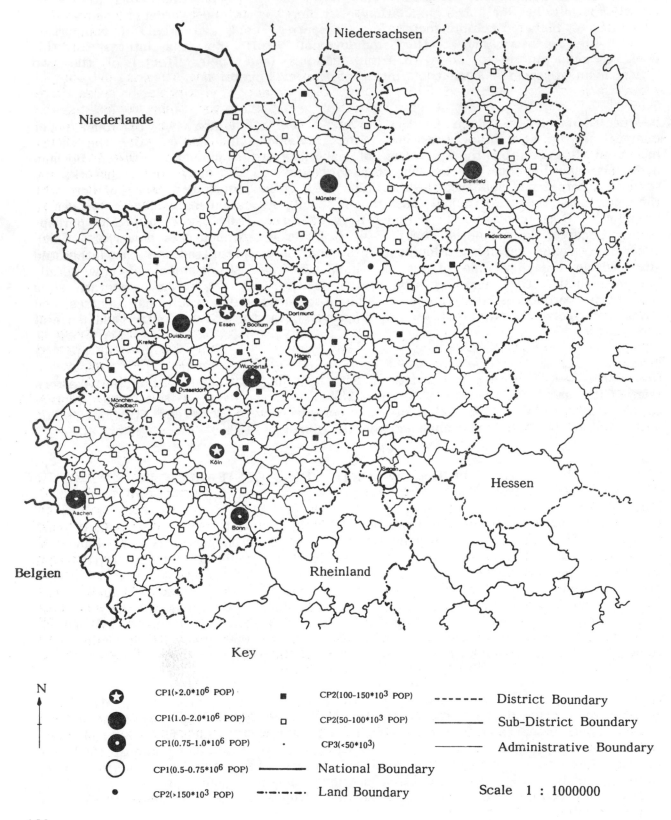

Key

⭐	CP1(>2.0*10^6 POP)	■ CP2(100-150*10^3 POP)	- - - - - District Boundary
●	CP1(1.0-2.0*10^6 POP)	□ CP2(50-100*10^3 POP)	——— Sub-District Boundary
◉	CP1(0.75-1.0*10^6 POP)	· CP3(<50*10^3)	——— Administrative Boundary
○	CP1(0.5-0.75*10^6 POP)	——— National Boundary	
•	CP2(>150*10^3 POP)	-·-·-·- Land Boundary	Scale 1 : 1000000

7-06

The Ruhr region is Germany's largest conurbation, containing about 5.4 million people. Formation of the region goes back to the 1920s; the first regional body was the *Siedlungsverband Ruhrkohlenbezirk*, which was replaced in the 1970s by the *Kommunalverband Ruhrgebiet* (KVR). This organisation covers 53 independent local authorities and eleven large towns and cities, the four largest being Essen with 623 578 people, Dortmund (577 295), Duisburg (521 293) and Bochum (384 047). This area has an average population density about six times higher than the rest of Germany.

7-07

The Ruhr is the largest and one of the oldest industrial regions in Europe. About 80% of the coal and 60% of the steel produced in Germany comes from there. In addition 30 main power stations categorise the Ruhr region as the energy centre of Germany. Apart from coal and steel, the electrotechnical engineering, precision engineering and chemical industries are important. About 52% of all employment is in manufacturing industry. Since 1957 there has been a steady decline in the number of collieries (Dortmund being particularly hard hit, declining from upwards of 200 collieries to closure of the last one in the early 1980s): there has been a shift in mining to the north of the Ruhr, where opencast mining now dominates production. Industrial jobs have also declined, partly being replaced by jobs in the tertiary sector. As a result of economic recession there has been an above-average unemployment rate throughout the Ruhr area (KVR 1983).

7-08

There are several phases of shopping centre development in the Ruhr. The first, from 1964 to 1971, saw development of Germany's second major shopping centre close to the city boundary of Dortmund. The **Ruhrpark** shopping centre opened in November 1964. It is situated on the major E-W motorway (*Ruhrschnellweg*) (Heineberg & Mayr 1986), and was built in the middle of green fields, about 8 km from the centre of Dortmund. Though the Ruhrpark centre appeared to be a big threat, research showed that in reality only 9% of all customers came from Dortmund, whereas 55% came from Bochum (ibid p51).

7-09

The Ruhrpark started with 23 000 m^2 gross floorspace, and today has 89 000 m^2. It is now the largest out-of-centre shopping complex in Germany (Heineberg & Mayr 1986). It was quickly accepted by shoppers because of its easy access by car. In addition, Bochum's city centre, only 5 km away, did not provide sufficient parking spaces, according to Heineberg & Mayr. Starting from 2 500 spaces, the Ruhrpark now has 6 500. 77% of visitors arrive by car, though there are also bus connexions to parts of Bochum and Dortmund: 13% arrive by public transport and 10% by bicycle or on foot. The Ruhrpark generally has about 50-80 000 visitors, though on a Saturday before Christmas the number may rise to 100 000 (ibid, p47). Its popularity led to an expansion from 30 to 56 retail units; in 1972-74 the two department stores were enlarged as they were again in 1976-77, at which time a fitness centre and a small office complex were added. Table 7-2 displays this on the next page.

7-10

In 1969 the second shopping centre in the Ruhr area opened at Lippe, near Hamm - the *Lippe Einkaufs-Zentrum*. It has 10 700 m^2 gross floorspace and 7 200 m^2 net floorspace.

Table 7-2 : Development of the Ruhrpark Shopping Centre

	1964	1974	1984
Total area, m^2	120 000	325 000	325 000
Gross floorspace, m^2	23 000	70 000	c89 000
Parking spaces, no	2 500	6 500	6 500
Establishments, no	30	69	84
Employment, no	1 500	3 500	3 500
Turnover, DMmillion	70	320	480

Source: Heineberg & Mayr 1986

7-11
The Ruhr's shopping development progressed further in the period 1971 to 1975: this could be described as the boom period. In 1971 the *Bero-Center* opened in Oberhausen, with 33 000 m^2 gross floorspace, and the *Westfalen-Einkaufszentrum* opened in Dortmund with 23 500 m^2 gross floorspace. Some of the other centres are listed below.

Table 7-3 : Some Shopping Centres in the Ruhr 1973-1975

Centre	Location	Gross floor-space m^2	Comments
1973			
Rhein-Ruhr Zentrum	Mülheim-Heißen	68 500	Close to Essen; largest in Germany at the time
Uni-Center	Bochum-Querenburg	5 636	
Einkaufszentrum-Altessen	Essen Altessen	18 500	Integrated with existing retailing in the area
City Center	Herne	12 655	
1974			
City Centre	Mülheim a.d.Ruhr	27 500	
Marler Stern	Bergkamen	40 200	
City Center	Bergkamen	23 000	
1975			
Löhrhof-Center	Recklinghausen	36 000	

7-12
Since 1979 the only shopping centres which have opened have been integrated with existing town centres or district centres. Generally they are smaller than those which preceded them: the City Center in Essen's city centre was opened in 1979 with 23 919 m^2 gross floorspace and a further 2 035 m^2 office space. In 1980 there was the *Glück-auf-Center* in Gladbach, with 14 700 m^2 gross floorspace. In 1981 there were Bochum's *Hansa Center*, close to the city centre, with 6 090 m^2 gross floorspace and 2 141 m^2 office space and the *Lippetor Einkaufszentrum* in Dorsten (6 034/2 488 m^2 respectively). In 1982 the *Rathaus Center* in Bochum (22 000 m^2, 56% of which are retailing) and the *Bahnhof-Center* in Gelsenkirchen, near a railway station (13 000 m^2). In 1984 there were the *Averdunk Centrum* near Duisberg's city centre (7 000 m^2) and the *Drehscheibe* in Bochum (12 400 m^2, 9 271 of which are retailing).

7-13
During the period 1985 to the present several small, though integrated, shopping centres have opened, but the phase of large uncontrolled shopping centre developments in the Ruhr area is truly over.

DORTMUND

7-14
Dortmund is the second largest city in the Ruhr region with 577 295 inhabitants in 1985, forecast to be 508 000 in the year 2000. Unemployment is high with an 18% unemployment rate in 1986: it is expected to stay high until 2000 (Gellinek 1986). Dortmund is located in the eastern part of the Ruhr, on an old trading route (*Ostenhellweg*) between the rivers Rhine and Weser. Bochum is 12 km west, and Essen 33 km west of Dortmund. Its economy was founded on coal, steel and beer; with its *Dortmunder Union*, it is Europe's number one beer town. In 1968 the second university of the Ruhr was opened on a greenfield site near the western boundary. Dortmund is the dominant economic and retail centre of the eastern Ruhr, whereas Essen dominates the western part.

7-15
Dortmund is well integrated into the strategic transport network. Three motorways connect it with major West German cities - to the north with Hannover and Bremen, to the east with Kassel, to the south with Frankfurt, and to the west with Düsseldorf and Köln. The main railway network provides hourly connexions with major West German cities, and Dortmund is part of the Rhine-Ruhr S-Bahn system, a network of 541 km in length, Dortmund lying near the eastern end. In addition, Dortmund has its own small light rail system which was developed at high cost, and has shown some disadvantages when compared with the former tramway system. Both S-Bahn and light rail did not arrive until 1983 (Hall & Hass-Klau 1985).

DORTMUND'S RETAIL STRUCTURE

7-16
Dortmund's city centre originated in a mediæval core. It was largely destroyed during the second world war but was quickly rebuilt. During the 1930s, major street widenings took place outside the old wall, and these continued after 1945. Dortmund has traditionally had a strong commercial and retailing centre, and was known for its good value for money. Its popularity was partly caused by a large hinterland - which becomes less industrialised toward the east and south-east. About one third of all of Dortmund's visitors come from the hinterland (Hermanns 1986). In order to promote city centre retailing part of it was pedestrianised in 1963 and extended in 1976 (Hall & Hass-Klau 1985) though it was 'upstaged' by Essen which had some of the earliest pedestrianisation in Europe, dating from 1904 (Hass-Klau, forthcoming).

7-17
The major threat from superstores and shopping centres appears mainly to have come during the boom period of shopping centre expansion 1971-75. During this period the *Westfalen Einkaufs-Zentrum* was opened with 23 500 m^2 (Heineberg & Mayr 1986). It is located in an old industrial area north of Dortmund's city centre (Figure 7-4 shows the areas of Dortmund). The main shop is the superstore Allkauf, which accounts for 54% of the total floorspace; the centre has very few clothes or shoe shops, its second most important traders being DIY and household goods. Unlike the Ruhrpark, nearly all the customers came from Dortmund and about 60% of them by car (ibid p79).

7-18
The second major retailing development within Dortmund was the Indu Park which opened in 1974 with 45 different undertakings, 37 being concerned with

163

FIG 7-4   **DORTMUND PLANNING REGION**
Source: Stadt Dortmund (1980)

KEY

▬▬▬▬	City District Boundary
———	Statistical Boundary
———	Sub Boundary
▬·▬·▬	Autobahn(Motorway)
············	DB(Railway)

KM

0 ├————————————┤ 4

N

wholesale or retail trade (Hermanns 1986, p12). When it opened it had 34 000 m^2 net retail floorspace (Gellinek 1986) with a total of 80 000 m^2 (Hermanns 1986). The Indu Park first accommodated the Metro-SB Großmärkte GmbH + Co and one year later the SB Superstore Wertkauf followed. However it must be remembered that many department stores which traditionally only settled in city centres have also moved into unintegrated shopping centres (ie not planned by local authorities). Of Dortmund's 11 department stores in 1987, 5 were not in the city centre, being partly in subcentres and partly in unintegrated shopping centres. Over the years the number of superstores, hypermarkets and retail warehouses has increased dramatically, despite a change in the legal framework.

7-19
The City of Dortmund's policy on retailing has been outlined by Gellinek (1986). There are three main areas within the city in which new retailing developments took place. Normally these areas had a land use plan passed before 1977, which designated the area for industrial use (*Gewerbegebiet*: this automatically allowed superstore construction). The three areas are:

* Dortmund Oespel: Indu Park opened 1974 (see above)
* Dortmund Aplerbeck: superstore Plaza opened in 1974
* Dortmund Mengede: a superstore of 8 000 m^2 was planned in Breisenbachstraße
  but the plan was not accepted by the local authority after long discussions
  in 1984. Only smaller superstores will be allowed in Breisenbachstraße,
  according to the latest regulations of the *Baunutzungs VO*, whose maximum
  size is 1 200 m^2 gross floorspace.

7-20
In 1977 the political body of Dortmund decided to stop large-scale retailing development at non-integrated locations such as the Indu Park. This decision remains valid today. However, after the decision was taken, new retail units settled just outside the Dortmund boundary (see Regensburg, Chapter 9). A well-known example was Adler clothes warehouse which settled in Holzwickede and managed to have its own bus line from Dortmund. After serious political discussion the City decided in 1985 to free up further space (5 ha each) in the Indu Park and in Aplerbeck for new retail warehouses which cannot be integrated into any traditional shopping centre. The retail warehouses of this type are:

* DIY and construction markets
* furniture warehouses
* garden centres
* car and car equipment centres
* camping and caravan warehouses.

7-21
Both centres (Indu Park and the centre in Aplerbeck) have negatively influenced the development of the neighbouring traditional shopping centres in Lütgendortmund and Aplerbeck. Improvements have been carried out for the traditional shopping streets in Aplerbeck, such as the construction of a bypass to take traffic out of the centre and improvement of the urban environment. Similar improvements apply to Lütgendortmund which will soon also have a new S-Bahn line to Dortmund's city centre.

Dortmund's Large Stores

7-22
In 1987 Dortmund had 83 superstores, hypermarkets and retail warehouses greater than 1 000 m^2 net floorspace. In particular, the retail warehouses had become particularly dominant, accounting for 64% of all new forms of retailing and 55% of the total sales area of retail units >1 000 m^2 net floorspace. In more detail, Dortmund has 19 superstores with more than 1 000 m^2 net floorspace, of

which five are located at the edge of the city (*Randlage*). There are 53 retail warehouses of which 36 are at the city edge. However 15 of the warehouses are in the statistical district Innenstadt (a total of 60 230 m^2 net floorspace) but not in the city centre (Stadt Dortmund 1988). The development of new forms of retailing has clearly affected Dortmund's city centre, as can be seen from Table 7-5 which compares the HGZs of 1979 and 1985. No comparative data for the city centre are available; the statistics for Innenstadt West have to be used, though this is clearly a much larger area (see Figure 7-4).

Table 7-5 : Comparison of HGZ 1978/79 to 1984/85 for Dortmund's Districts, 1984/1985 figures with percent change on 1978 and 1979

Districts	Establishments 1985	% ch.	Employment 1985	% ch.	Gross floorsp. 1000 m^2 1985	% ch.	Turnover Million DM 1984	% ch
Innenstadt-West	717	-10.2	9 246	-21.0	4 688	23.9	1 746	-3.4
City Centre	361	–	7 402	–	3 391		1 399	–
Innenstadt-Nord	386	-6.3	1 658	-15.1	1 007		343	10.5
Innenstadt-Ost	328	-5.7	1 875	15.6	954		362	3.7
Total Innenstadt	1 431	-8.2	12 779	-19.5	6 649		2 452	-0.7
Eving	152	-16.5	797	-15.8	438		170	15.4
Scharnhorst	157	-16.9	781	-20.1	451		169	7.0
Brackel	241	-12.4	1 310	-25.1	714		279	5.6
Aplerbeck	243	-3.6	1 593	1.3	1 273		377	35.0
Hörde	253	-23.6	1 463	-16.6	824		272	22.3
Hornbruch	222	-10.8	1 463	3.6	764		286	18.0
Lütgendortmund	287	0.7	1 882	37.3	1 363		513	122.0
Huckarde	155	-15.8	699	-14.1	416		134	14.5
Mengede	181	-6.2	864	-16.0	359		149	-2.3
Total Außenstadt	1 891	-11.6	10 852	-6.6	6 602		2 348	29.5
Total Dortmund	3 322	-10.2	23 631	-14.	13 251	5.8	4 800	12.1

Source: Stadt Dortmund 1988

Table 7-5 shows that retail turnover fell in the Innenstadt West (the enlarged city centre) by 3.4% in current terms, but by 23.5% in real terms. In comparison, the fall in turnover, in real terms, for the city centres of Bonn and Stuttgart 1978-1984 was -12%, for Hannover -10%, and for the City of Freiburg -15%; comparable data are not available for the city centre of Köln (TEST 1988). Dortmund Centre's decline is probably the most dramatic of any large city centre in Germany and is partly the result of the growth of shopping centres, superstores and retail warehouses, and partly high unemployment and an inadequate public transport system. It suggests that pedestrianisation by itself is not enough to counteract declining retail trends, neither is the provision of car parking spaces. Even in the town as a whole there was a decline in turnover, in real terms, of 11.5%.

7-23

When the HGZ is analysed in detail one can see that Dortmund has relatively large retail stores. The average size of all establishments is 400 m^2 and the mean employment is 7.1 people, compared with North Rhine Westphalia as a whole with means of 375 m^2 and 5.7 people employed. This is particularly true for

166

the Innenstadt (465 m^2/8.9 employees) and even more so for the city centre (939 m^2/20.5 employees) (Stadt Dortmund 1988 pp11,15). Large shops in Dortmund's city centre indicate a totally different retail structure from Köln - see Chapter 8; many shops in the city centre belong to international chains.

The Rôle of Transport

7-24

The BAG surveys show that 44.6% of Friday shopping trips to Dortmund's city centre from the rest of the city and its hinterland were made by car in 1980; by 1984 this had risen to 49.5%. 38% and 34% respectively came by public transport, and 13.7% walked all the way, the same in both years. We repeat that caution is needed with these data as they were collected in seven department stores, and only four other shops. Department stores normally have a large number of car parking spaces of their own, within the building. The rather specific BAG surveys also showed a decline of 1.4% of visitors to Dortmund on a Friday - 423 842 in 1980, 418 104 in 1984.

The Future

7-25

The future of Dortmund's city centre is suggested in a city planning document (Stadt Dortmund Stadtplanung 1983) and by Gellinek (1986). The connexion for pedestrians between the Hauptbahnhof and the shopping centre will be improved, as will the station itself. Some traffic calming is to be introduced (seen to be very important in housing areas close to the city centre), together with an extension of the pedestrian zone. Cycleways are planned, but so are extra parking spaces at three locations in or very close to the city centre. An electronic parking display will show available parking places in the various multi-storey car parks and this should reduce traffic looking for a place to park. A large tree-planting programme is planned for the city streets.

CONCLUSIONS

7-26

Dortmund, while one of a string of four 'upper centres' (according to Central Place Theory) with a catchment of over 2 million in *Nordrhein Westfalen*, nevertheless is situated in an area of economic decline, with some of the highest unemployment in West Germany. Furthermore, the Theory now has less relevance in view of new out-of-centre shopping centres, of which Dortmund has an inordinate share. Most notable of these is the *Ruhrpark*, between Bochum and Dortmund, the largest centre of this kind in Germany, with 89 000 m^2 gross floorspace in 1988.

7-27

Unlike most other cities, Dortmund's City Centre is not a statistical unit. It is contained within the western Inner City. That zone's retail turnover, 1978 to 1984, declined in real terms by 23.5%. This may approximately be compared with Bonn and Stuttgart, whose city centres each declined by 12%, and Hannover, whose city centre's retail turnover declined by 10%. The decline appears to be attributable less to the Ruhrpark than to other new centres within and close to Dortmund, and to its declining economic situation. Research has shown that only 9% of the Ruhrpark's customers come from Dortmund against 55% from Bochum.

7-28

In 1977, doubtless stimulated by the changes to the *BauNVO* at that time, the City authorities decided to stop retail developments at non-integrated sites. As a result, new retail units settled just outside the Dortmund boundary, causing the City to relax its position and allocate 5 ha in each of two locations, for new retail warehouses that could not be integrated within a traditional shopping centre. This provides some contrast with Regensburg (Chapter 9), though the two cities have very different catchment areas. In Dortmund there was no site near the city centre like the *Donaueinkaufszentrum* in Regensburg that could be set aside, even if the Dortmund city council had wished to do so. However, there was also a modest overspill beyond Regensburg's city boundary. Despite these comments, Dortmund's Chamber of Commerce has not had the powerful influence on the city's, and its surroundings', retail development that has been the case with Köln, as we shall find in the next Chapter.

7-29
Another factor affecting use of the city centre by shoppers is transport. The S-Bahn arrived later in the Ruhr (it reached Bochum in 1983) than in many other parts of Germany. Having arrived at the Hauptbahnhof, two main roads have to be crossed to reach the core of the centre. And, establishing a light rail system which passed under the centre happened in 1983 too, with additions since that time.

REFERENCES

Gellinek, Ph-O (1986) Stadtplanung und Einzelhandel in Dortmund, Fakten, Perspektiven, Konflikte **Urbanicom IX 'Braucht der Handel Künftig noch die Stadt?** Dortmund

Hall, P and C Hass-Klau (1985) **Can Rail Save the City?** Aldershot Gower

Hass-Klau, Carmen (forthcoming) Thesis: **The Pedestrian and City Traffic**

Heineberg, H and A Mayr (1986) **Neue Einkaufszentren im Ruhrgebiet** Münster Münstersche Geographische Arbeiten

Hermanns, H (1986) Braucht der Handel künftig noch die Stadt? **Markt und Wirtschaft** No 7, pp12-16

Kommunalverband Ruhrgebiet (1983) **Revier Report 1983** Essen

Krockow, Albrecht (1988) Ergebnis der Handels- und Gaststättenzählung 1985 **Wirtschaft und Statistik** 1/1988 pp26-32

Stadt Dortmund Stadtplanung (1983) **City-Konzept Dortmund**

Stadt Dortmund Amt für Statistik und Wahlen (1988) **Dortmunder Statistik der Einzelhandel in der Stadt Dortmund**

8 KÖLN

SUMMARY

8-01

Köln (Cologne) is West Germany's fourth largest city. It also dominates the southern end of the Rhein-Ruhr conurbation, midway between the Federal and Land capitals. In 1987 its population at 915 000 was slightly higher than in 1961. Its unemployment rate (1982) of 10.6% was the highest in the Köln-Bonn region. In retailing terms during the period 1968 to 1985 it reduced the number of outlets and of employees, and gained in floorspace and turnover (in both of which it was far ahead of the other Köln-Bonn region local authorities), though at rates lower than Leverkusen and the surrounding *Kreise*. In 1985, the number of employees per outlet in Köln was lower than the Federal average, while turnover per outlet and per employee were both higher than the Federal average.

8-02

The Land (State) Development Plan for *Nordrhein Westfalen* optimistically (but without legal backing) called for a retention of the central place hierarchy - large centres having the widest range of cultural, commercial and trade facilities, with smaller centres being less comprehensive. New retailing should be fitted into these centres' hierarchy. In reality matters did not work out this way and many new large retail developments were not 'integrated' - they were relatively free-standing, often some distance from existing centres, but invariably well-connected to motorways and other strategic roads. The 1977 and 1986 amendments to the BauNVO contained this expansion, but another factor was the strength of the Köln Chamber of Commerce. A third factor was that Köln's Inner City lost population to the outer areas at a slower rate than, for example, Hamburg and Hannover. The City Centre has therefore retained its vitality and assured trading position, which would undoubtedly have been much poorer without these restraints. The Chamber of Commerce also influenced the construction of a new museum close to the main railway station, and the updating and extension of Köln's city centre pedestrian network.

8-03

Three studies of conflict are made. One concerns the development of a new shopping centre in Hürth, built in 1977 after 15 years of conflict between the local authority, aware of North American retail developments, and local and regional retail organisations. The second discusses the conflict that can arise between planning and legal consents/refusals for retail development, showing how the Land can overrule a locally-made decision: there is some affinity with the British appeal system. The third concerns a major proposal for Köln 9 which was abandoned as a result of vehement local protest. Then follows an examination of retail performance within Köln as a whole, within its City Centre, and within the remainder of the City, by District. This traces the history of retail development and of pressures for further development in non-integrated locations, and also within traditional retail locations - the District 'High Street' (*Hohe Straße*). On gross floorspace the City Centre performed worse than the City mean average, while the City as a whole increased its gross floorspace by 19% during the period 1978/9 to 1984/5 (unfortunately, no other comparisons are possible). Turnover for the City as a whole showed a reduction of 7.3% in real terms - Bonn did a little better with a reduction of -4.8%, but Leverkusen recorded -12.2% and Stuttgart -15.6%. The chapter concludes with an examination of means of transport used for shopping. It is shown that Köln had among the lowest use of public transport of the German city regions, possibly in part because its public transport network was less sophisticated than other large cities' transport (no U-Bahn, S-Bahn only

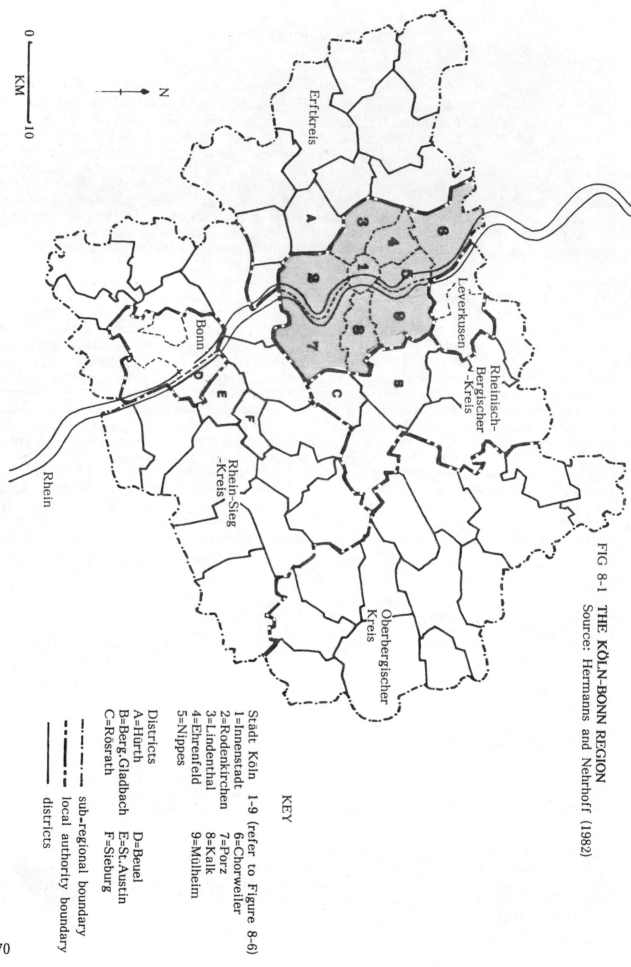

FIG 8-1 **THE KÖLN-BONN REGION**
Source: Hermanns and Nehrhoff (1982)

KEY

Städt Köln 1-9 (refer to Figure 8-6)
1=Innenstadt   6=Chorweiler
2=Rodenkirchen   7=Porz
3=Lindenthal   8=Kalk
4=Ehrenfeld   9=Mülheim
5=Nippes

Districts
A=Hürth   D=Beuel
B=Berg.Gladbach E=St.Austin
C=Rösrath   F=Sieburg

········· sub-regional boundary

━·━·━·━ local authority boundary

━━━━━ districts

introduced fairly recently, and far from complete as a network).

THE KÖLN-BONN REGION

8-04
Köln (Cologne) is the fourth largest city in West Germany, after Berlin, Hamburg and München. It is a strategic rail and road transport centre. Paragraphs 7-04 and 7-05 briefly discuss the *Land Nordrhein Westfalen*, and Figure 7-1 shows the position of Köln within the Land. It is the southernmost part of the industrialised area of the Land, with the Land capital, Düsseldorf, 26 km to the north; 18 km south lies Bonn, the Federal capital. To the west is Aachen, the Netherlands and Belgium, and to the east, the less-populated higher ground of the *Rheinisch-Bergischer Kreis* and the *Oberbergischer Kreis*. Figure 8-1 shows the Köln-Bonn Region and Table 8-2 shows how this Region has been increasing in population 1961 to 1987.

Table 8-2 : Population Changes in the Köln-Bonn Region

| | Population, thousand | | | | Percent change | | |
	1961	1970	1980	1987	61-70	70-80	80-87
Bonn	270.9*	274.5	288.7	291.8	1.3	5.0	1.1
Köln	909.1	994.7	976.7	915.0	9.4	-1.8	-6.3
Leverkusen	137.6	163.3	160.8	154.3	18.7	-1.5	-4.0
Erftkreis	279.4	335.8	399.3	406.6	20.2	18.9	1.8
Oberbergischer Kreis	206.9	227.2	247.3	247.0	9.8	8.8	-0.1
Rheinisch Bergischer Kreis	175.8	221.8	247.9	249.5	26.2	11.8	0.6
Rhein-Sieg-Kreis	301.0	376.8	463.5	483.8	25.2	23.0	4.4
Total	2280.7	2594.1	2784.2	2748.0	13.7	7.3	1.3

* Adjusted to accommodate later boundary change;   actual figure was 151 766
Source: Hermanns & Nehrhoff 1982, 1988

8-05
Unemployment was highest in Köln in 1982 with 10.6%. As unemployment statistics are not available on a Kreis basis, other figures within the surrounding area's employment districts (*Arbeitsamtsbezirke*) in 1982 were:

Bonn (Bonn + Rhein-Sieg-Kreis)	5.7%
Brühl (Erftkreis, Kreis Euskirchen)	7.9%
Bergisch Gladbach (Leverkusen, Rheinisch-Bergischerkreis, Oberbergischerkreis)	7.6%

Regional Results of three *Handels- und Gaststättenzählung* (HGZT) Surveys

8-06
Data are available from the 1967-68, 1978-79 and 1984-85 HGZT for the same regional breakdown as in Table 8-2 above (see Tables 8-3 and 8-4 on the next page). Readers should also refer back to para 6-38: the data in these two Tables are for gross floorspace and all retail trade. The Tables are therefore designated HGZT.

Table 8-3 : HGZT Data, Number of Outlets and Employees, for the Köln-Bonn Region

Area	Outlets			Employees		
	1968	1979	1985	1968	1979	1985
Bonn	2069	1949	1967	13514	14190	12927
Köln	7693	7136	6817	44737	44379	40607
Leverkusen	841	969	909	4979	7424	6207
Erftkreis	2199	2464	2343	7564	11550	11316
Oberbergischer Kreis	1765	1587	1511	6791	7972	7621
Rheinisch Bergischer Kreis	1456	1561	1579	5396	8154	8130
Rhein-Sieg-Kreis	2426	2659	2653	8207	12828	13277
Totals	18461	18325	17779	91188	106497	100088

Table 8-4 : HGZT Data, Floorspace and Turnover, for the Köln-Bonn Region

Area	Gross Floorspace 1000m^2 m^2/outlet m^2/employee			Turnover, million DM 1000DM/outlet 1000DM/employee		
	1968	1979	1985	1967	1978	1984
Bonn	409	609	675	982.8	2186.8	2628.5
	198	*312*	*343*	*475*	*1122*	*1336*
	30.3	42.9	52.2	72.7	154.1	203.3
Köln	1365	1990	2076	3483.2	7638.7	8944.9
	177	*279*	*305*	*453*	*1070*	*1313*
	30.1	44.8	51.1	77.9	172.1	220.3
Leverkusen	147	305	351	359.1	1140.5	1262.5
	175	*315*	*386*	*427*	*1177*	*1389*
	29.5	41.1	56.6	72.1	153.6	203.4
Erftkreis	249	617	762	488.6	1787.2	2178.6
	113	*250*	*325*	*222*	*725*	*930*
	32.9	53.4	67.3	64.6	154.7	192.5
Oberbergischer Kreis	250	455	465	416.7	1253.1	1560.1
	140	*287*	*308*	*234*	*790*	*1032*
	36.8	57.1	61.0	61.4	157.2	204.7
Rheinisch Bergischer Kreis	173	439	475	361.5	1219.5	1642.6
	119	*281*	*301*	*248*	*781*	*1040*
	32.0	53.8	58.4	67.0	149.6	202.0
Rhein-Sieg-Kreis	317	729	964	351.1	2084.1	3107.4
	131	*274*	*363*	*145*	*784*	*1171*
	38.6	56.8	72.6	67.2	162.5	234.0
Totals	2910	5144	5768	6443.0	17309.9	21324.6
	157	*281*	*336*	*346*	*945*	*1199*
	31.9	48.3	57.6	70.7	162.5	213.1

Source/Tables 8-3 & 8-4: adapted from Hermanns & Nehrhoff 1982, 1988

Before interpreting Tables 8-3 and 8-4 we should look at the general characteristics of the Köln-Bonn Region, comparing them with the Federal average. One problem with such a comparison is that the Federal statistics used by Krockow (1988) use *Verkaufsfläche* or selling area, whereas the Köln-Bonn data are for *Geschäftsfläche* or gross area. Number of outlets, employees and turnover are compared below.

	% change 1978/79 to 1984/85		
	Outlets	Employees	Turnover (current terms)
Federal	-1.4	-2.9	+29.3
Köln-Bonn	-3.0	-7.0	+23.2

8-07

The Köln Chamber of Commerce (see below) has powerfully campaigned to conserve the city's shopping and reduce competing out-of-town developments. These factors strongly influence the results in Tables 8-3 and 8-4, which are interpreted below:

* In terms of **outlets** there was a reduction overall 1968-85, the greater fall occurring 1979-85. Bonn shows less of a reduction than Köln, while Leverkusen rose to 1979 and fell to 1985, though not back to the 1968 figure. All the *Kreise* apart from *Oberbergischer Kreis* showed an increase 1968-85, in all three cases more pronounced 1968-79 than 1979-85.

* If these outlet figures are compared with **gross floorspace** per area the picture which emerges is that outlets have grown in size more than in number. Globally, the growth in floorspace was much greater 1968-79 than 1979-85, probably a reflection of the 1977 revisions to the BauNVO (see Chapter 6).

* In terms of **employees** Bonn and Köln both showed a reduction 1968-85, mostly occurring 1979-85. Leverkusen and all the Kreise showed an increase 1968-85, mostly occurring 1968-79 - in fact in all the Kreise apart from Rhein-Sieg-Kreis there was a modest reduction in employment 1979-85; in Leverkusen it was more substantial. Because of these patterns it is unrealistic to say there has been a redistribution of employment (as appears to be the case Federally) with urban areas losing to out-of-centre within a largely stable number of employees per sub-region. In fact the three urban areas had 52% of the employment in 1968, 62% in 1979 and 59% in 1985. 1979 was the peak for employment in the sub-region.

* More generally on turnover per outlet, Table 8-4 shows profound differences between the towns and the counties. Of the towns, Leverkusen did best in 1978 and 1984. *Rhein-Sieg-Kreis* started badly but had the highest rating of the counties in 1984. In all cases the change over the 11-year period 1967-78 was greater than in the 6-year period 1978-84.

* The floorspace data can be used to show growth comparatively between the cities and the Kreise. Bonn and Köln expanded by 49% and 46% respectively 1968-79, but Leverkusen's increase of 108% was more than twice as great. However, apart from *Oberbergischer Kreis* (+82%) the *Kreise* transcended Leverkusen with increases between 130% and 154%. In the period 1979-85 Bonn achieved an 11% increase, Köln only 4.3%, and Leverkusen 15%. The *Kreise* ranged between 2% and 32%.

* Finally, on Table 8-4, the significance of the turnover data for the whole of Köln needs to be emphasized. In real terms it lost 7.3% of turnover 1978 to 1984, but of the cities only Bonn did better, with -4.8%. Leverkusen lost 12.2%, and Stuttgart (TEST 1988) did even worse with -15.6%, largely explained by intense competition from four contiguous surrounding towns, as well as out-of-centre developments. Köln's Chamber of Commerce, as we shall see below, substantially contributed to Köln's good performance and to a lesser quantity of external competion.

8-08

It is possible to compare Federal and regional 'independent town' data from Table 6-5 (Chapter 6) in Table 8-5 below:

Table 8-5 : Comparison of HGZ Data, Federal and Köln-Bonn Region

| | Employees per outlet | | Turnover (1000DM) per | | | |
| | | | outlet | | employee | |
	1979	1985	1978	1984	1978	1984
Federal towns and cities	6.8	6.6	1026	1298	150.9	196.2
Bonn	7.3	6.6	1122	1336	154.1	203.3
Köln	6.2	6.0	1070	1313	172.1	220.3
Leverkusen	7.7	6.8	1177	1389	153.6	203.4

Köln did well against Federal averages: efficient use of employees per outlet, and considerably greater turnover per employee. It was close to the Federal average on turnover per outlet, but Bonn and Leverkusen were both above, particularly the latter.

PLANNING IN THE REGION

8-09

Planning in the Köln region has been determined both by the importance of nearby major local authorities and by the land development plans of *Nordrhein Westfalen* (NRW). There have been land development plans in 1960, 1970 and 1979. Between 1970 and 1976 there was a major reorganisation of local authorities - Köln more than doubled in size between those years, and lost some area in 1979 (Hall & Hass-Klau 1985). Some of the *Kreise* were totally new or reshaped, for example the *Erftkreis* was newly formed in 1975. In terms of population and employment, the forecast for 1990 for the Köln region was slightly more pessimistic than the reality. The forecast decline from 2.722 million in 1974 to 2.591 million in 1990 (-5%, similar to West German predictions) can be compared with the 1980 figure of 2.784 million (Table 8-2). Over the same period it was forecast that employment would increase from 1.168 to 1.183 million (+1.3% against a West German average of -1%) (BMBau 1976).

8-10

According to the land development plan (LDP), retailing and services of all local authorities have been classified into a hierarchy of basic, medium-sized, and major service centres. These are directly derived from Christaller's Central Place Theory. According to the LDP, which has no legal basis, the central place hierarchy applied to all large, medium and small centres: the largest having the widest range of culture, commerce and trade. These centres were inviolate, and new retail units were not to disturb this range of functions. In other words, new retailing had to be located in integrated centres (Der Minister für Stadtentwicklung etc 1986). The reality, however, has been rather different, with some new centres not integrated. The Köln region consists of two central places of the highest shopping & services order - the cities of Köln (first rank) and Bonn (third rank) - while 28 towns are centres of medium-sized goods and services, and 23 local authorities are classified as centres for basic goods and services (Hermanns 1982 and see Figure 7-4).

8-11

Infrastructure investments such as schools, hospitals, cultural facilities, roads and public transport were undertaken over recent decades according to these central place functions. In parallel with this, land use planners tried to control retail developments, and had reasonable success, from the 1960s onwards. However the reality for Köln changed when in quick succession the first large out-of-town shopping centres were established. These were the Main-Taunus-Zentrum near Frankfurt (1964) and the Ruhrpark Zentrum between Bochum and Dortmund in 1965 (Shaw 1983). It is strange that no centre of this size appeared at this time in the Köln-Bonn region. One reason may have been the presence of a powerful Chamber of Commerce (that of Dortmund was much less assertive). New shopping developments, with a few exceptions, appear to have been rather tightly controlled by planning authorities in agreement with representatives of commerce. The fact that Köln since medieval times has been an extremely strong and powerful commercial centre (including retailing) helps to explain this situation. Its commerce was largely formed by medium-size individual firms: these have been the backbone of successive Chambers of Commerce, a tradition which continues.

8-12

So, while new shopping centres do exist, they have not been developed on the scale they have in the Ruhr. As a representative of Köln's Urban Development Office (*Stadtentwicklungsamt*) pointed out, there have been no permissions granted in the Köln region for large 'wild' shopping centres. There have however been many small retailing 'sins' which are not so noticeable because of the large urban areas. In the hinterland there are many local authorities which have traditionally had a strong retail centre; in these locations new modern forms of retailing have had little chance to break in.

8-13

No large centres (above 10 000 m^2) were built outside Köln until 1976, the year before the legal restrictions on such developments. The largest was beyond the reach of Köln's Chamber of Commerce; it opened in St Augustin in the *Rhein-Sieg-Kreis* in 1976 with 35 000 m^2, 30 000 m^2 of which are a hypermarket. In 1977 the town of Hürth allowed an Allkauf store to open, with 12 000 m^2 (ISB 1986). A few other superstores and hypermarkets have been built which affect Köln: Siegburg, also in the *Rhein-Sieg-Kreis*, opened the Massa hypermarket with 13 000 m^2. A new furniture warehouse with 15 000 m^2 opened in Rösrath in 1968 and a 5 000 m^2 garden centre was added in 1984 (IHK zu Köln 1984). By and large, however, the Köln sub-region showed a rather controlled development in retailing and it appears that the time for getting approval for large shopping centres is largely over in West Germany. As some commentators mentioned, there are simply no suitable locations left within the cities.

8-14

We have noted above that Leverkusen has been more successful in some respects than Bonn or Köln. The local authority was formed in 1976 through an amalgamation of the towns of Leverkusen, Opladen and Schlebusch. The original Leverkusen built a modern shopping centre between 1969 and 1972, which today looks outdated. The total gross floorspace is 157 600 m^2. There are more local shopping areas in Opladen (130 400 m^2) and Schlebusch (61 000 m^2), and near to Schlebusch's centre is the Plaza hypermarket with 12 000 m^2; it is near the A3 motorway. In 1983 a 10 000 m^2 hypermarket opened in Langenfeld, close to Leverkusen (Gerhard 1986).

Conflict: Hürth

8-15

Hürth is located immediately south-west of Köln, adjacent to Köln 2 and 3. In 1962 an increase of 60-70 000 population was forecast by consultants, who suggested a shopping centre of about 14 000 m^2 gross floorspace. As US-style shopping centres had become popular in Germany at this time, the local authority decided they would like something similar, and modelled it on the Main-Taunus Centre on which construction had just started. Conflict soon arose

175

between the local authority of Hürth and local and regional retail organisa-tions and groups. Retail experts supported an increase in size to 55 000 m^2. It was not until 1970 that agreement was reached to build a shopping centre similar to Rødovre Centre in København, including several specialised shops and a large foodstore. However, the investor lost interest. Other firms moved in, one wanting to build 30 000 m^2 gross floorspace, including a department store and 40-50 specialist shops, with a second phase that had a further department store and 30 specialist shops. This firm lost confidence and withdrew.

8-16

In March 1973 three other financial groups wanted to invest and their concept of the centre varied from 9 000 to 50 000 m^2 gross floorspace. The local authority went for the largest, and preparatory work was carried out by inves-tor and local authority over the next two and a half years; the investor even-tually lost interest because of financial difficulties. Finally, Hürth's shopping centre was built, though smaller than originally envisaged - 28 000 m^2 gross, 15 000 m^2 net - and it opened in 1977, 15 years after it had been con-ceived. For the first time in Germany the main attraction was a 13 000 m^2 hypermarket instead of a department store though small branches of Kaufhof and Karstadt have located there (Hermanns 1977). The effect of this oversized shopping centre which did not fit in the central place hierarchy, was some decline in turnover, especially in nearby traditional shopping centres.

Conflict: Planning & Legal

8-17

Several conflicts are embedded in the legal procedure for new retail proposals. Normally every proposal goes first to the *Bauaufsichtsamt* (the Building Supervisory Board/Office of the Land, with a branch in most towns). This can happen in two ways, as a *Bauvoranfrage* or a *Bauantrag*. The *Bauvoranfrage* can be submitted by anybody involved in the project, the financier, the architect, etc. Different people can put forward a *Bauanfrage* for the same project - it is 'simply' an official form asking whether the project has any chance of being approved (though nothing is ever simple). If the project is larger than 1 000 m^2 it will go from the Building Supervisory Board to the Urban Development Office (*Stadtentwicklungsamt*), whereas if the project is smaller it will go to the planning department and the urban development office may not be informed about it. Köln has a two-tier planning system with both an Urban Development Office and a Town Planning Office. While responsibilities of the two offices is complex, generally speaking the Urban Development Office is responsible for strategic policy, and the Planning Office for detailed planning. However there is some overlap and relationships are sometimes strained.

8-18

A *Bauantrag* is needed to get the final permission, which can be given by the Urban Development Office or by the Planning Office, according to the project's size. About three quarters of all proposals to the Urban Development Office will not be given the go-ahead. That does not mean the proposal cannot prog-ress. If either office says 'no', the proposer can go back to the Building Supervisory Board (BSB) which is directly responsible to the Land Government, and is responsible for the **legal** procedure. Political aspects also play an important part: while North Rhine Westphalia's objectives are close to those of Köln, this is not always the case in a CDU Land like Bavaria. In the past, retail warehouses often received permission because they were regarded by the BSB as not easily integrated retail units which could be located without diffi-culty in industrial areas. Legal possibilities of obtaining permission are dis-cussed in Chapter 6 (for example, a development might gain planning permission if a local authority makes a mistake. Some entrepreneurs keep proposing their projects until a mistake is made: if this happens, permission has to be given.)

FIG 8-6 **KÖLN AND ITS NINE DISTRICTS SHOWING THE LOCATION OF RETAIL UNITS WITH MORE THAN 10,000m² OF SALES FLOORSPACE**
Source: Hermanns and Nerhoff (1982)

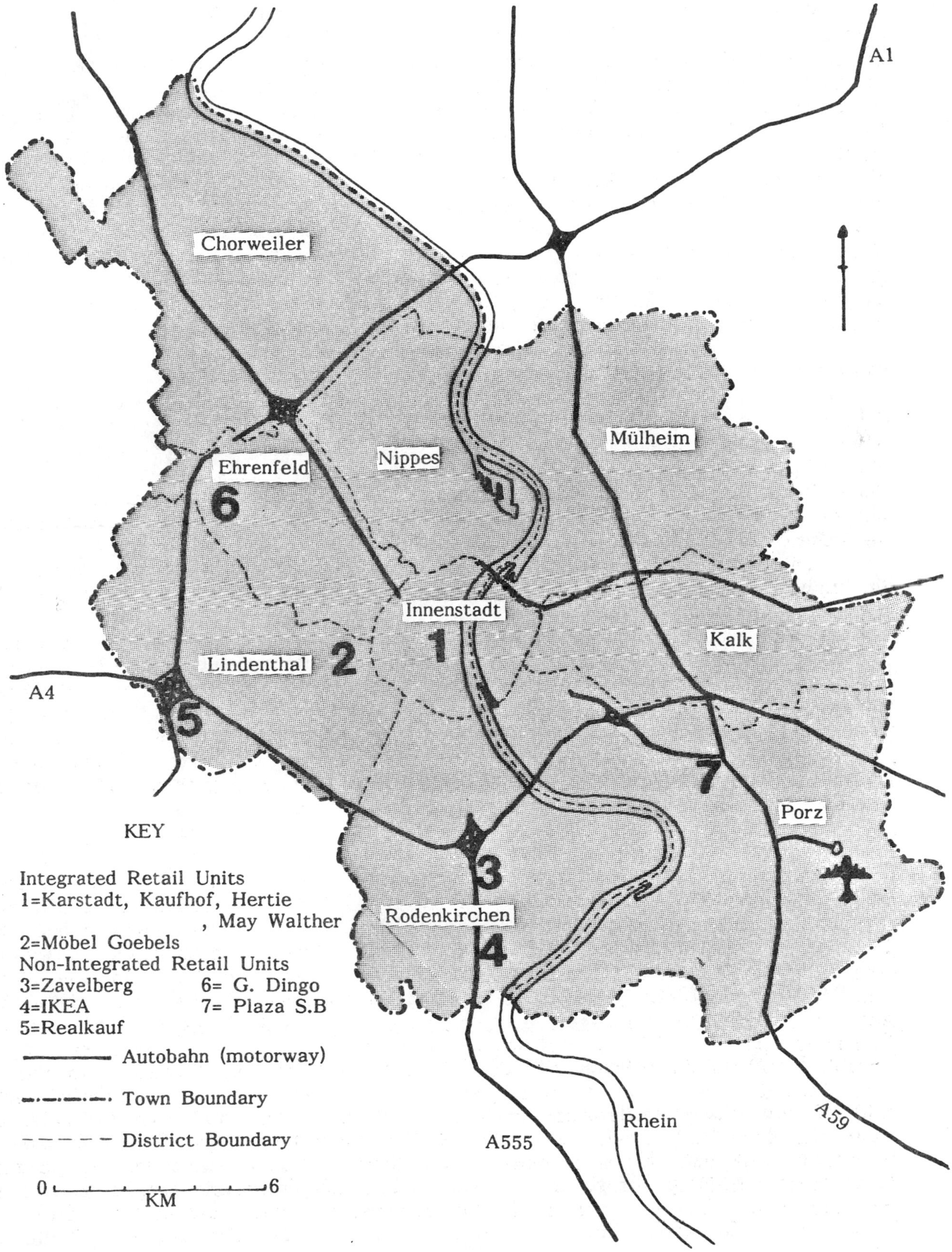

A1

Chorweiler

Ehrenfeld

6

Nippes

Mülheim

Innenstadt

Kalk

Lindenthal

2

1

A4

5

7

Porz

KEY

Integrated Retail Units
1=Karstadt, Kaufhof, Hertie
                  , May Walther
2=Möbel Goebels
Non-Integrated Retail Units
3=Zavelberg   6= G. Dingo
4=IKEA   7= Plaza S.B
5=Realkauf

Rodenkirchen

3

4

——————— Autobahn (motorway)

—··—··—· Town Boundary

— — — — District Boundary

0 |⌐———————————¬| 6
          KM

Rhein

A555

A59

177

THE CITY'S STRUCTURE AND RETAIL HIERARCHY

8-19

Figure 8-6 shows the City and its 9 Districts. Districts 2 and 3 do not have established District Centres while Districts 6 and 7 which do have them are designated as having good prospects for growth. The city centre still contains the largest shopping developments, with 93 300 m^2 in four retail units, each larger than 10 000 m^2. More information about these is given in Table 8-8. As well as the District Centres, Figure 8-6 shows the 'non-integrated' centres. Both types of centre may include retail warehouses, hypermarkets, superstores and supermarkets. It is interesting to consider the make-up of each district outside the city centre. Köln 2 Rodenkirchen has two middle-sized local centres and one non-integrated centre near the city boundary. Köln 3 Lindenthal has five middle-sized local centres and one non-integrated centre (see paras 8-26 and 8-27). Köln 4 Ehrenfeld has a main centre with integrated retail warehousing, a middle-sized centre and a non-integrated centre. Köln 5 Nippes has a main district centre with integrated retail warehousing. Köln 6 Chorweiler has a district centre 'with good prospects' and some integrated, smaller retail warehouses (see para 8-29). Köln 7 Porz has another district centre 'with good prospects', and a non-integrated centre (see para 8-28); the Köln-Bonn Airport is also in this District. Köln 8 Kalk has a main district centre. Köln 9 Mülheim has a main district centre with nearby retail warehouses, and a middle-sized centre. From this point on, only the District number is used.

8-20

The relative importance of Köln's 9 Districts, in retail terms, can be seen from the HGZ:

Table 8-7 : HGZT (gross floorspace) details of Köln's 9 Districts

District	Outlets 1985	Employees 1985	Gross Floorspace 1000 m2 1979	1985	% change	Turnover 1984 1000DM
1	2091	16636	681	721	6	3726385
2	554	2624	106	146	27	615043
3	943	4584	206	217	5	947061
4	623	3460	162	228	41	782354
5	569	2934	135	184	36	666297
6	259	1278	63	71	13	256781
7	455	2756	125	187	50	670410
8	548	2569	102	135	32	530494
9	750	3652	164	185	13	730515
All	6792	40493	1744	2074	19	8925340

Source: Hermanns & Nehrhoff 1982, 1988

The only comparable data 1978/9 to 1984/5 are for gross floorspace in these authors' publication. Outlets, employees and turnover are for *Ladengeschäfte* in 1978/9 and for all retail trade in 1984/5. There remains an unaccountable difference of DM18m for the whole of Köln between this Table and Table 8-4.

In six years the gross floorspace increased by 19% for the whole of Köln. The city centre (District 1) performed worse than the city mean.

8-21
The first large shopping centres were developed within Köln's borders. Those larger than 10 000 m^2 are listed in Table 8-8. Each is located on Figure 8-6 and it is interesting to note which are integrated (with existing shopping facilities) and which are not. Those in Köln 1 are all within the City Centre. In District 2, IKEA and Zavelberg are both not integrated. In District 3, M Goebels is integrated while Realkauf is not. In District 4 G Dinger is not integrated, neither is Plaza SB in District 7.

Table 8-8 : Retail Units in Köln with more than 10 000 m^2 of sales floorspace

District	Name	Size m^2	Year	Type
1	Karstadt	39 000	1963/72/83	Department store
1	Kaufhof	30 600	1891/1974	Department store
1	Hertie	14 300	1957/1965	Department store
1	May Walther	10 000	1936	Furniture warehouse
2	IKEA	15 100	1975	Furniture warehouse
2	Zavelberg	20 800	1970	Garden centre
3	Möbel Goebels	24 000	1962/1983	Furniture warehouse
3	Realkauf	13 000	1965	Hypermarket
4	G Dinger	10 000	1960	Garden centre
7	Plaza SB	14 773	1968	Hypermarket

Source: IHK zu Köln 1984

The City Centre (Köln 1)

8-22
Köln has always been an important centre of commerce and retailing. Its main shopping street, the Hohe Straße, is known to have been the main shopping centre even of the Roman town. It has long had a reputation as one of the most exclusive shopping streets in Germany, only comparable to the Zeil in Frankfurt or the Jungferstieg in Hamburg. The street was closed to wheeled traffic because of its narrowness. After the second world war it was again closed to vehicular traffic, its pedestrianisation then being seen as counteracting the new shopping developments taking place in the hinterland. Hermanns (1981) provides much information on the changes that have taken place in the Hohe Straße in recent years. During the 1970s, trading down of retailing in both the Hohe Straße and the Schildergasse occurred: it affected both the quality and the range of goods.

8-23
Trading down was expressed in a wave of sex shops, peepshows, etc, but discount shops also opened, selling cheap clothing, shoes and drugstore goods. A further manifestation of trading down was the fast food chain. In the 'old days' Hohe Straße and the city centre generally contained high quality cafés and restaurants; some moved out in the 1970s and were replaced by fast food outlets. Amusement arcades were added. Sex shops, discount stores, fast food and amusement arcades can all pay more rent than the traditional shops they replace, while eroding a street's character. The city centre's decline was summed up in the phrase 'one does not go into the city to buy something special.'

8-24

A significant reason for decline of the city centre was the expansion of retailing in the hinterland, which had been supported in the past by local government and the chamber of commerce. Writing in 1981, Hermanns noted that what used to be spent in the city centre was then spent in outer retail locations (though this needs to be qualified: Busse et al [1986] show that Köln's **Inner** City lost 20% of its population 1939-1985, while Hamburg lost 32% and Hannover 31%. This suggests that Köln has held more of its immediate catchment than some other cities). Hermanns further noted that Köln's city centre not only suffered from retail expansion at the edge of the city. The range of goods in the city centre was very often replicated in other retail centres; in his view there was not enough parking in the city centre, and vehicles were 'traffic-calmed' which he also did not approve. The old pedestrianised areas of the centre had become dated and needed reviving. And finally investment in large city centre projects was needed - other cities had done it.

8-25

From 1983 onwards Köln's city centre changed again. This followed from a number of events in which the Chamber of Commerce was vitally involved:

* enlargement of the pedestrianised area beyond the shopping streets to include large parts of the historic city centre
* creation of a traffic-free river bank by sinking the road and covering it
* construction of a new museum close to the station in the middle of the city centre; promotion of cultural activities in the city centre
* new initiatives by retailers, for example the Kölner Bazaar, arcades that are connected with existing pedestrianised areas
* refurbishment of established pedestrian streets - eg the Schildergasse - more style and the creation of better urban spaces
* new regulations controlling sex shops
* construction of new hotels and offices in the city centre.

Large Retail Developments in Köln excluding the City Centre

8-26

The first of the new form of hypermarket (*SB Warenhaus*) was built in Köln 3 in 1965 with about 13 000 m^2 net retail floorspace - it is called Realkauf, and is located at the junction of the A1 and A4 motorways. Köln 3 had already attracted a furniture shop in 1962 which expanded to 24 000 m^2 in 1983. A cluster of other shops developed around the furniture warehouse within easy reach of the B55 road; by 1982 the total net floorspace had reached 31 200 m^2 (IHK 1984), and a smaller cluster developed around the Realkauf hypermarket bringing its total net floorspace to 19 800 m^2.

8-27

Brandenburg (1985) discusses the Weiden Shopping Centre, and the Toom superstore, also in Köln 3 (see Figure 8-9). The Weiden centre is at the western end of the B55 within Köln 3, about 1 km from the A1. A planned S-Bahn station is 500m away and there are several bus stops. The Weiden centre, of 6 470 m^2, opened in 1972, 15 000 people live within a radius of 1 km, and the District has one of the highest population growths in Köln. The housing is of relatively high quality with purchasing power 20-30% above the Federal average. It has a high percentage of civil servants and a low percentage of lower-paid workers and self-employed people. The Toom superstore, of 4 300 m^2 is adjacent to Realkauf and included in the cluster around Realkauf described in the last paragraph. It is located in an industrial area, close to the motorway cross A1-A4, about 1 km from the housing in Junkersdorf and 2.5 km from the town of Frechen - which has another superstore. Junkersdorf is an exclusive housing area whose population has substantially increased since 1961. In 1981 it had 8 497 inhabitants.

FIG 8-9   DIAGRAMMATIC   MAP OF KÖLN 3 LINDENTHAL

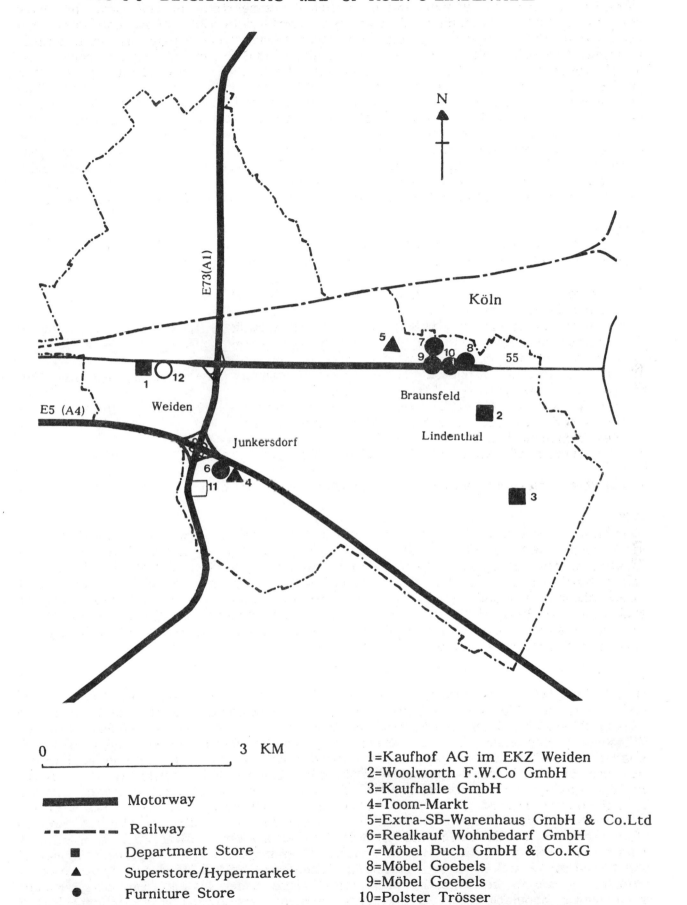

0   3 KM

━━━━━━━   Motorway

━·━·━·━   Railway

■   Department Store

▲   Superstore/Hypermarket

●   Furniture Store

□   DIY Store

○   Other large developments

1=Kaufhof AG im EKZ Weiden
2=Woolworth F.W.Co GmbH
3=Kaufhalle GmbH
4=Toom-Markt
5=Extra-SB-Warenhaus GmbH & Co.Ltd
6=Realkauf Wohnbedarf GmbH
7=Möbel Buch GmbH & Co.KG
8=Möbel Goebels
9=Möbel Goebels
10=Polster Trösser
11=Raab Karcher.Fliesenhandel
12=Wehmeyer im EKZ Weiden

181

8-28

The second of the large new hypermarkets opened in Köln 7 in 1968 with about 15 000 m^2 (Plaza SB). In 1973 a 7 500 m^2 furniture store opened close to Plaza, and Plaza garden centre of 8 500 m^2 opened two years later. By then the cluster had risen to 32 723 m^2 of net floorspace. These stores have another ideal location, close to the junction of the A59 with the B8.

8-29

In Chorweiler, Köln 6, a shopping centre opened within the town centre. It was planned in 1967 in connexion with a new housing estate for 92 000 people, later reduced to 80 000. The proposal was agreed with the Chamber of Commerce and the *Handwerkskammer*. A two-storey shopping centre with 28 000 m^2 gross floorspace was built, with connexions to S-Bahn and light rail stations. Some other shops were added so the new centre attained a total gross floorspace of 33 700 m^2 in 1976, when the main shopping centre opened (Hermanns 1976). The main shops consisted of a department store with nearly 11 000 m^2 + a superstore of 3 300 m^2.

8-30

The pressure to open new shops has been consistently strong over the years as can be seen from the Tables below. The tendency has been toward smaller (1 000-1 500 m^2) units.

Table 8-10 : Proposed Large Retail Units for Köln 1976 to 1987

Year	Number proposed	Total m^2 net floorspace	Average size of unit m^2
1976	2	15 500	7 750
1977	5	31 200	6 240
1978	21	105 600	5 029
1979	27	48 500	1 796
1980	8	9 200	1 150
1981	12	25 000	2 083
1982	18	37 600	2 089
1983	15	42 500	2 833
1984	23	64 100	2 787
1985	43	110 900	2 579
1986	35	63 000	1 800
1987 to 21.7.87	22	34 800	1 582

The average size of all proposals over the time period was 3 143 m^2
Source: Information from the Urban Development Office

The Table shows there has been no weakening in the number of large retail units proposed after 1977 and 1986, the years when changes in the BauNVO restricted locational potential of such stores (Chapter 6). As Federally, the average size of unit proposed reduced considerably from 7 750 to 1 582 m^2 of net floorspace. This is probably because of a combination of the restrictions on out-of-town development, and the scarcity of suitable sites within the total city.

8-31

Proposals are shown in more detail for three Köln Districts - 1 City, 5 Nippes, and 7 Porz - in Tables 8-11/8-13 below. These show 35% of the proposals in Table 8-10. Table 8-11 shows that 66% of applications were approved, representing 59% of the floor area requested. These are higher than for Köln 5 or 7 below, but are to be expected in a City Centre under attack from outlying, and out-of-town, shopping centres. However, there were far fewer applications for additions to the City Centre than to the other two Districts.

Table 8-11 : Proposed Large Retail Units for Köln's City Centre 1978-1987

Year (year area)	Number	Net floor-space m^2	Agreed	Not agreed	Type
1978	1	3 000		x	W
1979	1	5 000	x		SH
1980	1	935		x	F
1982	5	600Estimated	x		H
(9 200)		4 000		x	W
		2 000	x		S
		1 500	x		S
		1 100		x	S
1983	1	4 000	x		W
1985	2	4 400		x	H
(4 830)		430	x		F
1986	1	400E		x	S
1987	3	800	x		S
(5 100)		4 000	x		S
		300E	x		S
Totals 10 agreed of 19 030 m^2; 5 not agreed of 13 435 m^2					

Tables 8-11/13: E=enlargements; H=hobby market, garden centre, DIY; F=retail warehouse, furniture, fabrics, etc; W = department store, specialised shops, others; S = supermarkets, superstores, hypermarkets. Two 'x's mean Planning Department rejected a proposal, but the *Bauaufsichtsamt* agreed to it

Table 8-12 : Proposed Large Retail Units for Köln 5, Nippes 1978-1987

Year (year total)	Number	Net floor-space m^2	Agreed	Not agreed	Type
1978	2	5 200E		x	F
(9 600)		4 400	x		S
1979	3	2 000		x	H
		2 000		x	S
(4 900)		900	x*	x*	S
1982	3	1 000	x	x	S
		2 000	x	x	H
(7 000)		4 000		x	S
1983	2	3 500		x	S/H
(6 000)		2 500	x	x	?
1984	2	6 200	x		H
(10 400)		4 200		x	S
1985	2	1 000		x	S
(1 980)		980	x		S
1986	3	1 000	x		S
		3 700		x	W
(5 200)		500E	x	x	?
1987	2	2 200		x	W
(6 200)		4 000		x	H
Totals: 9 agreed of 19 480 m^2 (this would have been 4 of 12 580 m^2 without *Bauaufsichtsamt* intervention); 10 not agreed of 31 800 m^2					

Table 8-13 : Proposed Large Retail Units for Köln 7, Porz 1978-87

Year (year total)	Number	Net floor-space m^2	Agreed	Not agreed	Type
1978	5	3 500		x	S
		8 500		x	S
		2 500		x	W
		1 200		x	S
(16 700)		1 000		x	F
1979	4	4 500		x	F
		1 350		x	F
		1 000	?		F
(10 650)		3 800	?		S
1980	1	2 000E		x	W
1981	4	1 150	x		S
(14 850)		1 000E		x	H
		700	x		S
		12 000		x	W
1982	6	600	x		S
(10 150)		800	x		W
		900	x		S
		1 000	x		S
		6 000		x	F
		850E		x	W
1983	3	900	x		S
(4 100)		1 000	x		S
		1 200)	x	x	H
		1 000)		x	I
1984	4	1 200E	x		F
(24 270)		1 100	x		F
		1 270	x		W
		20 000		x	W
1985	9	15 000		x	W
(25 350)		1 000		x	S
		700		x	S
		1 500		x	W
		1 500E		x	W
		1 500		x	W
		1 300	x		W
		850		x	S
		2 000		x	H
1986	4	1 000		x	S
(9 800)		6 300	x3 300	x	H
		1 000	x		S
		1 500		x	S
1987	3	600	x		S
(2 200)		800		x	S
		800		x	H

Totals: 16 agreed of 18 020 m^2; 26 not agreed of 96 550 m^2

Of the three Districts examined, Porz was most successful in countering over-development, having had by far the greatest number (and area) of applications. Of those with clear decisions, 38% were approved, representing 15.7% of the applied-for floor area. Perhaps there was a strong desire to protect the attractive District centre.

8-32
Tables 8-12 and 8-13 are on the previous pages. Table 8-12 concerns Nippes, Köln 5. This District is north of the City Centre, west of the Rhine, and consists of 7 sub-districts and their sub-centres (Nippes, Mauenheim, Riehl, Niehl, Weidenpesch, Longerich, Bilderstöckchen). Its high density population was 117 587 in 1976 and 114 098 in 1984. The sub-district of Nippes could be described as an inner city area, a mixture of housing and manufacturing industries. This sub-district, located on Neußerstraße, expanded its net floor area from 20 400 m^2 in 1976 to 23 130 m^2 in 1983 (a fuller analysis of changes of this nature for all Köln's Districts may be found in Figure 8-16). Most of the other sub-districts used to be villages, and their enlargement started largely in the 1920s and 1930s. Niehl has had Ford car manufacturing since 1930.

8-33
The third of this set of Tables (8-13) is about Porz, Köln 7. It is located south of the city centre on the east side of the Rhine and has good light rail connexions with the city centre. The Köln-Bonn airport is within its area. The main shopping centre has been pedestrianised and is regarded as the most attractive shopping centre outside the city centre. The main attraction is a Karstadt department store of 6 000 m^2 net floorspace. There are many shops selling exclusive and luxury goods.

Conflict: Köln Mülheim

8-34
Mülheim (Köln 9) is situated east of the Rhine opposite Nippes. An old industrial area of 17 500 m^2 became available. Some private investors suggested a new shopping centre should be built with about 35 000 m^2, including a hypermarket with 9 000 m^2. Several large entrepreneurs were asked whether they would be interested - Karstadt, Allkauf etc. However, when the plan became known in 1986, protest rose from all sides. It was feared that such a centre would not only have negative effects on the district's traditional shopping centre, but also on the city centre, and on the towns of Leverkusen and Bergisch Gladbach. The protest was so vehement that all political parties agreed not to support a new shopping centre, and as a result the investor very quickly lost interest.

Changes in Köln's Local Centres

8-35
Köln, like most other medium to large cities, has many traditional sub-centres usually located on a local 'High Street'. The more important ones have a department store, and some now have superstores, hypermarkets, and discount furniture stores. Some attempt to portray these local centres may be found in Table 8-14 on the next page. Note that all of this section on local centres excludes the 'City' or CBD of Köln. The centres with Department Stores are shown, and District 9, Mülheim, has an *SB-Warenhaus* or hypermarket. Stores in the 500-999 m^2 bracket tend to be supermarkets, Woolworths, etc.

It can be seen that the majority of local centres are traditional High Streets at the core of a small network of shopping streets. Some have new large stores integrated with existing shops. Some are pedestrianised. One is the cluster of new large stores located at a motorway cross.

As might be expected, stores under 1 000 m^2 predominate, but there are 11 over 3 000m^2. Four Department Store firms are represented, though two Districts do not have one in their traditional centre (Köln 1 has many in the City Centre, not included here).

Table 8-14 : Characteristics of some of Köln's Local Centres

District/location/type		Dept.Store?	\multicolumn{4}{c}{No. of stores, of nett floorspace, m^2}			
			500-999	1000-2999	3000-4999	5000 +
1 Bonner/Sev.str.	1		4	3		
Neusser Str	1		6	3	1	
2 Rodenkirchen	2				1	
Zollstock	1		6			
3 Sülz/Lindenthal	1		5			
Sülz/Klettenberg	1		2	5		
Weiden	2	Kaufhof	5	2		1
Braunsfeld	1		3	4 >1000, no size given		
Lindenthal/Düren.	3		2	2		
4 Subbelratherstr.	1		2			
Venloer Str.	1	Kaufhalle	5	6		1
5 Weidenpesch	4	Globus	4		1	
Nippes Neußer Str	4	Kaufhof Kaufhalle	7	3	1	
6 Chorweiler	5	Karstadt	2	2		1
7 Porz	2	Karstadt	3			1
8 Kalk	1	Kaufhof	5	3		1
9 Dellbrück	1		5	1		
Mülheim	2		6	2	1	1

Key to type: 1 Two or more linked traditional shopping streets; 2 As 1, with an additional large store site; 3 Two traditional streets forming an L-shape; 4 Two or more separate, but adjacent, streets; 5 New shopping centre
Source: Amt für Standtentwicklungsplanung Stadt Köln

8-36
Table 8-15 shows the seven cases (of those on Figure 8-16) where most of the data are available for comparison between 1976 and 1983.

In each column, the amount in brackets beneath the two years is the percent change over those years. The Table shows that the District Sub-Centres for which there are adequate data increased their net floorspace between 11% and 26% (a mean of 15.1%) between 1976 and 1983. There is no clear pattern of change in the amount of floorspace devoted to convenience goods, though the four cases' floorspace devoted to comparison goods increased by a mean of 26.1%. The final two columns show a mean reduction in sales floorspace for convenience goods of -3.2% over the period. However, this smooths out the extremes - Rodenkirchen and Kalk each lost 13% and Sülz 9%, while Zollstock gained 10%. Figure 8-16 shows, for each sub-centre of Köln's 9 Districts, the net floorspace, and the proportion of convenience and comparison goods sold there, where it is possible to compare these data between 1976 and 1983. Source for Table 8-15 and Figure 8-16 is *Amt für Stadtentwicklungsplanung Stadt Köln*.

8-37
It is possible that the losses in Table 8-15, from sub-centres which are mainly traditional 'High Streets', were the gains of superstores or hypermarkets elsewhere in the District, in Köln as a whole, or in areas surrounding Köln, though it would be very difficult to corroborate this. As we have seen in Chapter 6, retail turnover, overall and in real terms, has been nearly static 1978 to 1984. But convenience goods turnover increased in real terms while comparison goods turnover declined, nationwide. Nevertheless, decline in a local centre may have been attributable to a preponderance of comparison goods

186

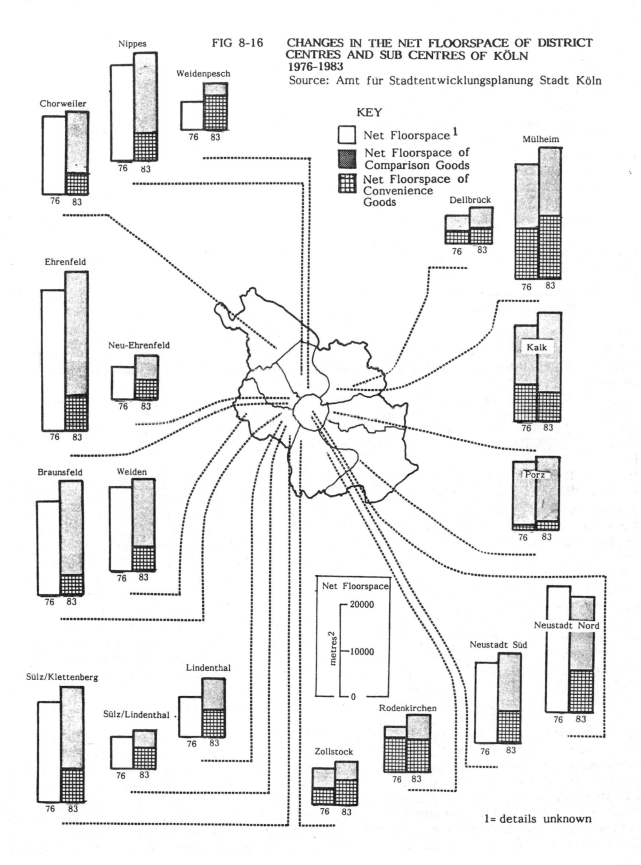

FIG 8-16 CHANGES IN THE NET FLOORSPACE OF DISTRICT CENTRES AND SUB CENTRES OF KÖLN 1976-1983

Source: Amt für Stadtentwicklungsplanung Stadt Köln

KEY

Net Floorspace [1]

Net Floorspace of Comparison Goods

Net Floorspace of Convenience Goods

1= details unknown

187

floorspace, while the reverse may have been true for convenience goods.

Table 8-15 : Sub-Centre Floorspace and Turnover Changes in Köln 1976 to 1983

District & Place	Net floorspace 1000 m^2		Convenience 1000 m^2		Comparison 1000 m^2		Convenience: Comparison %	
	1976	1983	1976	1983	1976	1983	1976	1983
2 Rodenkirchen	10.7	12.3	7.8	7.3	2.9	4.9	73:27	60:40
	(15)		(-5)		(68)			
Zollstock	8.0	9.3					47:53	57:43
	(16)							
3 Sülz/Lindenthal	7.0	8.8					64:36	55:45
	(26)							
7 Porz	14.6	16.9	1.2	2.2	13.3	14.7	9:91	13:87
	(16)		(80)		(10)			
8 Kalk	20.4	23.4	8.0	6.6	12.3	16.8	40:60	27:73
	(15)		(-18)		(37)			
9 Dellbrück Haupt.	6.9	8.0	2.8	3.3	4.1	4.7	40:60	42:58
	(16)		(18)		(14)			
Buchheimer Str	24.4	27.2					45:55	50:50
	(11)							

THE ROLE OF TRANSPORT

8-38
Table 8-17 shows public transport access to (mainly) department stores.

Table 8-17 : Percent using Public Transport to Reach Mainly Department Stores
Ranked by 1984 Weekday Percentage

City	Day	1976	1980	1984
München	Saturday	59	67	62
	Weekdays	73	76	73
Hamburg	Saturday	50	53	52
	Weekdays	66	70	67
Stuttgart	Saturday	30	47	46
	Weekdays	50	63	62
Hannover	Saturday	39	43	41
	Weekdays	57	50	54
Essen	Saturday	30	38	38
	Weekdays	43	54	52
Bremen	Saturday	39	40	35
	Weekdays	57	56	52
Köln	**Saturday**	**30**	**40**	**39**
	Weekdays	**47**	**52**	**45**
Düsseldorf	Saturday	37	37	33
	Weekdays	48	41	41
Dortmund	Saturday	26	31	27
	Weekdays	40	44	39
Duisburg	Saturday	33	25	24
	Weekdays	42	37	31

The Table (source: BAG 1985) only shows the proportion using public transport. Köln, with one of the less-sophisticated public transport systems (no U-Bahn, S-Bahn a late developer in comparison with other German city-regions, but an effective light-rail system) has among the lowest proportions of public transport use - though not as low as Dortmund.

In nearly all cases 1980 was the peak year with some deterioration after that, though often 1984 is an improvement on 1976. Köln is one of the poorer performers. As noted in Chapter 7, bearing in mind that Table 8-17 largely concerns department stores, which usually have substantial car parking of their own on the premises, and that many of these stores are in new out-of-centre shopping centres which also have substantial car parking, it is likely that public transport access to traditional 'High Street' stores will be at a rather higher level.

8-39
The full modal split for Köln, from the BAG surveys, is shown in Table 8-18:

Table 8-18 : Shopping Trips to the City Centre from Outside, and to District Shopping Centres, 1980 and 1984, column percent

| Mode | To City Centre | | | | To District Centres | |
| | 1980 | | 1984 | | 1980 | 1984 |
	Friday	Saturday	Friday	Saturday		
Car	32.7	44.9	43.4	51.7	33.0	34.0
Public transport	52.6	40.8	42.7	36.4	19.3	19.5
Motor/Bicycle	2.7	dk	2.4	dk	5.6	4.8
Foot	11.2	11.0	9.9	6.4	41.6	41.5
Park and ride	dk	1.6	dk	dk	dk	dk

Source: BAG Untersuchung Kundenverkehr Köln (not officially published)

City centre travel on Fridays showed a substantial increase in car use 1980-84. There was a lesser increase on Saturdays. These increases were partly at the expense of public transport, and partly those who walked all the way. Public transport reduced less on the Saturday. For the district centres the modal split was relatively stable over the four years.

8-40
The 1982 Kontiv research by Socialdata (1986/87) reinforced views about car use - 43.1% of all means of transport for Köln and 53.3% for the hinterland. This compared with car use in Hannover of 31%, München 40% and Stuttgart 44%.

CONCLUSIONS

8-41
While the Chamber of Commerce has maintained a strong grip on retail developments within its area, nevertheless a substantial number has been built. Demand for retail space is as high in the mid-1980s as it has ever been: even though the 1977 and 1986 amendments to the BauNVO have significantly contributed to the reduced size of proposed new stores (from an average size of 7 750 m^2 in 1976 to 1 582 m^2 in the first half of 1987). In the Köln-Bonn Region shopping developments are more evident within the three cities (including Leverkusen) than in the *Kreise* surrounding them. Another is the dominance of Köln's CBD: it has maintained and modestly enlarged its retail floorspace, added to its department stores, pedestrianised extensively, and the Chamber of

Commerce has also encouraged cultural enhancement (a new museum was opened recently) as part of the concept of a multi-activity city centre. Köln's Inner City lost less population to the Outer City (-20% in 45 years) than did Hamburg (-32%) or Hannover (-31%), which also helped maintain the City Centre's viability.

8-42

The third important characteristic is the control and selectivity exerted over those wishing to develop within the nine Districts of Köln. Between 1978 and 1987 in the City Centre an additional 19 000 m^2 of large retail units was approved, and 13 000 m^2 refused. In Köln 5 over the same period 19 000 m^2 were approved and 32 000 m^2 refused (and 7 000 m^2 of the approved total had been rejected by the City, but overruled by the Land). In Köln 7, with a very attractive pedestrianised District Centre, out of 9 proposals 1978 to 1981 only one was approved.

8-43

Köln is efficient in retailing. In 1985 it had less employees per outlet than the Federal Republic, Bonn and Leverkusen, and (in 1984) the highest turnover per employee of those places. In terms of turnover per outlet it ranked third of those four places. The Rhein-Sieg-Kreis, immediately southeast of Köln, has grown rapidly to be a competitor of Köln in several respects. Its population grew 61% 1961 to 1987, while Köln's rose and fell to be similar in 1987 to 1961. By 1985 Rhein-Sieg-Kreis had nearly half as much gross floorspace as did Köln (it had less than one quarter in 1968), and its turnover grew from about one tenth that of Köln in 1967 to more than one third in 1984. Immediately northeast, Leverkusen's retail capability (floorspace and turnover) has grown more rapidly than Köln or Bonn. Its numbers of outlets and of employees have grown while those of Köln and Bonn have declined.

8-44

However, without its powerful Chamber of Commerce there is little doubt that Köln's trading position would be much worse. Like many other cities, a certain number of improvements in retailing have to be (and should be) allowed. But control is not finely balanced, and the most likely outcome is that more new retailing premises will be permitted - because there are inadequate reasons for refusing them - than might be considered necessary. Then changes in the law, or a powerful Chamber of Commerce, emerge to reintroduce checks and balances. The main function of this case study has been to show that Köln has been more successful than most cities in achieving a rough balance between the satisfaction of need and greed. This is evident from the trading figures: Köln experienced a decrease in turnover 1978 to 1984 of -7.3% in real terms. However, Leverkusen showed -12.2% and Stuttgart -15.6% for that period. Only Bonn did better, but Bonn **is** the Federal capital with large government and diplomatic populations.

REFERENCES

BMBau (1977) **Raumordnungsprognose 1990** No 06.012 Bonn
Busse, Carl-Heinrich et al (1986) **Die Innenstadt: Entwicklungen und Perspektiven** Köln Deutsche Städtetag
Gerhard, BC (1986) Einkaufen: Das Umland lockt in **Markt und Wirtschaft, IHK Köln** No5 pp10-13
Hall, P and C Hass-Klau (1985) **Can Rail Save the City?** Aldershot Gower
HDE (1987) **Statistische Mitteilungen für den Einzelhandel** Special issue January Köln
Hermanns, H (1972) Fußgängerbereiche in Kölner Einkaufstraßen - Sonderdruck aus den **Mitteilungen der Industrie- und Handelskammer zu Köln** pp337-344
- (1976) Neues Einkaufszentrum in Köln-Chorweiler eröffnet in **Mitteilungen** etc as above pp752-754

Hermanns, H and U Nehrhoff (1982) **Die Entwicklung des Einzelhandels im Raum Köln-Bonn** Köln Untersuchung der Planungsstelle Gewerbliche Ansiedlung und Innenstadtsanierung

- (1988) do.

IHK zu Köln (1984) **Handelsatlas Standorte großflächiger Einzelhandelsbetriebe im Bezirk der Industrie-und Handelskammer zu Köln** Köln

ISB (Institut für Selbstbedienung und Warenwirtschaft e.V.)(1986) **SB-Warenhaus Report 1986** Köln

Krockow, Albrecht (1988) Ergebnis der Handels- und Gaststättenzählung 1985 **Wirtschaft und Statistik 1 1988** pp26-32

Markt und Wirtschaft IHK Köln (1986) **Der neue Frühling unserer Städte** No7 pp8-13

Der Minister für Stadtentwicklung, Wohnen und Verkehr des Landes Nordrhein-Westfalen (1986) Einzelhandelsgroßbetriebe und Stadterneuerung in **Kurzinformation No 6** Düsseldorf

Shaw, G (1983) Trends in Consumer Behaviour and Retailing in Wild, T (ed) **Urban and Rural Change in West Germany** London Croom Helm

Socialdata (1986/87) **Gutachten zur Verkehrsentwicklung und zum Verkehrsverhalten in Köln und seinem Umland** Köln

TEST (1988) **Quality Streets** TEST London

191

9 REGENSBURG

SUMMARY

9-01
Regensburg fortunately escaped destruction during the second world war. After the war it had one of the highest population densities in Germany; the population had also increased when accommodating refugees. Urgently needed urban renewal had to balance modern retailing demands with conservation of an historic core, and it was not until 1975 that conservation won, after several historic buildings had been demolished. In that year the whole of the city centre and an area on the north bank of the River became conservation areas. Regensburg shares the same central place level as München and Nürnberg, and is intended to act as a relief for those cities: it lies between them on the Danube.

9-02
64% of the population work in the tertiary sector - the recently-established University brought up the proportion to this level. However, it had a higher unemployment rate (12%) than Bavaria (8%) in 1983; the rate is higher still in the very rural, agriculturally-based, hinterland. The city centre claims about half of the retail turnover of the whole city; nevertheless, retail land use occupies only 20% of the city centre. Regensburg is extraordinary for the residential land use of its city centre, amounting to 49%, including a large area bordering the River and immediately west of the substantially pedestrianised shopping core. The residents and the high quality urban environment have been the greatest constraints on retail expansion; this was futher checked through the city's ownership of much of the land zoned for industry or mixed use - they could then decidc whether they wanted to let new retail developments be built on their own land.

9-03
However, the point was reached where pressures for expansion of the city centre's retail floorspace had to be acknowledged. In 1967, on the other side of the Danube and north east of the city centre, the *Donaueinkaufszentrum* (DEZ) was given planning permission. Initially it had 24 000 m^2 gross floorspace, 10 000 m^2 of which was taken by Quelle, Woolworth and the Coop, and the rest by 54 smaller shops and services. Two expansions have followed, permitted after large stores were also persuaded to expand in the city centre, resulting in DEZ having 56 000 m^2 gross in 1987. Provided the DEZ expansions do not continue to the extent they disturb a balanced relationship with the city centre, the latter has been given a trading security that can be found in few other locations. Regensburg's retail turnover has expanded remarkably, and comparison is made with München, which performed far better than other large cities 1978-1984.

INTRODUCTION

9-04
Regensburg is the only large city of the German medieval period which remains intact; its history can be traced back for nearly 2000 years. During the 12th and 13th centuries, Regensburg was one of the richest and most populous cities in Europe and an extremely important commercial centre. At the beginning of the 19th century it became part of the Kingdom of Bavaria but stayed for decades a poor provincial town. Where other large Bavarian cities more than doubled in population during industrialisation, Regensburg hardly changed (Keßler 1978). The construction of both the Bavarian railway network and a harbour established national and international trading links with Regensburg. It was only after 1850 that the population started slowly to increase. However even in 1850 Regensburg had a population no more than 29 000. It increased to

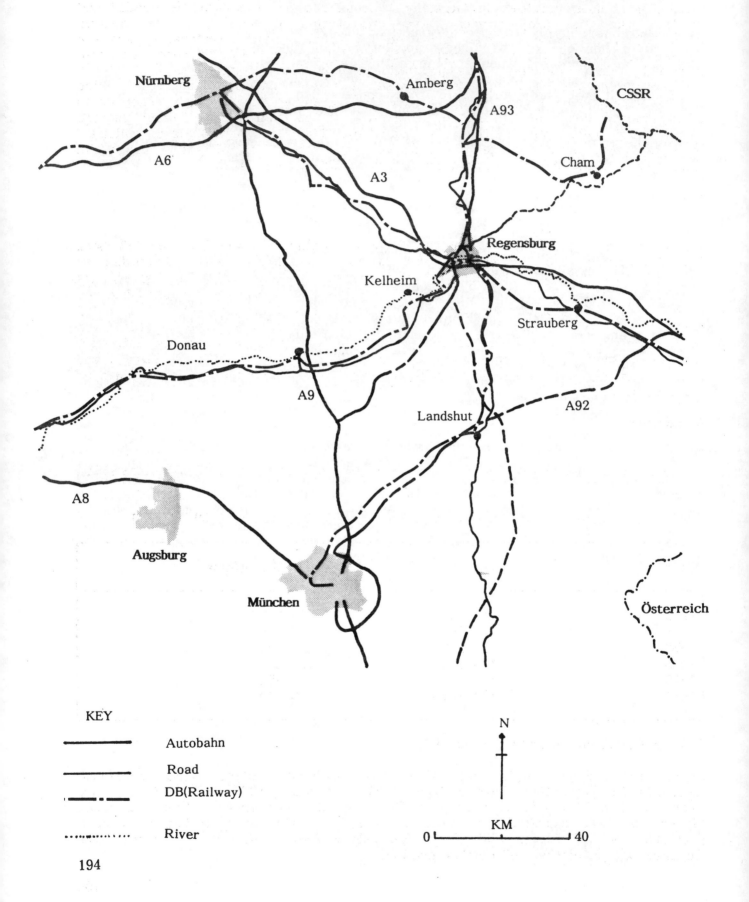

FIG 9-1   **LOCATION OF REGENSBURG**
Source: Stadt Regensburg Stadtplanungsamt

KEY

—————   Autobahn

—————   Road

—·—·—·—   DB(Railway)

·····•·····   River

N

KM
0 ———————— 40

194

95 000 by 1939, partly because the previous year the city had doubled its area. In 1986 its population was 124 000.

9-05
After the second world war the preserved historic city centre had one of the highest population densities in Germany. Urban renewal was urgently needed and in 1955 the first project was started, restoration of housing in the historic core. Conflicts arose between the need for urban renewal, restoration and the modern demands on the city centre. The need for more retailing space was also caused by higher demand - the population had increased largely as a result of refugees from the East, but also because of raised consumer standards. Some fast decisions were made to free space for retailing, such as the construction of a modern department store for Horten. In addition, several other modern shops were built, all at the cost of demolishing valuable historic buildings. It is said that more damage was done to the historic city (*Altstadt*) during the thirty years after 1945 than in several centuries (Steinbauer 1978).

Location

9-06
Regensburg is located in east-central Bavaria, roughly mid-way between Nürnberg (100 km distant) and München (120 km distant - see Figure 9-1). According to the Bavarian land development plan (*Landesentwicklungsplan*), Regensburg has been regarded as a main centre in the central place hierarchy for shopping and other tertiary sector activities. Its function has been to act as a relief centre for Nürnberg and München with whom it shares the same central place level (as does Augsburg), a position which was strengthened when its university was established. The hinterland has no towns of any significant size; the middle-sized Kelheim is 20 km from Regensburg, while the remainder arc 40 km or more distant.

Population

9-07
The change in population of the city and the hinterland (*Landkreis Regensburg*) are shown in Table 9-2:

Table 9-2 : Population of Regensburg and Landkreis Regensburg, 1950 to 1985

Year	Regensburg	Landkreis Regensburg
1950	119 633	104 272
1961	127 343	103 698
1970	133 066	120 290
1975	136 490	130 587
1980	132 604	138 352
1985	124 480	143 649

Source: Regierung Oberpfalz et al 1987

Since 1975 Regensburg's population has declined whereas the hinterland increased its population steadily from 1961. Between 1980 and 1985 the city experienced a considerable decline - 6% - in its population. This was much higher than was expected, for calculations in the land use plan had forecast a population of 127 121 in 1992 (Stadt Regensburg 1981). Now it is expected that Regensburg's population will further decline.

Employment

9-08
Table 9-3 shows Regensburg's city and hinterland employment structure in 1985:

Table 9-3 : Employment in Regensburg and its hinterland, 1985

	Regensburg		Landkreis Regensburg	
	No.	%	No.	%
Agriculture	110	0.2	1 109	5.3
Energy	1 134	1.7	131	0.6
Manufacture	18 177	26.7	9 079	43.0
Construction	4 790	7.1	3 362	15.9
Trade	12 500	18.4	2 424	11.5
Transport	5 664	8.3	495	2.3
Other services	25 599	37.7	4 174	19.8
Total	67 974	100.0	21 118	100.0

Source: as Table 9-2
Note: Because the Table does not include the independent workforce, the actual employment in agriculture is far higher than shown.

Most people in Regensburg work in tertiary activities (64.4%) and 25 000 jobs (about 35% of the total) are located in the city centre.   Manufacturing employment accounts for only about 27% whereas in the hinterland it is as high as 43%.   In economic terms the city and its hinterland have suffered from their location close to the East German and Czech borders.   Regensburg's unemployment rate was 12% in 1983 whereas in Bavaria as a whole it was 8.1%, and in the Federal Republic 9.1% (Stadt Regensburg 1984).   The hinterland is still very rural, agriculture accounting for 24% (1983) and unemployment is even higher than in the city, and very seasonal: in 1986 it varied between 8.8% and 18.3% (Regierung der Oberpfalz 1987).

9-09
The city of Regensburg received new economic incentives from the establishment of a university in 1967.   By 1986 it had about 12 000 students.   Its expansion includes a large university hospital, now being built.   In 1986 the BMW car manufacturer opened a new factory with 3 200 jobs, and the firm of Siemens substantially enlarged two of its plants.   Further economic incentives are expected with the opening of the Rhein-Main-Donau Canal, reconnecting Regensburg with the North and with the Black Sea, though the economic importance of this canal may have been overrated.

THE CITY CENTRE

9-10
Regensburg's city centre (see Figure 9-4) at 284 ha is larger than those of München (208 ha) and Nürnberg (159 ha). In 1983 over 15 000 people were still living there.   Over several decades the city centre experienced a drop in population density.   In 1950 the average density was 97 persons/ha which had declined in 1970 to 69/ha and 54/ha in 1983 (Höller 1978, Stadt Regensburg 1981 and 1984).   Despite this, population density in the city centre remains high in comparison with British city centres (York in 1988 has about 4-5000 inhabitants in its city centre).   In Germany as elsewhere in Europe smaller households, and a general demand for more living space, tend to reduce density. Similarly, it

FIG 9-4 REGENSBURG CITY CENTRE
Source: Stadt Regensburg Stadtplanungsamt

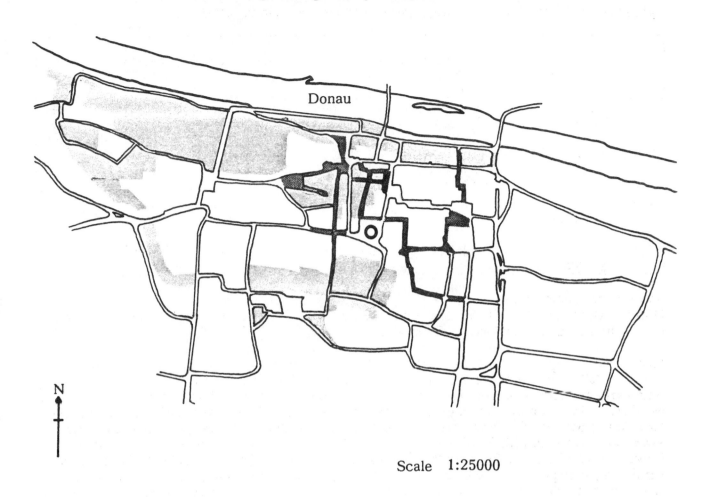

Donau

N

Scale 1:25000

Key

 Residential Land Use

 Pedestrianised Areas

 O Market Area

 DEZ Location

 City Centre

INSET :
DONAUEINKAUFSZENTRUM (DEZ) and
its relationship to the City Centre

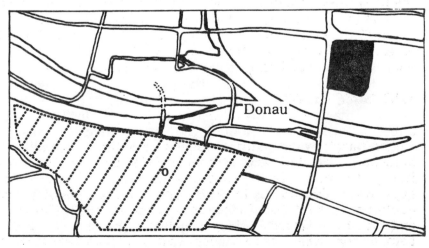

Donau

Scale 1:50000

is expected that Regensburg's city centre density will further decline because of an increased demand for larger flats. A detailed study showed that only about 15% of out-migration from the city centre was caused by a change in land use - change from housing to retail or other tertiary activities - while about 77% moved because they wanted more living space (Höller 1978).

9-11
Retail turnover in the city centre is about half that of the whole city and it has been estimated that the retail net floorspace is 100-120 000 m^2 (Stadt Regensburg 1986). The city centre still encompasses a variety of land uses. While retailing and office use dominate the central core and eastern parts of the city centre, the western part of the centre is primarily housing. The study by Höller (1978) showed that city centre land use has not much changed since the 11th century. Even today, 49% of available space in the city centre is still used residentially while only 20% is for retail use, 23% for public and private services, 3% for handicraft and industries and 5% for 'other'.

City Centre Retail Policy

9-12
The retail centre was historically located close to the Danube. When the railway station opened the centre moved south, closer to it. This change in location solved the modest problem of adding retail space to the city centre. Regensburg was still a small city and its population and employment expansion was very slow: therefore little additional space for retail purposes was required. The outcome of these slow changes was that Regensburg avoided the large-scale demolition of the 19th century in fast-growing cities.

9-13
After the second world war a serious attempt was made to expand retailing in the city centre, to service a substantial increase in population in the city and its hinterland. Such attempts were immediately faced with problems that hardly any other German city had. Its high residential proportion was unique; every house was several centuries old and if pulled down Roman remains were certain to be found - when that happened, archaeologists would delay new building often for several months. Not the ideal conditions for a fast-growing, profit-oriented sector like retailing. During the late 1960s and early 1970s, retailers were supported by a new planning concept which emphasized the importance of the city centre as a place to accommodate the sale of all types of goods, and services, which indirectly implied the creation of the space needed, even at the cost of pushing residents out of the centre. In the past, highest quality goods and specialised services had only been available in München and to an extent in Nürnberg. It soon became evident that making sufficient space available for such retailing and services was unrealistic for Regensburg.

9-14
After some demolition took place, destroying irreplaceable historic monuments, opposition quickly grew: the planning department had to change its objective. It became obvious that restoration of the city centre and preservation of its unique character had to have priority. In 1975, the whole of the city centre and an area opposite on the other side of the Danube (Stadtamhof) became conservation areas, with 1 200 listed buildings (Stadt Regensburg 1981).

9-15
Despite pressure by retail firms, the possibilities of developing any large modern forms of retailing have always been very much restricted in the city centre, because of lack of space. Even so, housing at ground floor level has been converted into retail space. This process was encouraged by the planning department as these flats did not have sufficient light - many streets are narrow and the buildings are tall. With the declaration of a conservation area

large retail changes have become even more difficult. Pressure was released in 1967 when a new modern shopping centre was established northeast of the historic centre. The new centre strengthened Regensburg's overall function as centre for the region, and the new centre has been enlarged several times.

9-16

In places, the city centre's physical character restricts car traffic, helping to protect its historic heritage. Many of the smallest streets have never allowed any car traffic. Large areas of the historic Altstadt are today pedestrianised (see Figure 9-4), but there remain too many parts where car traffic is allowed. Perhaps through traffic is still penetrating the historic city centre because the southerly bypass remains to be built. The traffic situation is worsened by the location of the city centre: few bridges link it to the north, the largest one dating from the 12th century and still open to motorised traffic. Traffic entering the historic city centre from the north visually and physically impairs several major historic monuments including the cathedral.

Retail Structure

9-17

Table 9-5 shows the development of retailing from 1978/79 to 1984/85, in comparison with München. Unlike other German cities, Regensburg showed increases in employment, outlets, gross floorspace and turnover during this time period. The increase in turnover in real terms appears to be very high in comparison with other German cities of similar size. When compared with München, Regensburg shows a much higher growth for all these indicators. It is also interesting to note that the increase in real turnover between the hinterland (44.6%) and the city of Regensburg (32.3%) was not as marked as in most other German cities, or as can be seen in München (9.8%) and its hinterland (64.3%) during the 1978/79 to 1984/85 period. Real turnover growth in both cities is still remarkable when compared with other cities (see para 8-03), and the 'poorer' achievement of München may simply relate to its much higher base.

Table 9-5 : Retailing in Regensburg, München and their Hinterlands

	City of Regensburg			Landkreis Regensburg		
	1978/9	1984/5	% change	1978/9	1984/5	% change
Employment	7 030	7 897	12.3	1 701	2 433	43.0
Outlets	842	1 046	24.2	587	792	34.9
Gross floorspace	317 000	449 000	41.6	118 000	169 000	43.2
Turnover 000DM	1 066 315	1 651 057	54.8	224 642	410 569	82.8
1984 at 1978 prices		1 306 216	32.3		324 817	44.6
	City of München			Landkreis München		
	1978/9	1984/5	% change	1978/9	1984/5	% change
Employment	59 031	61 899	4.9	4 994	7 397	48.1
Outlets	8 925	10 738	20.3	1 138	1 675	47.2
Gross floorspace	2 248 000	2 782 000	23.8	246 000	421 000	71.2
Turnover 000DM	10 228 586	14 190 528	38.7	876 068	1 819 032	107.6
1984 at 1978 prices		11 226 684	9.8		1 439 108	64.3

Source: Bayerisches Statistisches Landesamt 1981, 1987
Notes: The 1978/9 HGZ only includes outlets with a turnover of DM2 000 and over, while the 1984/5 HGZ includes all outlets. 1978=100, 1984=126.4

9-18
There are many reasons to explain the more equal growth between the hinterland and the city. One of these could be the recent increase in the city's land area (in 1977-78 Oberisling, Burgweinting, Harting and parts of Barbing became parts of Regensburg - Stadt Regensburg 1980). Clearly the opening and subsequent enlargement of the large shopping centre *Donaueinkaufszentrum* (DEZ), and sufficient space close by for other superstores has helped to discourage both large shopping centres in the hinterland, and to keep a substantial part of the purchasing power within Regensburg. The difference in income structure between hinterland (high unemployment, largely agricultural) and city is not as marked as it is in the larger cities like München, as those larger cities generally have a greater degree of suburbanisation of their high income residents.

Retail Policy and its Conflicts

9-19
The main conflicts in Regensburg became apparent after the opening of the DEZ, in relatively close proximity to the city centre, in 1967. This resulted from the initiative of an entrepreneur, Dr Vielberth, and followed a visit to the United States in 1962 from which he brought back the idea of building a covered shopping centre. After three large retailers (Quelle, Woolworth and Coop) agreed to become tenants, the idea went ahead. These three firms had been searching for a suitable city centre location, without success. The DEZ was the first fully air-conditioned shopping centre on two floors in Germany, and it attracted many visitors from all over Germany and Europe. During its first stage the shopping centre opened with about 24 000 m^2 gross floorspace, of which 10 000 m^2 were taken by Quelle while Woolworth and the Coop together rented 6 600 m^2. The rest was subdivided between 54 smaller shops and service sector activities. It took 18 months to rent the smaller units (DEZ 1984).

9-20
In 1970 there were plans to expand the DEZ centre. The department store Kaufhof wanted to move into it, and additional retail space was wanted by other firms. At that time the city of Regensburg had already become aware of the possible impact an enlarged shopping centre would have on retailing in the city centre. While in 1965 permission for the shopping centre was given in three months, in 1974 it took two years to get final approval. Opposition came mainly from retailers in the city centre who feared they would lose out. Only after major firms there - Horten, Benninkmeyer, Wöhrl etc - were willing to expand and invest further in the city centre could the plan go ahead.

9-21
A third expansion was planned and built in 1982/3 to accommodate some of the many firms in the shopping centre who wanted to enlarge. The permitted addition was relatively modest (about 6 000 m^2 plus a large multi-storey car park with space for 3 400 cars). In 1987 the DEZ had 56 000 m^2 gross floorspace, and included 100 retail units and other tertiary activities. In total, 22 000 people were employed. Activities in the shopping centre also include exhibitions and other cultural events. The design is attractive, there are many places to rest and the restaurants and cafés are of a high standard. There are plans for further expansion and there is no doubt the DEZ shopping centre has become the second main retail centre in Regensburg after the city centre. Another reason for this is that superstores and retail warehouses located in close proximity to the DEZ, in what had been designated an industrial area (*Gewerbepark*). For many it has become the main shopping centre as a survey has shown - only 30% of DEZ shoppers also visited the city centre (DEZ 1984).

9-22
Several retail warehouses and other new forms of retailing have settled next to the DEZ, and another shopping centre (the Alex Centre) has opened. The follow-

ing list shows the extent of retail settlement next to the DEZ:

* superstore 3 000 m^2, expanded in 1985 to 3 700 m^2
* in 1977 two furniture stores with about 3 176 m^2 net floorspace
* in 1979 the Alex Centre, a shopping centre with a DIY warehouse, textiles, café, bank, food store, drug store - totalling 13 500 m^2 net floorspace
* in 1982, an 800 m^2 net floorspace Aldi foodstore
* BLV (*Bayerische Lager Versorgung*) furniture and DIY store of 3 059 m^2 net and 6 759 m^2 gross floorspace.

The total net floorspace of the DEZ and the other retail stores in the Gewerbepark account for about half the available floorspace in the city centre. Finally, apart from the Gewerbepark, a new superstore (Neukauf) with 5 600 m^2 net floorspace, opened in 1975 southeast of Regensburg next to the B15 major road.

9-23
The land use plan of 1983 made it clear that no further space would be available for large-scale retailing in the city, though the demand is still very high. By and large the city of Regensburg has been rather restrictive in giving permission for new retail developments and/or expansions. If the policy against new shopping centres or other forms of retailing had not been so restrictive then the DEZ would have been expanded even further and would really have been a danger for the city centre. One of the most positive features of city centres is that they are not locked up at night or on Sunday like shopping centres or arcades. Thus the 'real life' is still taking place in the city centre. Today Regensburg's city centre appears still to have an attractive assortment of housing, retail outlets, restaurants and other tertiary activities. Some further small expansion in the city centre is possible, but it has to take into account the specific historic environment. A small shopping centre is planned in the western part of the city centre, totalling about 6 000 m^2, at the Arnulfsplatz. A much smaller development is possible in the form of an arcade in the Glockengassenviertel - of 2 100 m^2.

9-24
Regensburg has therefore restricted its space for retailing city-wide: one reason is that it did not designate many areas for industrial use in its land use plan (possibly in the past it was assumed no industries would want to settle there), and furthermore many industrial areas were bought by the city. Therefore the city is flexible and can sell to whom it wants (note the difference from Britain where local authorities are being forced by central government to sell unused land they own). Industrial space is becoming scarce and is used for new industries rather than retailing. There have been protests from new retail chains which want to locate in industrial areas, but the planning department wants them to locate (if anywhere) in residential areas. Often these firms had to learn the hard way. The planning department were in a powerful position: one official said they could work at an extremely slow pace - so slow it would affect the enthusiasm of firms to settle in Regensburg. 'Our working speed is improved considerably when they have agreed to settle where we want them, if we want them here at all.'

9-25
However, this type of policy has another side to it. Small local authorities just outside Regensburg have attracted some new retail investment. In Pentling to the southwest on a motorway intersection a new shopping centre with 3-4 000 m^2 opened in 1973; it was enlarged to 7 600 m^2 in 1986. A further superstore opened in Neutraubling (which has about 10 000 inhabitants) with 20 000 m^2 gross floorspace, about two-thirds of which are used for selling furniture, and one-third for food, shoes and carpets.

CONCLUSIONS

9-26

Regensburg shows best of all the German case studies the conflicts which can occur with new forms of retailing. It also highlights the positive and negative aspects of new retail developments. Regensburg is in many ways a unique case, but even so, many lessons can be learnt from it. Its retailing situation today resulted from a specific historical development, strengthened by the preservation of the city during the second world war. Such continuity introduces its own problems, though - retail expansion is difficult to accommodate, for example.

9-27

Regensburg also demonstrates a mix of land uses in its city centre, a characteristic which has been lost in many other German city centres. Because of its unique historical character it avoided the low quality pedestrianisation which can be found in some other German cities. Expansion of retailing in the other city centres, especially early developments, has often diminished the urban quality of town centres. In the case of Regensburg little expansion was possible despite high demand from retailers and developers. Construction of the DEZ shopping centre was a good solution, in particular because there were few traditional retail sub-centres which could realistically have taken up the demand. The city's policy both to be restrictive yet allow for expansion at a particular location just outside the city centre, appears to have worked very well: its success is shown by the HGZ results in Table 9-5.

9-28

The future of Regensburg's city centre, in terms of retailing, appears to be secure. Expansion outside the city is still possible, but in a relatively limited form. The only threats to Regensburg appear to derive from international tourism causing retail change along the lines experienced in York (see Chapter 5), or from an acceptance of pressure from the DEZ Centre for excessive expansion.

REFERENCES

Donaueinkaufszentrum (DEZ)(1984) **Journal, Information & Unterhaltung, Tips & Termine, Erlebnisse & Ereignisse** Regensburg

Höller, HE (1978) Bedeutung und Grenzen der Bestandsaufnahme für die Erneuerungsplanung historischer Altstädte in R Strobel (ed) **Regensburg: Die Altstadt als Denkmal** München Heinz Moos Verlag

Interview with the City of Regensburg Planning Department, September 1987

Keßler, W (1978) Zur Wirtschaftsgeschichte Regensburg in R Strobel pp 27-36 (see Höller above)

Regierung der Oberpfalz, Regionaler Planungsverband Oberpfalz-Nord, Regionaler Planungsverband Regensburg (1987) **Datenhandbuch Fortschreibung 1986** Regensburg

Stadt Regensburg (1981) **Flächennutzungsplan, Erläuterungsbericht,** Regensburg (the land use plan was officially approved in 1983)
    - (1984?) **Informationen zur Stadtentwicklung, Statistisches Jahrbuch 1982-3**
    - (1986) **Einzelhandelszentrum Arnulfsplatz Projektbeschreibung**

Steinbauer, C (1978) 20 Jahre Altstadtsanierung Regensburg Planung, Durchführung, Ziele in R Strobel pp 17-26 (see Höller above)

10 CROSS-CULTURAL PATTERNS

SUMMARY

10-01

This chapter assembles information about Britain and Germany in order to high-light the two countries' differences and similarities. Information regarding each country's administration, population, and economy is examined first. Next comes an historical comparison of the planning framework designed to highlight structural differences in decision making. Focussing more sharply on retail trends, the chapter examines the relative structures of the retail industry, together with the extent of out-of-centre retail development. Fundamental differences in the importance of particular interests and lobbies are discus-sed. Finally, a range of different town centre strategies is compared to see how local authorities and other interests are responding to the development of out-of-centre retailing. At that point the original hypothesis and objectives of the study are reviewed.

CROSS-CULTURAL COMPARISONS

ADMINISTRATION

10-02

Britain is a constitutional monarchy, with legislative power being passed from the monarch to the leader of the majority party in the House of Commons (the Prime Minister). Parliament consists of 650 elected Members who form the House of Commons, and about 1000 hereditary and life peers and bishops who form the House of Lords. While all legislation is initiated in the House of Commons, the House of Lords has the power to delay all but financial or budgetary matters. Although a limited amount of control has been devolved to Wales, and in particular to Scotland, Parliament remains the supreme decision making body. Welsh and Scottish Offices are the closest that Britain has to any form of regional government. Local government has no such tier, the largest authorities being county councils. Each county is comprised of a number of district councils. Both county and district councils are locally elected. In 1986 the metropolitan county councils were abolished, leaving the largest urban areas without any county level administration, and meaning that decision making is passed to district (or central government) level.

10-03

West Germany is a federal parliamentary democracy. The supreme legislative body is the *Bundestag* (Federal Parliament) which comprises 520 Members who, with the exception of those from West Berlin, are elected by a combination of plurality and proportional representation. The 22 Members from West Berlin are elected by proportional representation only, and have limited voting rights. The Federal Parliament has sole legislative responsibility for foriegn affairs, defence, currency, customs, air transport and the postal system. Education is the responsibility of West Germany's 11 *Länder*, or States. These States form the *Bundesrat*, which must approve about half of the federal laws. The Federal President is elected by the Federal Convention which is formed by all the members of the Federal Parliament together with an equal number of represent-atives of the *Länder*. The President appoints the Federal Chancellor, who selects Ministers to form the Federal Government (The Courier 1988). Below the *Lände* level there are *Regionalverband* bodies who coordinate groups of *Kreise* (county districts) and *kreisfreie Städte* (independent urban areas).

10-04

The most significant conclusion that can be drawn from this comparison is that the West German Government has a far stronger regional emphasis. Thus the *Lände* act as a second house when it comes to many aspects of national legislation. In addition they provide an important regional tier of administration, and help to limit the conflict caused by policies of different *Regionalverband* and *Kreis* governments. In Britain there is no such level of administration. National legislation is determined by Central Government, and counties and districts operate within this context.

POPULATION AND ECONOMY

10-05

In 1983 the UK's population was 56.4 million. With a land area of 244 111 km^2, this gives a population density of 231 persons per km^2. In 1985, West Germany's population was 61.2 million with an area of 246 687 km^2, giving an average density of 246 persons per km^2. While the populations and land areas of Britain and Germany are similar, in economic terms the West German economy is the stronger. While the British per capita gross domestic product stood at ECU 10 509 in 1985, the West German figure was ECU 13 543 (1984 1 ECU = £0.59 or DM 2.2381). The comparative economic strengths of the two countries are reflected in indices such as consumption and car ownership.

Table 10-1 : Private National Consumption Per Head (Purchasing Power Standard)

	GREAT BRITAIN	WEST GERMANY
1975	4 072	4 831
1980	4 456	5 714
1984	4 725	5 790

Note : At 1980 prices
Source : Eurostat 1986

Table 10-1 shows that the gap between British and West German private national consumption has been widening during the last decade, with German consumption running ahead of British. The strength of the German economy is also reflected by higher levels of car ownership, shown in Table 10-2.

Table 10-2 : Car Ownership in Britain and West Germany

	GREAT BRITAIN		WEST GERMANY	
	Cars	Per 1000 popln	Cars	Per 1000 popln
1975	14.0	310	18.0	340
1985	17.3	380	26.0	490

Source : Department of Transport 1987

URBAN STRUCTURE

10-06

The United States has several large cities with two or more 'downtowns'. All large cities have major retail malls on their periphery or in adjacent cities, and some have these in their original CBD. The flight from US centres to the suburbs or beyond has been extensive. Britain and Germany (apart from London

204

and the abnormality of Berlin) remain true to the traditional central city concept. Germany still adheres to the principles of central place theory though it has been distorted with the rather arbitrary location of major new retail centres. Similar things have happened to Britain which has not overtly subscribed to central place theory, even though the hierarchy of its shopping centres clearly reflects the theory.

10-07
Germany has four cities with populations over one million, but none comes anywhere near the population of Greater London. London dominates much of the administration of retailing and its share of the country's turnover is substantial. Until recently however it has not been in the forefront of new retail development, presumably because of its powerful base. One reason for out-of-town retailing demand is the completion of the orbital motorway, the M25.

10-08
London has a complex metro system supplemented by an equally elaborate suburban rail system; it also has one light railway, in Docklands; this is currently being extended and Parliamentary powers are sought for further extensions. There are metros or light rail systems in Glasgow, Tyneside and Liverpool. Birmingham and the West Midlands are remarkably deficient in rail systems considering Birmingham's population of about one million. The larger German cities (Berlin, Hamburg and München) - and Nürnberg with less than 500 000 people - have U-Bahn as well as S-Bahn. Cities in Britain larger than or the same size as Nürnberg, and which rely primarily on deregulated buses include Manchester, Leeds, Sheffield, Bristol and Edinburgh. Köln has no U-Bahn, but S-Bahn is under construction and it has an elaborate light rail network as well as surface trams. Frankfurt, Dortmund, Essen and Stuttgart have S-Bahn and light rail. Table 10-3 shows investment in urban and national rail systems in the two countries.

Table 10-3 : Investment in Urban and National Rail, Britain and Germany, 1975 to 1984, in ECUs and 1975 prices

| | Million ECU, 1975=100 | | | |
| | Suburban Rail & Subways | | Railways Generally | |
	Germany	Great Britain	Germany	Great Britain
1975	387	36	1 253	250
1978	396	23	1 254	239
1984	354	12	1 076	236
% change 75-84	-8.5	-67	-14.1	-5.6

Source: ECMT (1988)
Note: GB 'subway' is London Regional Transport only, so misses the Glasgow, Liverpool and Tyne & Wear systems.

The Table shows that absolute investment in West Germany for urban rail is greatly higher than it is in Great Britain, even allowing for some missing data. Taking railways as a whole, West Germany invested 5 (1975) to 4.6 (1984) times as much as Great Britain. Expenditure in both countries has fallen 1975 to 1984 - eight times as much in GB as FRG on subways (not allowing for the GB missing items), two and a half times as much in FRG as GB on railways generally - but in both cases FRG starts from a far greater base.

10-09

Some further comparisons of the rail systems may be quoted. FRG's rail network was 30 800 km in 1985 (124 km/1000 km^2) against UK's 17 100 km (70 km/1000 km^2) (DTp 1988). Both countries support public transport revenue costs, but there are substantial differences again. For Germany, all Federal expenditure on railways amounted to DM13.431 x 10^9 in 1986 (Der Bundesminister für Verkehr 1987). The British figures, for the same year for all rail subsidies and capital grants, excluding only the Tyne & Wear metro, were £1.050 x 10^9 (Department of Transport 1987). In ECU, these figures were respectively 1.554 and 6.310 x 10^9. Thus the Federal German expenditure on capital and revenue for all railways was four times that of the British Government.

10-10

While the German urban public transport system is generally more sophisticated than Britain's, its urban motorways and high capacity roads also outrank Britain. Köln for example has an internal ring motorway and nine radial motorways leading from or penetrating it. A favourite location for a large retail development is at a motorway cross.

10-11

The Association of German Cities' 1984 concept of traffic policy for its cities and towns is quoted in Pflaumer (1988):

> 'Public passenger transport and individual transport, either on foot, by cycle or in a car, must be seen as a whole system and each mode needs to be promoted where it offers the greatest advantages in economic, urban planning and social terms. With the help of development policy decisions, urban planning, building, traffic regulation and other organisational measures we must help to achieve a reduction in avoidable transport needs and so shape the traffic that is essential, in all its various forms, so as to improve the living and environmental conditions for our people.'

PLANNING FRAMEWORK

10-12

There are substantial differences in the British and German planning systems. These differences relate both to the overall structure of the systems and to specific laws and regulations that apply to retail development. Thus while Britain has experienced a relaxation of its planning framework since its inception in 1947, West Germany has strengthened its system in order to cope with different forms of development. These approaches are echoed in specific policies for retail development. While the British Government has weakened many of the controls on retail development during the last decade, in West Germany, the opposite is true as laws have been tightened better to control new forms of development, and thus limit their impact on existing retail provision.

10-13

The British 1947 Town and Country Planning Act required counties and county boroughs to draw up Development Plans. These plans, which consisted of a zoned land use map and supporting written statement, showed all important developments and intended landuse changes over a twenty year period. Landuse maps were known as 'town maps' and 'county maps'. The Development Plan then formed the basis for the consideration of applications for planning permission, and the local planning authority could reject a scheme if it departed from the approved plan. Applicants could of course appeal against such a decision to the Secretary of State, though the fact that he had approved the Development Plan meant that he was less likely to allow the appeal.

10-14

The 1968 and 1971 Town and Country Planning Acts reduced the importance of land zoning as an element of planning. The old-style county-level Development Plan was replaced by Structure Plans administered by the county, and Local Plans which are drawn up by districts. Unlike development Plans, where the main body of the plan consisted of a landuse map, the Acts placed emphasis on the Written Statement which was to be supported by a map. Thus the emphasis on a strict zoning of land was reduced.

10-15

More recently, the importance attached to Structure Plans has been reduced. Whereas previously they formed the basis for determining planning applications, Circular 14/85 stressed that development plans were now 'one, but only one' of the material considerations that related to an application. Circular 22/80 suggested that permission should always be granted to an application unless there are clear cut reasons for refusal. As regards retail planning more specifically, local authorities have been advised that the issue of competition is not a planning issue (Parliamentary Written Answer 5 July 1985), and that detailed assessment of retail impact was not usually necessary, and that the effects of a proposals on nearby facilities can usually be judged (Planning Guidance on Major Retail Development 1988). It was suggested that only where a development affected the viability of a nearby centre **as a whole**, were there grounds for refusal because of retail impact.

10-16

While in Britain there has been a substantial reduction in the importance attached to landuse plans and landuse zoning, and local authorities have lost much of their ability to control development, in West Germany the picture is very different. While local authorities in Britain are encouraged to abandon their adherence to Central Place Theory, in Germany it is recognised as a cornerstone of planning law. Much of German planning law is embodied in the *Bundesbaugesetz (BBauG)*, or Federal Construction Law, which is complemented by the *Baunutzungsverordnung (BauNVO)*, or Construction Use Regulation. BBauG requires local authorities to draw up two types of development plan. The first, the *Flächennutzungsplan*, shows the main landuse functions, effectively zoning land for uses such as housing, industry, forestry or retailing etc. The second type of plan is the *Bebauungsplan*, or construction plan, which focusses on smaller areas, and, like the *Flächennutzungsplan*, is legally binding. Land-use zoning is further defined by BauNVO which describes in detail the possible uses for each area of land, together with building heights and plot ratios.

10-17

The BauNVO was substantially tightened by amendments in 1977, and again in 1986, specifically to deal with new types of retail development. However the amendments only apply to construction plans approved after these dates. The 1977 amendment said that retail establishements with less than 1 500 m^2 could not locate outside designated or central areas if adverse effects on urban structure were likely, though the local authority had to prove this. Retail developments larger than 1 500 m^2 were subject to the same constraints, except that the onus of proof fell on the developer (who could also be the retailer) who had to prove that the impact would not affect urban structure. The rules for determining developmental appropriateness originate in Federal law; that is interpreted by the *Lände* and passed to the local authorities, who are able, within limits, to add local regulations: some variation therefore occurs in different parts of the country.

10-18

The BauNVO also applied to change of use to retailing from another category. A number of locations were excepted from these strict zoning regulations, such as areas deficient in a particular type of retailing, where there is no other planned retail development in a nearby centre, or where the development is in a central location easily accessible to the whole of the area's population. Since 1986, the critical size for retail developments has been reduced from 1 500 to 1 200 m^2.

10-19

For projects over 1 000 m^2 there are further problems of political differences between city and *Land*. The Urban Development Office (*Stadtentwicklungsamt*) may refuse permission to develop, but appeal can be made to the *Land* Building Supervisory Board (*Bauaufsichtsamt*) who can overturn the refusal. There seem to be some affinities here with the British appeal system, where the Secretary of State can overturn a local planning refusal.

10-20

This brief comparison of British and West German planning law has highlighted a number of important differences. While Britain has moved away from strict zoning of landuses, in Germany this method is still rigidly adhered to. And while British local authorities have been encouraged to adopt a more flexible approach to new types of large retail development, German law has increased the ability to control such development. Other European countries - France, Sweden, Belgium, and the Netherlands for example - have also tightened their planning laws to allow greater control over development. British *laissez faire* policies create conditions more akin to those which allowed retail decentralisation and downtown decline to occur in the US from the 1950s onwards.

10-21

Another legal difference which is important for setting the context for retail change is the difference in trading hours permitted in the two countries. In Britain, most shops are legally required to close at 20.00 and not to open on Sundays. In reality this law is subject to widespread abuse, with many stores trading late at night and on Sundays. There have been attempts to reform the law to remove the legal restrictions on Sunday trading. In Germany, by way of contrast, trading hours tend to be 09.00 to 18.30 on weekdays, and 09.00 to 14.00 on all but the first Saturday in the month which has the same hours as a weekday. There is little or no Sunday trading.

STRUCTURE OF THE RETAIL INDUSTRY

Table 10-4 : Retailing in Britain and Germany 1978-1985 (1984 prices)

	Great Britain			Germany		
	1978	1984	% change 78-84	1978/9	1984/5	% change 78/9-84/5
Outlets (10^3)	389.6	343.2	-11.9	412.7	406.8	-1.4
Turnover(ECU 10^9)	135.6	139.6	+2.9	206.9	211.7	+2.3
Turnover per Outlet (ECU 10^3)	348.0	406.7	+16.9	501.3	520.4	+3.8
Turnover per Capita (ECU)	2 495	2 542	+1.9	3 337	3 459	+3.6
Population per Outlet	139.4	160.0	+14.7	148.3	150.4	+1.4

Sources : Central Office of Information 1979 p237, 1987 p267 (based on data from VAT returns); Table 6-2; Eurostat 1987

10-22

Table 10-4 contrasts British and German retail trends between 1978 and 1984. The first observation is that in Germany retail turnover, as a whole, and per capita was higher than in Britain. Change in total turnover between 1978 and 1984 was fairly similar in the two countries, though when per capita turnover change is considered, growth in Germany was almost twice that in Britain. Yet when turnover per outlet is considered, growth in Britain far exceeds that in Germany. This, combined with the British decrease in the number of outlets and the corresponding increases in the population per outlet, clearly reflect a process of concentration within the British retail sector. The table, together with evidence from national and case study chapters, shows that similar changes in total turnover have been accommodated in different ways. In Britain, out-of-centre development has often been justified by the growth of consumer expenditure, yet the German experience suggests that growth can be accommodated within existing provision (bearing in mind that a certain amount of new expenditure would have been absorbed by new developments allowed before planning laws were tightened in 1977).

10-23

As Table 10-4 suggests, the most significant feature of the British retail industry has been the concentration of market share among fewer and fewer firms. While the number of independent and small retail firms has fallen, the size of the largest has grown significantly, competitive advantage ensured by economies of scale. As numbers of retail companies have fallen, the size of individual stores has grown. Thus in the convenience goods sector, there has been a progression from small, counter service shops through selfservice supermarkets to superstores and hypermarkets. Looking at the operations of Tesco (Tesco PLC 1986), one of Britain's largest convenience retailers, between 1977 and 1986, these trends can be seen clearly. Thus while the number of Tesco stores has fallen from 722 to 395 (-45%), the average floorspace per store has increased from 672 m^2 to 1773 m^2 (+164%). These changes are reflected by a 43% increase in turnover per employee and an increase in turnover of 118% (both in real terms).

10-24

Retail firms have expanded in a number of different ways:

- by organic growth - incremental expansion into new locations - (eg Dillons bookshops)
- by consolidation - replacing small exisiting outlets with new larger ones (eg Tesco and Sainsbury)
- by takeover - merging with or absorbing a competitor (eg Tesco takeover of Hillards)
- by diversification - this can be by organic growth (eg Sainsbury spawning of Homebase) or by takeover (eg WH Smith takeover of Paperchase and Our Price Records).

10-25

The end result is the creation of very large trading empires. The Burton Group, for example, owns Burton, Debenham, Top Shop, Top Man, Dorothy Perkins, Principles and Champion Sport. Often the general public are unaware of the concentration of ownership since a firm trades under a number of different names, and even in different retail sectors. Howard and Davies (1988) showed that in 1986 in Northumberland Street in Newcastle, 74% of shops were branches of multiples, while 41% were owned by firms with at least one other outlet in the street, usually trading under different names. Broadbridge and Dawson (1988) estimated that concentration will continue within retailing until each market sector is dominated by 5 to 10 firms accounting for between 70 and 80% of sector sales. They suggested that by the mid 1990s, 50% of sales would be in the hands of the 60 or so largest firms.

10-26

The US and Germany have each parallelled Britain in having the same number or fewer firms with a larger number of outlets. In the US the number of firms was fairly stable 1963 to 1982 but the number of multiunit establishments nearly doubled. In Germany the number of firms with 1-49 outlets all decreased 1979-85, but those with 50 or more outlets increased by 13%, but the overall change was less dramatic - from 1.19 outlets per firm to 1.20 outlets per firm.

10-27

In terms of larger stores, department stores remain very important in the German shopping scene. Their turnover has declined until very recently in city centres, but they have taken the opportunity to move to out-of-centre developments or to district centres; coping with out-of-centre competition meant they first went downmarket, but more recently they have gone upmarket again. Firms with the largest turnover have been the most successful. Firms with a turnover of 250 million DM to more than 1 bn DM have increased turnover 1978 to 1984 by 64% in current terms, whereas all other firms achieved only 18% (in real terms the former is a more modest gain, the latter a loss).

10-28

The US built their first out-of-town store in 1926. By 1984 there were 24 717, 86% of which were less than 200 000 square feet in size. Germany built shopping centres well before Britain. The Main-Taunus-Zentrum was opened in 1964 and Brent Cross in London in the late 1970s. The Caerphilly hypermarket opened in 1972. In Germany there were 66 hypermarkets in 1966 and 1 408 in 1977. By 1980 their market share was 15%, and about 65% were edge-of-town. German retail warehouses appeared in the early 1970s, with a wider range of goods than was the norm in British stores.

OVERSUPPLY OF OUT-OF-CENTRE STORES?

10-29

Redistribution of retail supply can take place at various levels - from the marginal problem where all existing stores continue to operate, though with lower turnover, alongside a new store to the other extreme where existing stores start to close down. Lacking both definitions and data, it is difficult to estimate whether there will be an oversupply of retail facilities in Britain or Germany, though some inferences can be drawn. In terms of impact, many studies have been done.

10-30

Chapter 2 explored the impact of recent British shopping developments. It was seen that most impact studies described falling trade in the surrounding catchment, although in some cases a concrete link between a new store's opening and surrounding stores' decline was hard to establish. Analysis of Tesco's performance between 1974 and 1984 showed that as store size has increased so has efficiency, with turnover per m^2 increasing from £2 312 to £3 568 in real terms. Since the convenience goods market remains static, gains in Tesco trade must represent losses elsewhere, both in terms of trade, and floorspace. Many observers have concluded that much of the impact of new stores is accommodated by lower turnover and profit margins in surrounding stores, with some small firms trading long after they cease to be profitable, often simply because they represent the owner's established pattern of daily life.

10-31

The impact of out-of-centre regional shopping centres is even more uncertain. As yet only two have been built and information regarding their impact is limited. However, there is agreement that it is this form of development which most closely resembles that of the town centre and thus poses the greatest threat to its survival. It was shown that the Merry Hill centre in Dudley will comprise almost 90% national mutliples. This compares with 55% in Wolverhampton. Consultants estimated the trading impact for Wolverhampton would average 9.5% by 1990, though some key anchor stores could lose up to 20% of their trade. The impact of the nearer Sandwell Mall, should it be developed, would be even greater.

10-32
Britain's wide range of **proposals** cause more concern than existing new retail developments. It may be, where a group of proposals has been made or is contemplated, that if one or two are given planning permission, endorsed by the Secretary of State, the others will withdraw. Certainly Tesco's policy is not to establish superstores where others are operating. German data permit more probing. We have noted that Germany's population has actually started to fall, and also that retail turnover in real terms has been static 1978-84. While out-of-centre retail stores are far less space-intensive than city centre ones, it does seem notable that the Köln-Bonn region's floorspace increased by 99% 1968 to 1985.

10-33
In Chapter 1 there were less equivocal data for the US. In one location during the period 1972-84 population grew by 13%, personal income by 44%, but planned shopping centres by 86% and their floorspace by 80% or more.

INTERESTS AND LOBBIES

10-34
In contrast to their European counterparts, most British Chambers of Commerce are relatively weak associations of small retailers, and as such, rarely have any significant influence. Branches of multiple retailers are answerable to their head offices, and almost all policy decisions are made at a national level. While, individually, large retailers can be powerful voices, rarely do they enter into local Chambers of Commerce. An exception to the general weakness of Chambers of Commerce in Britain however is in Wolverhampton, described in Chapter 4. Here, the landlords of one of the town centre shopping centres, key local employers, are an important influence in the Chamber of Commerce which in turn lobbies the Council. Multiple retailers tend to form national rather than local trade organisations. Examples include the Retail Consortium and the British Retailers Association (formerly the Multiple Shops Federation).

10-35
Chapters 2-5 have shown that local authorities, either in groups or individually, have little influence outside that bound up in their statutory functions. Thus both the Association of Metropolitan Authorities and the Association of District Councils criticised the lack of guidance emanating from Central Government but had little effect. Southampton's campaign to mobilise local authority opposition to out-of-centre retailing also appears to have been ineffective.

10-36
In a *laissez faire* economy, where planning has been weakened, it is logical to conclude that the most powerful actors in the retail field are the large, multiple retailers and the developers. The German situation is dissimilar. First of all the Chambers of Commerce are often (but not always) very powerful in all aspects concerning a city centre, and their influence often spreads to beyond the city boundary. Their voice is potent on the local Council, and, taking the example of Köln, they have been instrumental in constraining out-of-town developments (even in adjacent Kreise, which are separate authorities); they have significantly affected decisions on extensions of pedestrianisation, upgrading of earlier foot streets, introducing a new museum in the centre, pressuring for car parking and public transport. Chambers of Commerce are

supported by the trade associations, for example the *Bundesarbeitsgemeinschaft* (BAG), and the *Hauptgemeinschaft des Deutschen Einzelhandels* (HDE), both of whom are based in Köln. These bodies carry out careful research and employ large technical staffs skilled at projecting the demands of the industry. BAG promotes a very large survey of users of stores within its membership, about every four years; the enormous data set is analysed by the University of Köln.

10-37
Germany also has associations of different kinds of stores. There is a Federal Organisation of Retailers and an Association of Superstores. A representative of the latter considered that hypermarkets and superstores were what modern people wanted.

TOWN CENTRE STRATEGIES

10-38
Local authorities in Britain have reacted to the prospect of out-of-centre retail developments in a variety of different ways. Their strategies may be divided into five main groups, though none is necessarily mutually exclusive:

1. **Accept the workings of the 'free market'.** This approach is usually adopted by local authorities on the edge of large urban areas, but who lack any substantial retail provision. By allowing a major out-of-centre development within their boundaries, they will secure a larger share of the local retail market. Examples include Sandwell and Dudley MBCs in the West Midlands who gave permission for the Sandwell Mall and Merry Hill schemes. This approach results from a lack of regional coordination, causes damage to existing centres, and may start a development 'bandwagon' as other local authorities try to limit damage and trade draw by permitting similar schemes in their areas.

2. **Adapt town centres in an attempt to make them compete on equal terms with out-of-centre developments.** Sometimes local authorities follow policies to make town centres seem the equal of out-of-centre schemes. The most common approach is to make efforts to accommodate more cars by roadbuilding and the provision of more car parking spaces. This is the approach that many US downtowns pursued in the 1950s, and actually hastened the decline of retailing there as the environment became less attractive to shop in. Other attempts to mimic out-of-centre developments include the introduction of climatically controlled shopping environments, even the glazing-over of existing streets. To differing degrees this is the approach being adopted by Birmingham, Portsmouth and Southampton.

3. **Adapt, (or encourage change in) the function of the town centre.** This strategy is only practical when the town centre has some other function apart from traditional retailing. The best examples are towns such as York which combine a fine urban environment with history and heritage, and which are able to attract large numbers of tourists. Taken to its logical conclusion, local shopping needs would be sated by out-of-centre shopping, while the town centre would survive as a historical theme park with speciality retailing geared to the demands of the tourist. Such a strategy can only work in a very small number of locations in Britain, and even there provides no solution to the problems of access and inequality that out-of-centre developments engender.

4. **Resist out-of-centre development where possible, emphasise the inherent qualities of the town centre by environmental and public transport improvements.** This approach attempts to reinforce and exploit the existing features of town centres. Environmental improvements such as widespread pedestrianisation improve a centre's attraction to the shopper, while improvements in public transport, such as the introduction of light rail, reinforce the town centre's position at the centre of the town. At the same time, unavoidable out-of-centre retail development should be accommodated as close to the existing centre as

possible, capitalising on any spin-off trade for existing shops, while ensuring the maximum possible access for all. Examples of local authorities pursuing this approach include Wolverhampton and Halifax. Given the current context within which retail planning must operate, it would seem the most rational strategy.

5. **Resist out-of-centre development absolutely, do little else.** In the current political climate, such a policy would be unlikely to survive the appeal system. Local authority control over that which was won on appeal would be limited. It is likely that trade would be drawn to surrounding districts where new development did occur.

10-39

In Canada, Toronto has always protected the interests of its centre, but for a while had a liberal attitude to out-of-centre schemes. That changed toward one which endeavours to locate them where the city would benefit most, and the city centre be affected least. The German response is most likely to be one of nos. 2, 3 and 4. However, with reasonable legal backing, the Germans are less fearful of the future of city centres than other countries. At least, planners are less fearful: the traders make a lot of fuss to ensure they continue getting what they want. It has been said the crisis of the city centre is the crisis of the department store; indeed, that seems to be the only retail outlet to be at all strongly affected.

10-40

Given that some think German city centres have a problem, their solutions are not particularly innovative. They want more pedestrianisation, more car parking, improved public transport, the creation of urbanity, facilities that pull people in, arcades, glassing over streets. Stores should add specialisms, selling a wider range of goods. There should be further concentration, not just in food. Hannover, more radical than most, wants more traffic calming as well as more pedestrianisation, encouragement of bicycle and pedestrian access to the centre. The optimistic view is that the decline of town and city centres has ceased, that department stores are on the upturn, and that stores are moving back in. Contrarily, one commentator said that while the BauNVO laws would allow a 25 000 m^2 new retail development in a city centre, the shopkeepers, via the Chamber of Commerce, would stop it.

THE HYPOTHESIS AND OBJECTIVES

10-41

The first part of the hypothesis ('Very substantial investment in German city centres will not be adequate to counter the competitive pressure from non-city centre [mainly out-of-town] mega shopping centres, and from down-market trends within parts of large and medium-sized city centres') was certainly true, according to HGZ data, until quite recently. Now the tide may well have turned, as was noted in the previous paragraph, above. The objective required answers to seven questions; they are attempted below:

a. How does the extent of outer shopping developments in Britain compare with Germany and how far have pressures been resisted in each case? This is adequately answered in the text above.
b. Is the pressure for outer shopping development a phenomenon which cannot be stopped? (Does it cater for everyone's needs?) Germany have shown that some control is possible, given that a local authority wishes to exert this control. Outer shopping developments could theoretically cater for every-one except the extreme immobile poor.
c. While German public sector policy toward its city centres is to invest heavily in them, can they continue to resist the pressure for more outer

centres, and their competition when built? They have done so to a reasonable extent, though the competition from outer centres is clearly having some adverse effect on city centres.

d.   How far can pedestrianisation and public transport investment maintain the city centre's competitiveness? Are new policies needed? They appear to have been important for the larger cities, and pedestrianisation on its own has enhanced the attractiveness of medium and small cities and towns. Retail associations are urging further rehabilitation of Köln's central environment. New policies seem to be much more needed in Britain than in Germany, though we suggest in Chapter 11 that policies which reduce urban travel demand are urgently needed everywhere.

e.   When should an administration act to have most likelihood of success in countering such pressures? If it has legal backing, when proposals are first made. Otherwise it is a longer term campaign to strengthen the law.

f.   What are the broad social (employment, accessibility, residential change, loss of services), economic, environmental and energetic consequences of a laissez-faire attitude toward outer centres? Who pays these costs? These topics are widely discussed in Chapters 2-5.

g.   Following from the answers to the above questions, are there in fact inalienable reasons for underpinning the city centre's economic viability? In Chapter 11 we make proposals to underpin all traditional urban centres because of the ease of access to them.

REFERENCES

Broadridge, AM and John A Dawson (1988) **Retailing in Scotland 2005** Institute for Retail Studies University of Stirling

Central Office of Information (1973,1979,1987) **Britain 1973/1979/1987 : An Official Handbook** London HMSO

Central Statistical Office (1986) **Annual Abstract of Statistics 1986 Edition** London HMSO

The Courier (1988) **Dossier** Issue 107 January-February

Department of Transport (1987) **Transport Statistics Great Britain 1976-1986** London HMSO

 - (1988) **International Comparisons of Transport Statistics 1970-1985** London

Der Bundesminister für Verkehr (1987) **Verkehr in Zahlen 1987** Bonn

European Conference of Ministers of Transport (1988) **Investment in Transport Infrastructure in ECMT Countries** Paris

Eurostat (1986) **Review 1975-1984** Luxembourg

 - (1988) **Eurostat 25th Edition** Luxembourg

Howard, EB and Ross L Davies (1988) **Change in the Retail Environment** Harlow Longman

Pflaumer, Hans (1988) The Development of Urban and Transport Planning in West Germany in Carmen Hass-Klau (ed) **New Life for City Centres** London Anglo-German Foundation for the Study of Industrial Society

TESCO Plc (1986) **Annual Repoort and Accounts 1986**

11 ISSUES & RECOMMENDATIONS

THE FUTURE OF URBAN CENTRES

11-01

The term 'urban centre' is intentionally a catch-all phrase. It refers to city and town centres of widely different ages and quality, and to the range of facilities on offer. It also refers to inner city and suburban shopping streets or sub-centres. It refers to centres which have been pedestrianised, have trees, elegant shops, theatres, historic churches, to centres which are clean and have little vandalism. It is usually, but not always, the good quality streets that have integrated large new retailing - covered shopping malls or single superstores. But, 'urban centres' also refers to shopping areas where pedestrians have to fight vehicular traffic, which have little intrinsic historic interest, where many traditional shops have disappeared and been replaced by banks and building societies, estate agents and sex shops, amusement arcades and betting shops; their users fall over broken paving stones, are surrounded by graffiti, and have a higher expectancy of being mugged. The middle-class shopkeeper, shopper or town planner, when wanting to protect existing centres, is usually referring to the former type, but **all** types are important, as we show below.

11-02

This book has been pervaded with a sense of the sacrosanct. As Brand (1987) has abrasively pointed out, urban and regional planners (and politicians with these constituencies) are obsessed with several sacred cows, the first of which is protection of the countryside, and the second is protection of traditional town centres. Any readers who have reached this point will have noticed the nagging presence of the latter, overtly or subliminally. In the public debate, protection of traditional shopping areas has been argued on several bases: because they're there, because they have economic significance, because they are important for the exchange of goods and ideas, because of their diversity, because this is where the town's roots are. But surely their primary importance is contextual: they perform a particular rôle within a distribution and information network that spreads well beyond the town. Christaller recognised this in 1933.

11-03

In order to present a rational and cogent argument for retaining and enhancing existing centres, we have to look at the urban context. In all countries the distribution of services should ideally mesh with the distribution of people's residences, so as to minimise travel (except for ceremonial and élitist reasons, the invention of mechanised means of transport was to accommodate journeys that could not be made on foot or horse; travel has since become detatched from these principles, often being made for its own sake). Such an ideal has never been attained because of several constraints, not least of which is the unwillingness of private investors and public transport operators to meet its demands. Travel, in urban terms, can more easily be accommodated as a need than as a desire, to paraphrase Maslow (1954). Traditionally, in many countries, services were concentrated at the urban core; not surprisingly, urban cores were densely occupied places until recently. Then, as urban areas grew in physical size, sub-centres, corner shops etc all helped to minimise travel, which for most people remained on foot.

11-04

The advent of public transport, and then the motor car, has greatly increased the distance people are prepared to travel to satisfy consumerist needs (and desires). For a long time public transport radiated from preeminent urban

centripetally - the retail explosion (fission) rather than implosion (fusion). Orbital movements are also important, to district centres and large stores which have established where sufficient land was available for them to spread on one level and have hundreds, if not thousands, of associated parking spaces.

11-05

Arguably this allows a great freeing of the human spirit, choice and comparison of prices and quality - not simply between competing stores in a town centre, but between shopping centres. Yet, a societal, environmental and energy price has to be paid for the new flexibility. In Chapter 1 Orski (1987) was quoted, showing how locational flexibility was creating massive problems in the US. Development of sub-centres large enough to rival downtown, suburban and ex-urban shopping malls ... was creating orbital and outward movements in cities designed for radial movements. So, change the network to accommodate these new movements? At phenomenal expense, Orski said, because the desire lines passed straight through the most expensive residential areas. Also in Chapter 1, we saw how the car, given full rein so to speak, could bring Atlanta's downtown to its knees - from a 1954 share of the region's turnover of 29% to 4% in 1977. Or Seattle as a whole from 72% of the area's sales in 1954 to 34% in 1982; its downtown fell from 31% of the area's sales to 10% over the same period.

11-06

But the issue is not just the travel demand of **new** shopping locations. Existing travel in many urban areas is nearing saturation on many of its streets. In Britain, and probably elsewhere, it is recognised by all politicians that urban road congestion is creating major problems which are difficult to solve. There is a prolific literature on this topic (eg Thomson 1977, OECD 1979, Adams 1981, Hamer 1987). Road building is largely unacceptable because of its appetite for residential property, which can threaten the political careers of its proponents (the Conservatives lost the GLC 1973 election to Labour on such a platform). Some cities, eg London and München, are also finding their public transport systems running at high capacity levels.

11-07

Each traditional shopping area built up a clientele from its catchment area. These people travelled in different ways as new forms of movement were devised. Despite the advent of trams, other rail systems, buses, cars, taxis, bicycles, motorcycles, it is extraordinary to see the proportion who have continued to walk to the shops through this period. Hurdle (1986), using data from the 1981 Greater London Transportation Survey, calculated the modal split for every one of London's 139 town centres outside the West End. No less than 46.7% of visitors to these centres walked all the way. Brög in his Kontiv research (ECMT 1985) showed that 39% walked to shops throughout Germany in 1976; there was even a slight increase to 40% in 1982.

11-08

If all these streets and centres fit an important distributional pattern, then we suggest they should be made as attractive as possible and their use encouraged, providing a context in which the market could operate acceptably. The reasons for doing this would be partly those suggested above, though one of importance is perhaps inadequately considered. We have termed this **trip degeneration**. By this we mean the antithesis to 'trip generation', the technical term which describes the establishment of new demand for travel. As a general principle, we suggest that nothing should be done which adds further travel demand to that which already exists: land uses should be clustered and densities increased so that work, shopping, educational, pleasure, etc trips are shortened in length, and some will not be needed at all.

This introduction has set a context for the following analysis of the report's content and for a number of recommendations.

216

IS CONVENTIONAL WISDOM VALID?

Earlier chapters have amassed a great deal of evidence with which it is possible to challenge the stance of some retailers, some developers, some politicians ... that is frequently used to support out-of-centre retailing. This section attempts to summarize and challenge this position. Each response has one or more paragraph numbers cross-referencing to the main text, where fuller evidence may be found; occasionally new material is introduced, and referenced.

A The public needs a wide range of shopping facilities, and benefits from competition between them (2-11)

*** Consumers able to use many new retail facilities benefit from the advantages of a wide selection of goods, competitive prices, one stop shopping and sheer convenience (2-107). However many recent trends actually operate against the best interests of the consumer. So, while a consumer benefits from a wider range of goods within a store, the choice of store has narrowed; a large number of small stores is replaced by a small number of large stores operated by only a handful of firms. The large catchments of many new stores mean the consumer has a limited choice of shops. In addition, they are likely to have to travel further to get there (Chapter 2).

*** Often the kinds of goods sold in retail warehouses and superstores are available in traditional centres and do not require a car to carry them away (6-13).

*** The capitalist tendency toward monopoly is well advanced within the British and German retail sectors. At the turn of the century about 80% of convenience goods retailers were independent; by the late 1980s the British market has become dominated by five large firms, with further concentration predicted (2-37 to 2-43).

*** While a few companies in each sector may increasingly compete for new sites (5-11), this may lead to unnecessarily high prices. Once one supermarket chain has developed a superstore in one location, it is unlikely that another will attempt to rival it - leading to 'spatial monopoly.' (2-108) While this was Tesco's view, sometimes the opposite happens, reflecting a chain's need for 'presence'.

*** Through examination of the prices charged by large supermarket chains, it does not seem that savings in operating costs (resulting from internally efficient superstores) have been passed on to the consumer.

*** Higher than necessary prices might be termed 'monopolistic profit'. Very high profit levels have been common across the British retail sector (2-48), and rather than being used to lower prices, they may well have been used to sustain further corporate growth, by new store openings or take-over (2-49 to 2-52). Many large British retailers, facing market saturation have moved into other retail areas or abroad in order to sustain their corporate need to grow. Whether such processes best serve the consumer is open to doubt.

B Out-of-centre retail development is necessary to accommodate the growth in consumer expenditure

*** Comparison of expenditure trends in Britain and Germany shows that similar rates of growth in Germany have been accommodated without recent expansion out-of-centre (T10-4).

*** Despite the relative importance of German department stores, comparatively few have located out of centre (6-14). While the number of German shopping centres (in an out-of-centre location) increased from 3 in 1965 to 72 in 1982, their average area has consistently reduced over that time (T6-5).

*** Location of German shopping centres 1970-82 has moved from urban fringe/ green field toward new housing and suburban areas (T6-6). Yet, stores outside built-up areas still had the greatest turnover per outlet and per employee in 1985. Turnover per m^2 of sales outside built-up areas was the **lowest** of all locations, however, which reflects the lowest efficiency of land-use - a condition not necessarily to be applauded in low density countries like the US or Canada; it appears distinctly profligate in high density countries like Britain and Germany (T6-7).

*** Retail warehouses have lured trade away from traditional centres, not created it (6-80)

*** While Köln to some extent refutes Assertion B, Regensburg does so very decisively (comparisons with München in T9-5, 9-12 *et seq*). Perhaps the most significant weapons Regensburg had were: (i) ownership of land by the City (9-24); (ii) large numbers living in the City Centre (9-10); (iii) the availability of a large area close to the City Centre on which much of the Centre's expansion could take place without imperilling the historic core (9-03); (iv) the City's requirement that City Centre department stores should be enlarged before permission to expand the DEZ Centre would be given (9-20). München and its hinterland are so prosperous that retailing in both has expanded.

C A Government's powers do not allow out-of-centre retail trends to be brought under control

*** Evidence from North America and Europe does not support this assertion. While the British Government has reduced local planning authorities' ability to control retail development, it has retained control of large developments via the 'call-in' procedure (2-12). The Government's oft-stated commitment to the Green Belt shows how much control is possible (2-07, 2-14). Advice from the English DoE has reduced local government's control over retail development (2-10).

*** The strength of German retail planning control has increased over the years, with amendments to the law in 1977 and 1986 to make large out-of-centre development more difficult to achieve. This is expressed in the recent development of large stores closer to existing centres (6-13, 6-51). Nevertheless, an 'appeal system' also operates in Germany, where an office of the *Land* can overturn decisions of a local authority (8-17 to 8-18)

D Market forces are the most efficient means of allocating space to retail provision

*** Many large British retailers complain that the lack of guidance from central government is creating uncertainty and increasing the trend toward out-of-centre development (2-17, 2-18)

*** The interests of retailers do not necessarily coincide with the interest of town centres (2-18)

*** Current levels of investment and consumer expenditure cannot support both the growth of out-of-centre retailing and simultaneous improvement of in-centre floorspace (2-50). Retailers and developers have planned for continued growth, yet recent increases in interest rates show how unreliable spending prediction can be (2-59)

*** Small retailers' concern about retail trends caused them to lobby Hampshire

218

CC, influencing the policies of the South Hampshire Structure Plan (3-1
similar lobbying, beneficially influencing Wolverhampton MBC's attitude
the future of its town centre.

*** The relative freedom to develop in integrated situations in Germany
fact strongly influenced by the established retail lobby (6-27). Dortmund's
policies argued for development in three areas designated for industrial use;
in 1977 it abandoned this policy of permitting development on non-integrated
sites and would-be developers moved to a different local authority outside the
city. Dortmund then partly reversed its policy: here, it seems the market pre-
vailed, though not operating **efficiently**, in Dortmund's view (7-19 to 7-20).

*** Retailers see a dangerous situation arising in traditional centres; plan-
ners and academics think this fear is exaggerated (6-45 to 6-48). However, the
strength of German Chambers of Commerce has greatly contributed to the country's restrictive policies toward retailing (6-59). And yet, there are considerable differences between Chambers of Commerce: that in Köln has been more
influential than the one in Dortmund, for example (7-02, 8-11, 8-41). In
Britain, Wolverhampton's Chamber of Commerce is forthright (4-17).

> E 'The limited number of superstores in inner-city areas today is
> not due to inherent preference among retailers for out-of-town or
> edge-of-town sites. It is caused by the web of complex planning laws'
> (Retail and Distribution Management [1986])

> F It is not the rôle of the planning system to inhibit
> competition (2-07)

*** Many British local authorities are keen to accommodate new retail
development in town centres as a means of pre-empting competition from outside
(3-16, 3-21, 3-41, 3-49, 3-50, 4-08, 4-29, 5-13).

*** Retailers' preference for out-of-centre locations probably owes more to the
fundamental principles of their operations than to constraints imposed by an
overbearing planning system. Most out-of-centre retailing has two basic requirements. 'Extensive' methods mean a large, single level unit with a relatively
low turnover per square metre. The second, and related, principle is the need
to gear operations to the car user since they tend to purchase larger amounts,
and are often more affluent. This need is expressed in large surface level car
parks, and locations connected to the strategic road system (2-45 to 2-46).

*** The belief that retail development in town centres is stifled by planning
regulations tends to suggest that the British planning system is still a force
to be reckoned with. Chapters 2-5 have shown that this is no longer the case
(2-27). In South Hampshire retail developers can play one local authority off
against another (3-06, 3-28). In the West Midlands, Wolverhampton is unable to
resist out-of-centre retailing (4-26, 4-31 to 4-37). In York, an apparently
strong retail policy developed by neighbouring local authorities was shattered
when one authority decided to grant permission for a large out-of-centre
development against the agreed policy (5-40, 5-41).

*** Examination of British planning appeals suggested that **non-retail** issues
are most often the key features of their dismissal. Questions about the Green
Belt or about immediate effects of traffic generation appeared to be more
relevant than specific retail issues. Advice from the Department of the
Environment has reinforced this tendency. This contrasts strongly with Germany
where most retail applications are determined on retail grounds alone, but
local authorities have the option of refusing consent on, say, traffic grounds
(2-22, 6-23).

*** Planners in Köln operate quite differently from Assertion F: they have inhibited retail expansion considerably and turned away many would-be developers who do not fit the City's concepts (8-19, T8-11 to T8-13)

> G *The concept of a retail hierarchy is outdated and no longer has*
> *any relevance in retail planning* (2-30, 2-31)

*** Hampshire CC put forward several reasons to justify retention of Central Place Theory, as established by Christaller in Southern Germany, in 1933 (3-15)

*** Strength of adherence to the theory explains why level of investment - particularly in roads, parking and pedestrianisation - in German trade centres is higher than in Britain (6-35)

*** A map of *Nordrhein Westfalen* shows the established structure of Central Place Theory (F7-1). The theory's relevance has been diminished in the Dortmund area because of its inordinate share of out-of-centre developments (7-26). In Köln, the *Land*'s optimistic call for adherence to the theory was in some disarray until the City and its Chamber of Commerce firmly applied the 1977 and 1986 amendments to the BauNVO, thus allowing a degree of respect for the theory to continue (8-02). Lack of adherence to the theory led to existing store losses in Hürth (8-16). However, the theory remains strong in Bayern (9-06).

> H *Retailers design their operations to accommodate car users*
> *who wish to use their cars*

> J *'If cars are designed out of commercial areas, people may*
> *prefer out-of-town shopping complexes where they can take*
> *their cars' Nicholas Ridley cited in The Surveyor (1986)*
> *(similar opinion in 3-15, 5-09)*

*** While retailers may be selecting out-of-centre locations in response to rising levels of car ownership, they are also influencing behaviour and generating a large amount of new traffic; many of these people used to walk to the shops (5-08). The effects of a new superstore opening in an already highly congested area such as London may therefore be particularly acute. Other effects include increases in energy use, pollution, noise and accident rates (transport is generally discussed in 2-104 to 2-106, T2-18).

*** In Germany, transport issues are viewed as an integral part of any planning issue (10-11). The centre of München is remarkably successful, has one of the highest shopping turnovers/m^2 and one of the lowest provisions of car parking in Germany - and has highly developed U-Bahn, S-Bahn and tram networks (6-55)

*** Mr Ridley's view of the rôle of transport in retail planning suggests that retailers are dependent on car users for their trade, and that town centres should be geared to the needs of car-borne shoppers to prevent them being lured to out-of-centre complexes. Research in Germany disagrees (6-54). The Ridley assertion seems also to apply predominantly to smaller towns: the 1978/79 National Travel Survey states that **for Britain as a whole** car use for shopping amounts to 68% of all modes (Lester & Potter 1983). In Greater London it was 29%, excluding the West End, where car use was very much smaller (Hurdle 1986). Yet, very often local authorities try to improve their town centres by accommodating larger numbers of vehicles (3-35, 3-39): the effects of accommodating this minority are out of all proportion either to their number or to their contribution to retail turnover.

*** Where this imbalance of allocation has been recognised and rectified by pedestrianisation, or some other form of traffic restraint, the shopping centre usually becomes more popular with shoppers, and retail turnover is boosted as a result (3-35, 3-38, 4-09, 5-10, 5-44, 5-45).   Sometimes, in-centre pedestriani-sation is not sufficient in itself to counter out-of-centre development and other incentives, or the application of the law, may be necessary (T7-5).   And, different shopping modal splits occur in different cities, usually connected with the level of investment in public transport.   Thus, Köln on a 1984 weekday showed that 45% of visitors to department stores used public transport, while in Dortmund the proportion was 39% - in München the proportion was 73%! (T8-17)

*** Several authorities argue against further car parking in traditional centres;   TEST's earlier work in 10 German cities showed little relationship between the quantity of car parking and retail turnover (6-54)

*** The experience of the United States must form the final argument against the accommodation of cars 'at any cost'.   Downtowns were modified to cater for the massive increases in car ownership experienced during the 1950s and 1960s. New roads and car parks were provided to serve downtown and relieve road congestion.   These new roads quickly filled with newly generated traffic, which then made these centres less attractive to shoppers and thus to retailers. Many retail firms then abandoned downtown to develop new stores on the periphery of urban areas where motorists could easily reach them using the freeway system.   In many cases offices followed suit, and some 'suburban down-towns' developed close to freeway intersections.   A few downtowns have partial-ly recovered through speciality retailing.   But US cities have not achieved a new equilibrium based on the new decentralised downtowns served by the car. Road congestion has followed retail decentralisation.   The situation appears ripe for another wave of retail decentralisation - hardly a rational form of urban management (1-04 to 1-18).

*** Evidence from Britain, Europe and North America indicates that cars and shopping areas do not mix well. Attempts to adapt traditional centres to the motor car affect the quality of the shopping environment and often discourage consumers from using it (Chapters 1 and 7).

K   New retail development acts as a valuable source of new employment (2-22, 2-29, 2-99)

*** When retailing as a whole is considered, jobs tend either to be redistri-buted or there is a net loss;   net additions to an area's jobs are less evident (2-100, 2-101, 4-40, 6-70).   In Germany, there was a net 2.9% loss of retail employment 1979 to 1985 (6-78).   Employment change 1979-1985 showed losses for small retailers and department stores totalling 182 000 jobs.   Supermarkets, other food stores, superstores and hypermarkets together gained 93 000 jobs, and a category which includes filling stations gained 62 000 jobs.   The 27 000 jobs outstanding either went to other classes of employment or represent jobless people (T6-11)

*** The nature of employment 'created' in new superstores and retail warehouses deserves close attention (T2-17).   A high proportion of staff are employed on part-time contracts, management is very often dominated by males, while sales staff, specially on checkouts, are invariably female (2-102, 2-103).

L   Detailed calculation of retail impact is not usually necessary

*** The quantity, quality, characteristics and frequency of collection of German retail statistics enable trends to be understood and remedial action taken where necessary (6-39, 6-40)

*** In Britain the lack of statistical information is criticised by retailers, consultants, academics and planners alike (2-13, 2-15, 2-17, 2-18)

221

THE MAIN ISSUES AND RECOMMENDATIONS

We have seen that in Britain (at least where there is still considerable out-of-centre pressure) there is no clear set of criteria with which to evaluate a retail planning application. Chapter 2 showed that large retailers are often as concerned about this lack of guidance as local authorities: the national guidance which is available tends to be qualitative rather than quantitative. There is a demonstrable need for a set of clearly defined criteria relating to effects on trade, employment, access for those without use of a car, and of conflicts between transport and the environment. We would argue that planning's rôle should extend beyond land use issues toward the social effects of different forms of development. There is a need for a holistic planning approach. We believe that if all the effects of retail development were taken into account, Central Place Theory would be the optimum way of achieving a rational distribution of retailing facilities.

We therefore recommend :

1 A STANDARD SET OF CRITERIA FOR EVALUATING RETAIL PLANNING APPLICATIONS SHOULD BE ESTABLISHED.

2 NATIONAL PLANNING POLICY AND ADVICE SHOULD BE BASED ON CLEAR DEFINITIONS OF ACCEPTABLE LEVELS OF IMPACT ON TRADE, EMPLOYMENT, ENVIRONMENT AND TRANSPORT

3 NATIONAL PLANNING ADVICE SHOULD ENCOURAGE RETAIL APPLICATIONS TO BE EVALUATED HOLISTICALLY, WITH REFERENCE TO SOCIAL AS WELL AS LAND USE EFFECTS

An important difference between British and German planning is the use of land zoning. Whereas British planning has consistently moved away from the strict land use zoning of the 1947 Town and Country Planning Act, Germany has developed a zoning system which reduces uncertainty yet retains a certain degree of flexibility. However, in both countries the most effective form of land use control has proved to be local authority land ownership.

We therefore recommend that

4 CLEAR BUT FLEXIBLE LAND USE ZONING POLICIES TOGETHER WITH THE POWERS TO IMPLEMENT WOULD REDUCE UNCERTAINTY AND COULD BENEFIT SOCIETY, RETAILERS AND DEVELOPERS ALIKE

5 WHERE LOCAL AUTHORITIES OWN LAND, THEY SHOULD BE GIVEN REASONABLE DISCRETION TO USE THIS IN THE BEST INTERESTS OF THE LOCALITY

We believe that uncertainty and bias have resulted from a lack of up to date national retailing data. With the cancellation of the British Census of Distribution scheduled for 1981, data relating to retailing have either been based on the results of the 1971 Census of Distribution, or have been derived by a number of different methods the accuracy of which cannot be easily assessed. The effects of this lack of data are twofold. First, as time passes so the importance attached to quantitative assessment of retail impact diminishes as the data become less certain. This inevitably increases the subjectivity of the decision making process. The second effect is to give retailers and developers an advantage over local authorities who do not have access to the same internal sources of data, and who have to prove that a development will undermine the vitality of existing shopping (in Germany the onus of proof is on the local authority for developments of less than 1 500 m^2, and on the shop owner for developments over that size). The situation in Germany is better as retail censuses are undertaken fairly regularly, although inconsistencies in the way data are presented can increase the difficulties associated with comparative analysis.

We therefore recommend that

6 A QUINQUENNIAL RETAIL CENSUS (SOLD BY H.M.S.O.) SHOULD BE REINTRO-DUCED IN BRITAIN TO LESSEN PLANNING UNCERTAINTIES AND REMOVE THE ADVANTAGE ENJOYED BY DEVELOPERS AND RETAILERS. IN GERMANY, RETAIL CENSUS DATA SHOULD BE AVAILABLE IN A NATIONALLY CONSISTENT MANNER.

An important difference between local authorities in Britain and those in Germany is the existence of regional planning bodies in Germany which are able to overrule the decisions made by districts. Several times it has been shown that in Britain district authorities act with only their own interests at heart. This is specially true for metropolitan areas which now lack county planning bodies and tend to rely on non-statutory cooperation between dist-ricts. Thus Sandwell MBC in the West Midlands is keen to secure a large out-of-centre retail and leisure development which will have serious implications for neighbouring centres. Despite Hampshire County Council's attempts to limit the amount of out-of-centre retail development, Eastleigh BC is not averse to permitting development that would take trade from nearby Southampton city centre. County councils' ability to strategically control retail development has been reduced by the Secretary of State's criteria for approving Structure Plans, together with Department of the Environment advice that Development Plans are 'one, but only one' of the factors affecting an application. With the coordinating control of counties reduced, only the Secretary of State has the choice of whether to call-in a large retail sheme.

We therefore recommend that

7 COUNTIES OR NEW STATUTORY SUB-REGIONAL OR REGIONAL BODIES SHOULD INVARIABLY CONSIDER APPLICATIONS WHOSE IMPACT EXTENDS BEYOND THE BOUNDARIES OF AN INDIVIDUAL DISTRICT

We have seen that in both Britain and Germany the most significant trend within the retail sector has been toward concentration. In both countries this has been most marked in the convenience goods sector. While some observers such as NEDO (1988) argue that retail competition always endeavours to meet the needs of the customer, we argue that in many cases such concentration may be opera-ting in the trader's corporate interests rather than those of the consumer. As firms get larger so they are able to benefit from economies of scale, and implement new efficient operating methods. These lead to high profit levels which, rather than being passed on to the consumer in terms of lower prices, are often used to finance expansion programmes. As store size increases, so the choice of goods within the store increases, though the choice of which store to use may have become more restricted. We argue that the effect of retail concentration, together with new forms of retailing like superstores and retail warehouses, has been toward the creation of spatial monopolies, since a local market is dominated by the existence of such a store.

The move toward a smaller number of larger stores has undoubtedly benefited the retailer, through cheaper land and the effects of concentration. It is also generally held that the consumer benefits through lower retail prices. However, what has really happened is that the retailer's benefits have become societal and consumer costs. In more detail, retailers benefit from the higher returns that extensive methods allow, together with lower land costs and lower distrib-ution costs which result from a reduced number of stores being operated. Consu-mers have to pay for higher transport costs since on average they travel fur-ther to get there, and probably spend more time getting there. Society has to pay for more transport infrastructure (invariably roads) to facilitate this movement, and suffers from environmental deterioration brought by higher traffic levels, and a loss of land.

To ensure that the consumer and society are not disadvantaged by retail concentration and its consequences, we recommend that

8   TRENDS TOWARDS RETAIL CONCENTRATION AND SECTORAL AND SPATIAL MONO-POLY SHOULD BE CAREFULLY MONITORED TO ENSURE THEY ARE NOT AGAINST THE PUBLIC INTEREST. THE REMIT SHOULD BE KEPT AS WIDE AS POSSIBLE TO LOOK AT INDIRECT EFFECTS WHICH MAY RESULT FROM CONCENTRATION

A key difference between Britain and Germany appears to be differing attitudes towards town centres. In Germany, most town centres were substantially damaged during the Second World War and almost all were subsequently rebuilt along traditional lines. This rather traumatic experience may have heightened public awareness and concern regarding the fate of the town centre. Certainly, German Chambers of Commerce are generally well organised and voluble defenders of such centres. In Britain, few city centres were devastated to the same degree, and often these were rebuilt on modern lines which have not rallied the same degree of public support.

The taking of town centres for granted by the British public is parallelled by generally weak and unorganised Chambers of Commerce. It has been shown that they   usually only represent local traders; the national multiples tend not to get involved in local issues and instead form their own national organisations. It seems likely that if public awareness of the benefits of town centres were raised, and Chambers of Commerce were roused, the lobby to save town centres could become more powerful. As well as providing a voice to defend traditional centres, such mobilisation could work positively to improve town centres. We argue that local authorities have a key rôle to play in bringing various bodies together. By encouraging national multiples to get involved in local issues, obtaining advice and support of national tourist boards and historic building organisations, and by raising the profile of the local Chamber of Commerce, local authorities could gain public support, and develop a coherent improvement plan for the city centre.

Possible moves could be the appointment of town centre managers (as in Ilford, East London), or the commissioning of local architects and urban planners to devise a plan to make a coherent centre and to capitalise on its heritage and variety. The aim would be to protect the town centre's range of functions while making it a more attractive place to be. Strong local influence could help temper the trends towards retail 'gentrification' evident in York and other historic town centres. It is also of crucial importance for medium sized towns, often the centres most threatened by out-of-centre retailing.

We therefore recommend that

9   RETAILERS SHOULD FORM STRONG CHAMBERS OF COMMERCE, ON THE MODEL OF KÖLN AND WOLVERHAMPTON, TO PROTECT THEIR INTERESTS, AND TO LOBBY FOR SENSITIVE CONSERVATION OF TRADITIONAL TOWN CENTRES

10 LOCAL AUTHORITIES SHOULD BRING TOGETHER LOCAL AND NATIONAL AGENCIES SUCH AS CHAMBERS OF COMMERCE, TOURIST BOARDS AND HISTORIC BUILDING AGENCIES TO DEVELOP A TOWN CENTRE'S CHARACTER, TO RAISE PUBLIC AWARENESS AND TO DEVELOP INTEGRATED LOCAL DESIGN SCHEMES

Many local authorities who perceive a threat from out-of-centre retail develop-ment are already embarking on improvement schemes for town centres. Such schemes frequently include plans to refurbish dated shopping centres, to introduce or extend pedestrianisation, and even to glaze over existing shopping streets to provide comfortable shopping environments. Where these improvements are sensitively carried out town centres undoubtedly benefit, but all too often 'improvement schemes', in Britain at least, hinge on the need to gear town centres to the needs of the car. Many German local authorities are recognising that building larger car parks and access roads can affect the town centre's environment to the point where they are no longer attractive places to be. This process has been taken to its logical conclusion in the United States where town centres responded to rising levels of car use by road and car park building programmes. New facilities quickly became congested with traffic, and the impact on the environment grew until a point was reached when traders and customers abandoned downtown for freeway locations.

Many US downtowns exist only in name. While such a process might not proceed as quickly and as far in Britain, lessons can be learnt about the effects of obsessively catering for the car. An alternative that has been implemented by many European cities is to actively restrain car access to the city centre, and to capitalise on the central location by substantially improving public transport. There is evidence that the environmental improvement derived from largely traffic free environments makes the centre more attractive to shoppers, enhances trade, and enables it to resist competition from out-of-centre retailing (TEST 1988).

We therefore recommend that

11 LOCAL AUTHORITIES SHOULD BE WARY OF REDESIGNING THEIR TOWN CENTRES TO ACCOMMODATE THE CAR, IN AN ATTEMPT TO COMPETE WITH OUT-OF-CENTRE RETAIL SCHEMES. ON THE CONTRARY, THEY SHOULD INTRODUCE TRAFFIC RESTRAINT, ENVIRONMENTAL IMPROVEMENT AND BETTER PUBLIC TRANSPORT. A SUBSTANTIAL RESIDENTIAL POPULATION, WITHIN WALKING DISTANCE, COMPLEMENTS SUCH POLICIES.

REFERENCES

Adams, John (1981) **Transport Planning: vision and practice** London Routledge & Kegan Paul

Brand, Peter (1987) 'What are you doing here?' asked Milligan in **The Planner** 73,4 pp23-26

Christaller, W (1933) **Die zentralen Orte in Süddeutschland** Translated by CW Baskin (1966) **Central Places in Southern Germany** Prentice Hall

Council of the European Communities (1985) Council Directive of 27 June 1985 on the effects of certain public and private projects projects on the environment in **Official Journal of the European Communities** No L 175/40

ECMT (European Conference of Ministers of Transport) (1985) **Changes in Transport Users' Motivations for Modal Choice: Passenger Transport** Paris

Hamer, Mick (1987) **Wheels within Wheels – a study of the road lobby** London Routledge & Kegan Paul

Hurdle, D (1986) **Shopping Trips to Town Centres** GLTS Analysis Report No 15 Greater London Council

Lester, Nick and Stephen Potter (1983) **Vital Travel Statistics** London T2000

Maslow, AH (1954) **Motivation and Personality** New York

National Economic Development Office (1988) **The Future of the High Street** London NEDO

Organisation for Economic Cooperation & Development (1979) **Managing Transport** Paris

Orski, C Kenneth (1987) 'Managing' Suburban Traffic Congestion: A Strategy for Urban Mobility in **Transportation Quarterly** 41,4 pp457-476

Plowden, Stephen (1988) Superstores in **The Lata Review** No 66 p8 Winter

TEST (1988) **Quality Streets** London TEST

Thomson, J Michael (1977) **Great Cities and their Traffic** Harmondsworth Penguin

INDEX

230